Educational Leadership and Critical Theory

Educational Leadership: Innovative, Critical and Interdisciplinary Perspectives

Series Editors: *Jeffrey S. Brooks, Alan J. Daly, Yi-Hwa Liou, Chen Schechter and Victoria Showunmi*

The Educational Leadership series provides a forum for books that push the conceptual boundaries of educational leadership and that introduce novel perspectives with the promise of improving, challenging and reconceptualising the field of study and informing practice. Books in the series take a global, interdisciplinary focus and cover educational phases ranging from early years to higher education. They aspire to be field-leading innovations that advance new theories, topics and methodologies. The series will be of interest to those working across disciplines such as educational leadership, school leadership, teacher education, sociology, anthropology, economics, psychology, political science, philosophy and public policy.

Also available in the series:
The Relational Leader: Catalysing Social Networks for Educational Change, edited by Yi-Hwa Liou and Alan J Daly

Forthcoming in the series:
Women Navigating Educational Research, Jana L. Carlisle

Educational Leadership and Critical Theory

What Can School Leaders Learn from the Critical Theorists

Edited by
Charles L. Lowery, Chetanath Gautam,
Robert White and Michael E. Hess

BLOOMSBURY ACADEMIC
LONDON • NEW YORK • OXFORD • NEW DELHI • SYDNEY

BLOOMSBURY ACADEMIC
Bloomsbury Publishing Plc
50 Bedford Square, London, WC1B 3DP, UK
1385 Broadway, New York, NY 10018, USA
29 Earlsfort Terrace, Dublin 2, Ireland

BLOOMSBURY, BLOOMSBURY ACADEMIC and the Diana logo are trademarks of
Bloomsbury Publishing Plc

First published in Great Britain 2024
Paperback edition published 2025

Copyright © Charles L. Lowery, Chetanath Gautam, Robert White, and
Michael E. Hess, 2024

Charles L. Lowery, Chetanath Gautam, Robert White, and Michael E. Hess have asserted
their right under the Copyright, Designs and Patents Act, 1988, to be identified as Editors
of this work.

Series design by Tjaša Krivec
Cover image © YAY Media AS / Alamy Stock Photo

All rights reserved. No part of this publication may be reproduced or transmitted
in any form or by any means, electronic or mechanical, including photocopying,
recording, or any information storage or retrieval system, without prior
permission in writing from the publishers.

Bloomsbury Publishing Plc does not have any control over, or responsibility for, any
third-party websites referred to or in this book. All internet addresses given in this
book were correct at the time of going to press. The author and publisher regret any
inconvenience caused if addresses have changed or sites have ceased to exist, but can
accept no responsibility for any such changes.

A catalogue record for this book is available from the British Library.

A catalog record for this book is available from the Library of Congress.

ISBN: HB: 978-1-3503-5342-8
PB: 978-1-3503-5346-6
ePDF: 978-1-3503-5343-5
eBook: 978-1-3503-5344-2

Series: Educational Leadership: Innovative, Critical and Interdisciplinary Perspectives

Typeset by Newgen KnowledgeWorks Pvt. Ltd., Chennai, India

To find out more about our authors and books visit www.bloomsbury.com
and sign up for our newsletters.

Contents

Series Editors' Foreword	vii
List of Contributors	xi
Introduction: Why Critical Theory and Educational Leadership? Charles L. Lowery	1

Part 1 Critical Educational Leadership for Understanding School and Society through the Theoretical and Reflective Lenses   15
Chetanath Gautam, Robert White, and Michael E. Hess with insights from contributors

1	Educational Leadership through the Lens of Critical Theory *Chetanath Gautam*	21
2	Understanding the Role of Education in Emancipation, Liberation, and True Democracy *Robert White*	37
3	Educational Leadership as a (Consumer) Culture Industry *Richard Niesche*	57
4	Is Transformational Leadership One-Dimensional? *Robert E. Kirsch*	75
5	Cultivating Relations of Freedom through Education Leadership by Drawing from the Critical Theory of Herbert Marcuse *Patrick M. Jenlink*	95
6	How Educational Leaders Make Better Decisions through a Frankfurt School Understanding of Rational Decision-Making *Chris Brown*	113

Part 2 Critical Educational Leadership for Improving School and Society through the Pragmatic and Active Lenses   133
Charles L. Lowery with insights from contributors

7 Competitive Character in Education and the Frankfurt School's Theory of a New Anthropological Type   139
Taylor Hines

8 Marcuse's Critical Theory for the Educational Practice of Critical Media Literacy   155
Steve Gennaro and Douglas Kellner

9 Perspectives of the Relationship as an Enduring Message of Hope through Dialogue, Reflection, and Action in Freire's *Pedagogy of the Oppressed*   171
Betty J. Alford, Rene Levario, Sergio Chavez, and Alberto Medina

10 Unpacking the Intersections of Habermas's Critical Theory and Ladson-Billings's Culturally Relevant Practice   189
Anthony Walker

11 A New Critical Theory and the Black Divide   201
Rhonda T. Humphries

12 African American Education for Liberation in Twenty-First-Century America: From Critical Theory to Black Power   213
Bakari K. Lumumba

Conclusion: Fromm's Productive Love as a Syndrome of Attitudes for a Moral Care and Ethical Respect in Educational Leadership   223
Charles L. Lowery

Index   243

Series Editors' Foreword

Jeffrey S. Brooks, Curtin University School of Education, Australia
Chen Schechter, Bar-Ilan University, Israel
Alan J. Daly, UC-San Diego, USA
Victoria Showunmi, UCL Institute of Education, England
Yi-Hwa Liou, National Taipei University of Education, Taiwan

The history of thought and practice in educational leadership can be conceived as a punctuated equilibrium (English 2008). The arc of the field's history is a steady evolution of traditional ideas centered around management, administration, efficiency, rational decision-making, authority, and power (Beck and Murphy 1993). Heavily influenced by business administration and management literature, the field is also shaped by sociology, anthropology, economics, psychology, political science, philosophy, and public policy. As an applied field, scholarship in educational leadership shapes—and is shaped by—developments in schools, universities, policymaking processes, and in other formal and informal education settings (Brooks and Miles 2006). This has meant that there is space in the field for both highly theoretical work and for research grounded in a specific context. Of course, quite a lot of scholarship in the field seeks these aims at the same time as a way of generating relevant knowledge in situ while also advancing thought and practice throughout the world (Gunter 2016).

Occasionally, ideas are introduced that compel scholars and practitioners to reconsider the foundations of "what they know" and adopt new ways of thinking about and practicing their work. Among intellectual movements that upset educational leadership's orthodoxy were postmodernism, critical theory, feminist theories, social justice, culturally relevant school leadership, distributed leadership, and more purposeful studies of the relationship between leadership and learning (Brooks and Normore 2017). Each of these domains of inquiry produced novel perspectives on educational leadership (to be sure there are others; we do not pretend this is an exhaustive list) that inform contemporary conceptual and empirical research. Additionally, each of these intellectual movements initiated a paradigmatic shift in the way people engage in the practice of educational leadership, think about their work, and conduct themselves as leaders and followers in formal and informal education settings.

For all this innovation, the arc toward improvement has been slow, and often the emphasis on the traditional has subdued the exploration of the radical. This book series seeks to establish a space for research that (1) explores promising concepts at the edges of the field, (2) encourages the publication of new ideas, and (3) critiques contemporary assumptions about educational leadership. Our hope is that the series may play some role in prompting future conceptual and empirical revolutions that will move the field forward via emergent scientific and artistic revolutions.

New perspectives are emerging from across the field and other disciplines that have great potential to influence, and be influenced by, educational leadership scholarship and practice. Among these are exciting developments related to sustainability and climate change, social networking, religion and spirituality, immigration and globalization, student-centered leadership, and innovative contributions to traditional topics such as community-school relations, gender, race, ethnicity, sexuality, diversity, intercultural/cross-cultural studies, globalization, early childhood and adult education, student voice, and activism. To be sure, there are others. While it is easy to point to individual articles or small groups of scholars working in these areas, there is no clear publication outlet for deeper, focused, and nuanced works that explore and challenge such ideas in the detail afforded by a full-length book or highly focused edited volume. Reaching out beyond the field of educational leadership, there are developments in sociology, anthropology, political science, policy studies, psychology, curriculum studies, brain-based research, environmental science, creativity studies, medicine, law, and other fields that have yet to be deeply explored or understood in terms of their possible applicability to educational leadership. We see the series as a place where such disciplines, ideas, and lines of inquiry can come into dialogue and create innovation. We see this book series as a forum for interdisciplinary, innovative, creative, and indeed controversial work.

In addition to providing a forum for such exciting ideas, we aim for this series to also include a diversity of authors and contexts underrepresented in many extant book series. This means a diversity of authors, geographical contexts, and perspectives. As this is a series of research books, we anticipate the primary audience being academics, but the topics will be of interest to practicing school leaders, teachers, policymakers, and scholars working across disciplines such as educational leadership, school leadership, teacher education, sociology, anthropology, economics, psychology, political science, philosophy, and public policy. We invite you to join us in the conversation—to share your work and your insights—as we explore and extend the field of educational leadership.

References

Beck, L. G., and J. Murphy (1993), *Understanding the Principalship: Metaphorical Themes, 1920s–1990s*, New York: Teachers College Press.

Brooks, J. S., and M. T. Miles (2006), "From Scientific Management to Social Justice … and Back Again? Pedagogical Shifts in Educational Leadership," *International Electronic Journal for Leadership in Learning* 4 (1): 2–15.

Brooks, J. S., and A. H. Normore (2010), "Educational Leadership and Globalization: Literacy for a Glocal Perspective," *Educational Policy* 24 (1): 52–82.

Brooks, J. S., and A. H. Normore (2017), *Foundations of Educational Leadership: Developing Excellent and Equitable Schools*, New York: Routledge.

English, F. W. (2008), *Anatomy of Professional Practice: Promising Research Perspectives on Educational Leadership*, Lanham, MD: Rowman & Littlefield.

Gunter, H. (2016), *An Intellectual History of School Leadership Practice and Research*, London: Bloomsbury.

Jackson, L. L., N. Lopoukhine, and D. Hillyard (1995), "Ecological Restoration: A Definition and Comments," *Restoration Ecology* 3 (2): 71–5.

Kensler, L. A. W., and C. L. Uline (2017), *Leadership for Green Schools: Sustainability for Our Children, Our Communities, and Our Planet*, New York: Routledge.

Kensler, L. A. W., and C. L. Uline (2019), "Educational Restoration: A Foundational Model Inspired by Ecological Restoration," *International Journal of Educational Management* 33 (6): 1198–218.

Senge, P. M., N. Cambron-McCabe, T. Lucas, B. Smith, and J. Dutton (2012), *Schools That Learn (Updated and Revised): A Fifth Discipline Fieldbook for Educators, Parents, and Everyone Who Cares about Education*, London: Nicholas Brealey.

Stafford-Smith, M., D. Griggs, O. Gaffney, F. Ullah, B. Reyers, N., Kanie, … D. O'Connell (2017), "Integration: The Key to Implementing the Sustainable Development Goals," *Sustainability Science* 12 (6): 911–19.

Contributors

Betty Alford is Professor of Education, Co-Director of the Doctoral Program, and Chair of the Educational Leadership Program at California State Polytechnic University (Cal Poly), Pomona. Betty has a wide breadth of experience in K-12 education, teacher preparation, and educational leadership programs. She taught for six years in Texas before serving as a high school counselor, elementary school principal, and junior high school principal. She then taught for twenty-seven years in the secondary teacher preparation and educational leadership programs at Stephen F. Austin State University before moving to Cal Poly. Her research interests include critical issues in educational leadership, culturally proficient leadership development, and improving access and equity in high-need schools.

Chris Brown is Professor of Education and Director of Research at the Department of Education Studies, University of Warwick. Chris is seeking to drive forward the notion of Professional Learning Networks (PLNs) as a means to promote the collaborative learning of teachers. Alongside his research into PLNs, Chris also has a long-standing interest in how research evidence can and should, but often does not, aid the development of education policy and practice. Over the course of his career, Chris has written or edited nineteen books and led/co-led research projects to the value of £6m across these two areas.

Sergio Chavez is Superintendent at Farmersville Unified School District. He earned his doctorate at California State Polytechnic University, Pomona. His professional interests include mentoring, staff development, dual language immersion, and school community engagement. He has served in the past as a teacher, a principal, and a district bilingual director.

Chetanath Gautam is an Associate Professor in the Educational Leadership Graduate Program at Delaware State University. Dr. Gautam holds two masters and an EdD degree in education, educational leadership, and educational research. He has authored several research articles, book chapters, and other scholarly reports. Scholar-practitioner educational leadership and research is Chetanath's primary focus of study that incorporates processes of theory–practice interaction. Dr. Gautam frequently examines the theory–practice continuum through perspectives of critical theories in educational leadership in P-20 settings, which includes equity, justice, and culturally relevant education and leadership. His research interest focuses on high-need school contexts. His primary research fields include the urban and rural United States as well as countries worldwide, as he partners with a global community of researchers.

Steve Gennaro is a critical theorist, philosopher of technology, and child rights activist with two decades of award-winning teaching experience. Dr. Gennaro is one of the founding members of the Children, Childhood, and Youth Studies Program at York University. He was named to the Child Rights Academic Network 2021 in Canada and appointed to the European Academy of Sciences of Ukraine in 2022. He is currently working with Henry Giroux on a collection titled *Transformative Practice in Critical Media Literacy: Radical Democracy and Decolonized Pedagogy in Higher Education* (co-edited with Nolan Higdon and Michael Hoechsmann) to be published in 2023.

Michael E. Hess is Associate Professor of Educational Studies in the Gladys W. and David H. Patton College of Education at Ohio University. Dr. Hess holds a PhD in cultural studies from Ohio University where he is a faculty in the educational leadership program. His background is critical and cultural studies in educational foundations, and his major research interests include social justice, rural Appalachia, democratic leadership, place-based education, qualitative research methodologies, and international service learning.

Taylor Hines is a Teaching Assistant Professor and faculty fellow at Barrett, The Honors College at Arizona State University, and an editor for *Damage Magazine* (Damagemag.com). He did his graduate work at Purdue University where he was a Ross Fellow in the Department of Mathematics, studying noncommutative algebraic topology. He is currently studying the psychoanalytic dimension of first-generation critical theorists to understand the role of science and technology on subjectivity and subjectification in the era of neoliberal capitalism.

Rhonda T. Humphries is an authentic and transformational school leader with more than a decade of service to private, public, and charter schools in the DC, Baltimore, and New York City areas. Rhonda is currently pursuing her doctorate at The George Washington University.

Patrick M. Jenlink is Regents Professor and has held the positions of E. J. Campbell Endowed Chair in Educational Leadership, Doctoral Program Coordinator, Department Chair, and Professor of Doctoral Studies in the James I Perkins College of Education, Stephen F. Austin State University. Dr. Jenlink's teaching emphasis in doctoral studies includes courses in ethics and philosophy of leadership, research methods and design, and leadership theory and practice. His research interests include neoliberal ideology and its impact on education, critical theory, democratic education, teacher preparation, and critical leadership. He has authored and/or edited twenty-three books and authored over a hundred book chapters. In addition, he has authored and published over 175 peer-refereed articles and over two hundred peer-refereed conference papers. His most recent books include *Multimedia Learning Theory and Its Implications for Teaching and Learning* (2019), *The Next Generation of STEM Teacher: An Interdisciplinary Approach* (2019), *The Language of Mathematics: How the Teacher's Knowledge of Mathematics Affects Instruction* (2020), *Teaching as a Clinical Practice Profession: Research on Clinical Practice and Experience in Teacher Preparation* (2021), and *Literacy in Teacher Preparation and Practice: Enabling Individuals to Negotiate Meaning* (2022).

Douglas Kellner holds the George F. Kneller Chair in the Philosophy of Education at the University of California, Los Angeles. He earned his PhD in philosophy from Columbia University. Dr. Kellner has taught philosophy for more than twenty years. He also has taught abroad in Canada, Taiwan, Sweden, and Finland, where he received a Fulbright Fellowship. He is the author and co-author of many books, including *Herbert Marcuse and the Crisis of Marxism* (1984), *Camera Politica: The Politics and Ideology of Contemporary Hollywood Film* (1988), *Critical Theory, Marxism, and Modernity* (1989), *Television and the Crisis of Democracy* (1990), *Postmodern Theory: Critical Interrogations* (1991), *The Postmodern Turn* (1997), and *Media Culture* (2020), coauthored with Steven Best.

Robert E. Kirsch is Assistant Professor of Leadership and Integrative Studies at Arizona State University. His research is primarily focused on critical theory as a lens to analyze organizational development and change, in particular contributions from the "Frankfurt School" of critical theory. He is the co-editor of *Marcuse in the Twenty-First Century: Radical Politics, Critical Theory, and Revolutionary Praxis* (2018), among other published works. He is also a board member of the International Herbert Marcuse Society and the Caucus for a Critical Political Science.

Rene Levario is Instructional Services Specialist in Riverside Unified School District in Riverside, California. He completed his doctoral studies in educational leadership at California State Polytechnic University, Pomona.

Charles L. Lowery is Associate Professor of Educational Leadership and Policy Studies in the School of Education at Virginia Polytechnic Institute and State University. His research interests focus on the impact of crisis, conflict, and controversy on educational decision-making for school leaders, particularly in rural, underresourced, and remote schools. He has published on democratic education and the impact of the opioid crisis on school and students. His most recent edited volume, a collaboration with his mentor Patrick M. Jenlink, is *The Handbook of Dewey's Educational Theory and Practice* (2019).

Bakari K. Lumumba is the Assistant Director of Community Standards & Student Responsibility at Ohio University. He has a background in African studies and international studies and also has an expertise in community engagement. His research focuses on critical advocacy and activism, pan-Africanist theory, Black Crit studies, and school–community partnerships to improve the quality of education for African American students in K-12 schools and beyond.

Richard Niesche is Associate Professor of Educational Leadership in the School of Education at the University of New South Wales, Sydney. His research interest is primarily in critical perspectives in educational leadership. He has published his research in a number of books and peer-reviewed journals, and he is also the founding co-editor of the Educational Leadership Theory book series with Springer. Recent books published include *Social, Critical and Political Theories for Educational Leadership* (2019), *Theorising Identity and Subjectivity in Educational Leadership Research* (2020), and *Understanding Educational Leadership: Critical Perspectives and Approaches* (2021).

Alberto Medina is an educational leader in the state of California, United States. He holds the earned EdD in educational leadership from California State Polytechnic University, Pomona.

Anthony Walker earned a BA degree in elementary education with a minor in special education from Northern Kentucky University. He holds a Master of Education in Educational Counseling from Texas Christian University and earned a Doctor of Education in Educational Leadership from Stephen F. Austin State University. Dr. Walker embraces his role as a scholar-practitioner with a sense of moral responsibility grounded in aspirations to change the lives of learners and help them become future scholars and leaders. His research interests examine topics such as intersections of difference, identity awareness, systems of privilege, equity-minded practice, and curriculum. He has authored and co-edited a series of books that address social justice and racial equity in schools, including *Un-American Acts* (2015), *Un-Democratic Acts: New Departures of Dialogues in Society and Schools* (2016), and *Quantum Realities: Educational Truth-Telling in an Era of Alternative Facts* (2017).

Robert White is the E. V. Wilkins Endowed Professor in Education at Elizabeth City State University. Robert earned his PhD in Special Education & Educational Psychology (Inclusive Practice) at Durham University, UK. He also holds a Master of Science in Psychology (Child Development) and a BSc in the Social

Sciences from the Open University and studied for his BEd in Special Education with Essex University in the UK. Before becoming an academic, he was an outdoor leadership educator, primary school teacher, county wide behavior support teacher, elementary school principal, and a system wide educational consultant. Robert currently works with several international colleagues on research exploring the intersection between school leadership, inclusion, equity, justice, peace-building, and sustainable development through emancipatory education. Robert has served as the Coordinator for the Inclusion and Equity Thematic Group of UNESCO Teacher Task Force, has published multiple books, many research articles, and his teaching focuses on school improvement and effectiveness.

Introduction: Why Critical Theory and Educational Leadership?

Charles L. Lowery

Critical Educational Leadership

Critical theory is not new to the conversation or field of educational leadership. However, arguably the field of educational leadership studies has suffered from a veritable lack of engagement—at least consistently—that has connected it to the Institute of Social Research at the University of Frankfurt (aka "the Frankfurt School"), or the broader development of critical theory since. The void of scholarship focusing on the nexus of critical theory and educational leadership is not without its reasons. Critical theory, particularly in countries with strong ties to capitalism, can be a sensitive subject. Although there have been many well-presented arguments and critiques of critical theory (e.g., Michel Foucault's or Chantal Mouffe's), many myths and misconceptions are associated with critical theory as a subject. In some countries, such as the United States, critical theory has been vilified and even *demon*ized in some public and political discourses.

Although this text is not concerned with dispelling this misinformation, it is hoped that this work can be presented to open-minded and critically oriented leaders and scholars who recognize that these are distractions that divert our attention away from ways of thinking that are critical and innovative. Fundamentally, this text is about just that—critical and innovative thinking. It is not about whether critical theory is good or bad, right or wrong. We take critical theory to simply be a set of frameworks or models for first considering issues and problems then applying moral judgment. That said, our collective goal is to deliver this work in the spirit of the Frankfurt School with a sound and relevant rationale for educational leaders to understand and improve the experiences of students while in school, and hopefully postgraduation in society.

However, while we embrace the spirit of the Frankfurt School scholars—many of whom stood up and spoke out against issues still relevant to life and learning today—we do not limit ourselves to only discussing critical theorists who were immediately connected to the Frankfurt School. The Frankfurt School scholars merely initiated a philosophy of understanding and improving the social sciences that has continued and evolved for nearly a century.

It would be easy to transition to a discussion of the connection of critical theory and education in a broader sense. After all, educational leadership cannot—or rather should not—be divorced from discussions about the broader fields of education, learning, pedagogy, and teaching. Any work concerning educational leadership must also consider education as a topic. We do not disagree that there exists a long tradition of educational scholars whose work has integrated the concepts and concerns of critical theorists (and many of the contributions to this text do emphasize that connection). However, there have been many education scholars (some of whom have contributed to this text) who have utilized the approaches of critical theorists that can certainly be located in the literature on education more broadly.

Educational leadership is more unique. Headteachers, principals, ministers, and superintendents (terms that shift from country to country) have unique responsibilities and roles, but ultimately set in a position to make and influence decisions, allocate resources, or engage in efforts to mobilize resources, and ultimately solve problems whether individually or by means of bringing the right constituents together. We cannot lose sight of the fact that the discussion of critical theory within the context of educational leadership for primary/secondary (UK) and K-12 (United States) schools is not only lacking but also mostly nonexistent.

Therefore, it is important to indicate early that this text is not primarily about *critical theory* in and of itself. It is foremost a work about educational leadership. We consider not only what are some salient points from the work of key critical theorists, but we also take a stance of criticality as educational leaders to understand what critical theory can mean for our discipline. For this introductory chapter, we have asked ourselves three important questions on this idea. First, "What can K-12 educational leaders learn from critical theory?" Second, "What should K-12 educational leadership learn, essentially, about critical theory?" And, finally, "Why should critical theory matter to educational leaders in schools around the world?" This chapter attempts to entertain those questions and as such serves to introduce the rest of the chapters comprising this book.

So, Why Critical Theory?

The social scientists and critical thinkers who formed the original Frankfurt School in Germany faced what has been called "some of the most compelling problems and questions of modern society" (Thompson 2017: 1). Thompson, in his *Handbook of Critical Theory*, went on to define critical theory in this way:

> It is a distinctive form of theory in that it posits a more comprehensive means to grasp social reality and diagnose social pathologies. It is marked not by a priori ethical or political values that it seeks to assert in the world, but by its capacity to grasp the totality of individual and social life as well as the social processes that constitute them. It is a form of social criticism that contains within it the seeds of judgment, evaluation, and practical, transformative activity. (1)

This definition is important in that it reveals that critical theory is a method of understanding "set with the task of uncovering the social conditions under which knowledge about itself is articulated, since the way we comprehend the objective world is related to the ways we conceive of ourselves" (2). It also brings to the forefront the fact that critical theory as a social science was not formed by already established ethical frames or previously politicized agendas. The purpose of the scholars shaping critical theory was to "grasp the totality of individual and social life" and the processes that create that totality.

To get at such a deep understanding of culture and society, one cannot be hindered by allowing the biases of politics to hinder the judgment or by being ideologically one-sided. The problems that have presented themselves in our social lives are human problems, not political or ideological ones. That is not to say these problems did not become politicized in the 1930s in the same way they do today; it is only to say that critical theory saw politics as simply another manifestation of the social realm and therefore secondary to the problems. For the critical theorist, the evils of fascism and the Nazi regime were syndromes of the human condition. Therefore, their critique of far-right authoritarianism was more an attempt to understand, analyze, and evaluate the situations and circumstances that allowed fascism to take its hold on so many people in their country. But perhaps more important to the *critique* of critical theorists than analysis and evaluation was and is still the concept of reflection (Freire 2005; Habermas 1971, 1973; Stromquist 2014).

Even more critically oriented is the concept of "self-reflection" or reflexivity. Horkheimer (1972: 11) defined self-reflection as "the consistent and radical questioning of subjective and objective data; the integration of all knowable reality into a unified whole; and the attempt to provide an ultimate and intrinsic foundation for the universal validity of knowledge."

These underlying assumptions about societal problems were not one-sidedly positive *or* negative, but instead were framed as being simultaneously positive *and* negative. "Negative and positive" at the same time, these assumptions offer a frame to critique that which exists in class society and an imperative for changing these conditions. As Fuchs (2015) pointed out, for the critical theorist, "concepts are negative and positive at the same time; they are an accusation of that which exists in class society and an imperative for changing these conditions" (2). Arguably, this could perhaps be a major reason critical theory is targeted by political elites and framed as such an evil to the average working-class citizen.

Take, for instance, the opioid crisis in America. This is a defining crisis for many, and it has a direct impact on our schools, communities, and health system (medical and mental). Some may singularly see the "pill mills" and overprescription of opioids as a root cause of the epidemic. Others may myopically lay blame on people's addictions and drug abuse as the defining factor.

But also, it may be due to the lower socioeconomic situation of working-class people in underresourced and vulnerable areas who may not have adequate or appropriate access to more affordable options for health care or less addictive medicines and treatments. These may also be areas in which the jobs and lifestyles of individuals are more hazardous and therefore see a higher number of pain-causing incidents. Also, other pain treatments that may in fact work better and have fewer risks than opioids may not be authorized because they are not as profitable to pharmaceutical companies.

Finally, a culture prone to a consumerism based on immediate and convenient gratification may very well be a culture with a tendency toward a need for immediate and convenient relief over drawn-out therapies. Availability of time and other resources may make convenience a necessity for some. Perhaps the critical theorist would look at this complexity of syndromes and say each of these persists due to division and alienation—the lack of connection to resources, capital, and assets; the absence of advocates; the scarcity of information about options.

A similar analysis of the decline in democratic faith occurred not only in the United States but around the world. Critical theory provides perspectives for us to look at the persistence of antidemocratic sentiments, and the recent rise of demagogues and authoritarians globally not only sees the lust for power on the part of the autocrat. The critical theorists would also see the historical tendency of those without power to yield to perceived strength, to abdicate personal responsibility to those seen as capable, or to have the means to get things done. These critical thinkers, like Adorno, Benjamin, Fromm, and Marcuse, would see the subjugated human being's desire to accept the will of one man or woman to rule for them by proxy, to vicariously achieve power through the "strong man" even when they themselves are left powerless. Strongman politicians and machine-loving antidemocratic representatives are the opiates of the populists.

The reflective gaze of critical theory looks at the sphere of conditions in which the problem is located. It is the tendency of Western thought to think of problems and dilemmas "radically"—that is, we look for *the roots* of the problem. Critical theorists viewed problems as rhizomes—vast systems of interconnected concerns from which issues stem. Many view problems as an oak tree, but critical theorists see problems as a forest of Aspens. Even the arch-nemesis of critical theory—unbridled "consumer capitalism," a product of what they termed the culture industry—was itself a product of systems. Capitalism was created by and shaped by a collection of interdisciplinary issues stemming from the economic, psychological, and social needs of individuals. The critique of critical theory was that unfortunately these individuals were mostly disinterested and disconnected from their fellowman. Disinterested as in disenfranchised. Disconnected as in we have lost our understanding of what it means to be individuals in a society. As Erich Fromm (1947) stated,

> [The] mature and productive individual derives his feeling of identity from the experience of himself as the agent who is one with his powers; this feeling of self can be briefly expressed as meaning "I am what I do." In the marketing orientation man encounters his own powers as commodities alienated from him. He is not one with them but they are masked from him because what matters is not his self-realization in the process of using them but his success in the process of selling them. Both his powers and what they create become estranged, something different from himself, something for others to judge and to use; thus his feeling of identity becomes as shaky as his self-esteem. (54)

Our public and political interests have devolved into often immature and frequently selfish desires and fears. Our civic responsibilities and community engagement have become inept. For many, civic participation is relegated to voting (where and when possible) not based on policies but on partisanship, watching commercialized corporate news outlets to be "informed," and social media rants. Our collective voice has been diminished to a meme—individualized and as disconnected from reality as it is from the source of who created the meme.

But this, although critical, is not a sufficient argument for critical theory. Critical theory is not simply being critical. It does challenge the status quo, but not simply to be challenging. Critical theory is about analysis and evaluation. It is about improving the human condition by exposing the elements of human interactions that alienate us from one another. Critical theorists would question why certain individuals remain socially inefficient, why some people become so politically selfish, why other citizens remain so civically irresponsible or so critically ill-informed.

The complexities around these perceptions are vast—and the lens of critical theory is flexible enough to examine the rhizomatic nature of the assumptions and attitudes that drive these phenomena. Yet a rhizome is still a rhizome—its capacity to sprout anywhere is still limited to the type of soil it flourishes in.

One such rhizome is that of individualization—the way in which certain individuals become increasingly alienated from other human beings and begin to reject the individual responsibility or any real effort at belonging. Fromm (1955) described it this way:

> We have reached a state of individuation in which only the fully developed mature personality can make fruitful use of freedom; if the individual has not developed his reason and his capacity for love, he is incapable of bearing the burden of freedom and individuality, and tries to escape into artificial ties which give him a sense of belonging and rootedness. Any regression today from freedom into artificial rootedness in state or race is a sign of mental illness, since such regression does not correspond to the state of evolution already reached and results in unquestionably pathological phenomena. (70)

Critical theorists did not reject individual freedom—they merely argued that many people never reached the level of personal maturity to understand what it means to be an individual. Individuals exist in the community of society and therefore have responsibilities to themselves and others.

In fact, this alienating individualization (this lack of brotherliness) was at the heart of the narcissism and destructiveness in fascism and authoritarianism. As Jason Stanley (2018) has recently stated, "The most telling symptom of fascist politics is division" (xiv). Failure to recognize the distinction between a mature, developed individuality and the individuality formed by division has impacted our ability for relatedness and rootedness. Relatedness is "the necessity to unite with other living beings, to be related to them" (Fromm 2002: 29). Fromm stated, "This need is behind all phenomena which constitute the whole gamut of intimate human relations, of all passions which are called love in the broadest sense of the word" (29).

But critical theory never allows us to examine only one side of the coin. Critical theorists acknowledged that the potential of our social, cultural, physical, spiritual, and emotional human needs manifests in positive and negative ways (perhaps even along a spectrum between these poles). Take Fromm's recognition of the imperative of relatedness for example. This desire to relate to others can have positive and negative outcomes:

> Man can attempt to become one with the world by submission to a person, to a group, to an institution, to God. In this way he transcends the separateness of his individual existence by becoming part of somebody or something bigger than himself, and experiences his identity in connection with the power to which he has submitted. Another possibility of overcoming separateness lies in the opposite direction: man can try to unite himself with the world by having power over it, by making others a part of himself, and thus transcending his individual existence by domination. (29)

Either way this type of individualization is what one might call "hard conformity." This causes individuals to reject reason and embrace irrationality.

This text proposes that critical education offers a framework in which self-actualization is possible. It is a concept already in the literature supporting meaningful and relevant curriculum and pedagogy. With the progress made in efforts to make schools democratic spaces where students are "reunited" with others in their communities, it also provides an authentic and (relatively) autonomous place to expose youth to "the optimum of truth attainable in a given historical period" (Fromm 1990: 184). The danger is that in many of our societies knowledge has become a commodity—valued not for fostering our power of self-realization but instead knowledge "has degenerated into an instrument to be used for better manipulation of others and oneself, in market research, in political propaganda, in advertising" (184). As Fromm warned us,

> Students are supposed to learn so many things that they have hardly time and energy left to think. Not the interest in the subjects taught or in knowledge and insight as such, but the enhanced exchange value knowledge gives is the main incentive for wanting more and better education. We find today a tremendous enthusiasm for knowledge and education, but at the same time a skeptical or contemptuous attitude toward the allegedly impractical and useless thinking which is concerned "only" with the truth and which has no exchange value on the market. (185)

Why critical theory? Schools, like democracies, fail only when we do not learn to operate in pluralistic and intercultural ways—to foster authentic inclusion and autonomy-building equity. We do not learn properly to function as a democracy or as an education system because we neither see such strategies frequently modeled in our agents of socialization (i.e., home, churches, schools), nor do we as developing citizens have ample opportunities to practice or engage in democratic endeavors as youth. To look at the reasons behind this from a critical perspective may be an imperative for school leaders moving forward.

Critical theory is a means to analyze the reasons behind this trend of anti-intellectualism and contempt for critical thinking. Unlike its late-in-life offspring—critical pedagogy—critical theory contemplates the relationship between knowledge and the globally accepted need for individuals with critical thinking skills and a deeper understanding of human interaction. Subjects and important themes for social interaction are being erased from schools because they are not viewed as expedient for progress of technological-industrial advancement. As a result, there is a risk that we will lose the motivation and capacities for personal growth as socially efficient and mature individuals. When in fact there remains a need for individuals who understand what it means to live in a community and can engage in both compromise and coalition-building. For students, it is key to understanding their condition as human beings in an ever-changing world and for providing them frameworks for understanding how their decision-making shapes the future and their problem-solving improves the future.

Why Is Critical Theory Important to School Leadership?

Critical theory is about the development and implementation of critical literacies. In an applied sense, people develop critical literacies to *read* the world—to decode and comprehend the domains and dimensions of the problems that confront them. Critical theorists shaped, and continue to shape, analytical lenses to look at particular problems (decoding), then work out systems of thinking to better understand those issues (comprehension), which also includes making moral judgments about those concerns (inference and conclusion drawing).

The critical theorists of the Frankfurt School were in no way singular or myopic in their topics or theories. They analyzed and critiqued geography, history, economics, art, literature, sociology, and anthropology. We might also add to this technology. As Kellner (2003) once pointed out, critical theorists in their writings confronted theories of monopoly capitalism, the new industrial state, the role of technology and giant corporations in monopoly capitalism, the key roles of mass culture and communication in reproducing contemporary societies, and the decline of democracy and of the individual. Critical theory drew alike on Hegelian dialectics, Marxian theory, Nietzsche, Freud, Max Weber, and other trends of contemporary thought. (2)

It is true that while many of them identified as liberal or "on the left," their form of liberalism would likely look quite different from the expressions of liberalism of today. Leading critical theorists Horkheimer and Adorno were avid critics of their contemporary culture. In their original 1947 publication, they lamented the loss of traditional expressions of film and entertainment that they considered high art (Horkheimer and Adorno 2002). It was not too far removed from some of the views held by conservatives now regarding postmodern and alternative expressions of art and music. Adorno and Daniel (1989) wrote this about jazz music in their era:

[The] use value of jazz does not nullify alienation, but intensifies it. Jazz is a commodity in the strict sense: its suitability for use permeates its production in terms none other than its marketability, in the most extreme contradiction to the immediacy of its use not merely in addition to but also within the work process itself. (48)

This was not necessarily the liberal defense of contemporary forms of musical expression one might read today. In light of this, Adorno and Horkheimer might by today's standards be thought of as conservative, at least in this regard.

Also, it should be recognized that the critical theorists were arduous critics of Freud and even Marx himself. They did not all agree—for instance, take the exchange of essays between Bertolt Brecht and György Lukács on expressionism (Adorno et al. 2007). Their work captured broad-brush perspectives of aesthetics and the spectrum of politics and public opinion. And, yes, they were staunch opponents of capitalism. But to fully understand their views and opinions on capitalism, one must understand that their critique was not merely concerned with capitalism as an economic model. They viewed capitalism as a model of human interaction and the impacts it had on the way people experience life, and therefore, they critiqued capitalism as much as a social and psychological model as an economic and political one.

Then, with this in mind, the work of the educational leader is one that both has been influenced by and furthermore integrates politics, economics, history, and other subjects examined by critical theory. Likewise, not everyone agrees on the purpose of education or a simple standardized approach to educational leadership. Therefore, we have much to gain in terms of thinking and theory from the challenges offered by the structure of critical theory. By structure here, I am referring to the nature and expression of critical theory as it relates to the various frameworks and models presented by the various theories of criticality and how they were presented in the work of critical theorists. It offers a very varied and nuanced demonstration of democracy. We can see elements of debate and dialogue; we also can find blatant examples of plurality expression and thought. There is not much difference in the competing values and public opinions with which school leaders everywhere must contend. Therefore, structurally there is much to be learned in how critical theorists engaged in these differences and managed them.

However, the issues that critical theorists addressed (i.e., social, economic, and political concerns; human behavior and psychology; the temporal aspects of history and sociology; the role that mass-produced culture plays in the way people think and interact) have implications in both schooling and education. How students, teachers, and parents interact in the schooling of a country's youth is a concern of human behavior and psychology. The way that curriculum is interpreted and transformed into pedagogical expression is influenced by local and popular culture—namely through our ways of thinking about technology and navigating digital habitats. An understanding of the historical and sociological contexts of school and learning is also implicit in educational leadership. Educational leadership is replete with related and relevant issues that connect critical theory with educators' application and implementation of learning and teaching.

To exemplify this idea, I will use a concept from my chapter on Fromm's productive love as a model for educational leadership (in Part II of this book). One aspect of this chapter is that I present the notion of producing citizens who are "Politically Literate" as an aim of productive love. This is only one aim, but it is an important consideration. Here I ask that the reader keep in mind that I personally try to neither confuse nor conflate politics with partisanship. I am not intending to discuss conservative vs. liberal parties. The scope of perspectives held by citizens of any nation-state is complex and, in my opinion, not as dichotomous as mediated narratives wish us to believe. Furthermore, just as voting is only one aspect of sociopolitical engagement, partisanship is merely one facet of politics. Human desires, values, and interactions—whether it be in local organizations such as schools, or at the federal level in Congress—are at the root of all politics. Therefore, school leaders must exhibit political literacy and work to create learning environments in which students learn political literacy as well as are conducive to the development of other critical literacies.

With that stated, the reason I see political literacy as inherent to productive love and an imperative for educational leadership is because politics is about human interaction and experience. Politics is the pitch and field in which competing views and values face off and vie for position and possession. Politics is as much about discussion and dialogue as it is debate. Partisanship is only about divisions—sometimes highlighted by debates and sometimes not. Although Schattschneider (2003) wrote in his 1942 publication, *Party Government*, that "political parties created democracy and … modern democracy is unthinkable save in terms of parties" (1), others like Dewey (1916) argued that democracy was more than a form of government, that is, it was "primarily a mode of associated living, of conjoint communicated experience" (84). Dewey (1954) also emphasized the political concern of individuals at the community level over national parties and partisan strongmen:

> A man who has not been seen in the daily relations of life may inspire admiration, emulation, servile subjection, fanatical partisanship, hero worship; but not love and understanding, save as they radiate from the attachments of a near-by union. Democracy must begin at home, and its home is the neighborly community. (213)

Dewey's idea of being democratically neighborly is synonymous with Fromm's notion of brotherly love. It is likewise, though indirectly and arguably so, implicated in Habermas's communicative action in the public sphere. Educational leaders are community—or neighborly—leaders. They often must serve as a voice of reason and being a firm but loving "brother" to parents, to teachers, to students, and to other stakeholders.

Critical educational leaders, then, desire neither fanatical or servile admiration nor hero worship. Instead, they must offer a humble and calming voice of reasoning even when other voices, in the efforts of those individuals to likewise be heard, are not so rational. They must be reflective and often revolutionary when others are being reactive and even rebellious. When leaders examine issues and concerns from a perspective of critical theory, they are trying to understand the roots of the situation. This is done out of a need to both understand and then improve schools as microcosms of society.

Conclusion and Volume Division

To reflect this twofold need, this book is divided into two parts. The first part, "Critical Educational Leadership for Understanding School and Society through the Theoretical and Reflective Lenses," presents chapters that focus primarily on *the theoretical*. This part underscores the philosophical or reflective dimensions of a critical educational leadership. Critical theory, first and foremost, was directed at fostering a holistic understanding of society that was both temporal (i.e., "historical") and dialectical (i.e., shaped by opposing forces) (Fuchs 2015). A critical educational leadership requires school leaders to have a grasp of the dimensions of society that shape and solidify knowledge and learning. Brooks and Normore (2010) proposed that leadership in today's schools needed a "glocal" (global + local) perspective grounded in various critical literacies. They asserted that leaders must develop "(a) political literacy, (b) economic literacy, (c) cultural literacy, (d) moral literacy, (e) pedagogical literacy, (f) information literacy, (g) organizational literacy, (h) spiritual and religious literacy, and (i) temporal literacy" (53–4). These literacies serve as theoretical frames to understanding both society and the role of schools and education within that society. Many of these chapters in this text focus on these same domains (i.e., political, cultural, moral, pedagogical, etc.) of education and educational leadership. As well each reveals a temporal aspect of where both the field of educational leadership and critical theory itself are situated in contemporary society.

The second organizational part, titled "Critical Educational Leadership for Improving School and Society through the Pragmatic and Active Lenses," offers insights into *the pragmatic* aspect of the discipline. This part underscores the active or practical dimensions of a critical educational leadership. It is grounded in the second core concept of critical theory: improving society. Stromquist (2014) stated, "At the heart of critical theory is the firm belief that human beings are perfectible (not easily perfectible but perfectible in the long run) and that the power of reason can help us improve ourselves as a collective" (1). This can only be achieved through the application of a societal critique that is sensible and realistic. Critical theorists are often known for their critique of the capitalist system—this is true as we've noted. However, this critique is underscored by their attempts to understand human nature—our behavior and psychology—within the political, economic, cultural, temporal, and spiritual structures of our lives and modes of living. Fundamental to this was their consistent analysis of human interaction to perfect or improve the human experience. Educational leaders hold the same obligation in an educational sense—to improve society through education. This begins with the integration of the reflective and active aspects of critical theory into an educational leadership praxis for improving the educational experience for students as human beings.

References

Adorno, T. W., and J. O. Daniel (1989), "On Jazz," *Discourse* 12 (1): 45–69.
Adorno, T. W., W. Benjamin, E. Bloch, B. Brecht, and G. Lukács (2007), *Aesthetics and Politics*, London: Verso.
Brooks, J., and A. H. Normore (2010), "Educational Leadership and Globalization: Literacy for a Glocal Perspective," *Educational Policy* 24 (1): 52–82.
Dewey, J. (1916), *Democracy and Education: An Introduction to the Philosophy of Education*, New York: Macmillan.
Dewey, J. (1954), *The Public and Its Problems*, Athens, OH: Swallow Press.
Friere, P. ([1970] 2005), *Pedagogy of the Oppressed*, London: Continuum.
Fromm, E. ([1947] 1990), *Man for Himself: An Inquiry into the Psychology of Ethics*, New York: Henry Holt.
Fromm, E. ([1955] 2002), *The Sane Society*, Oxfordshire: Routledge Classics.
Fuchs, C. (2015), "Critical Theory," in G. Mazzoleni (ed.), *The International Encyclopedia of Political Communication*, 1st ed., 1–13, Hoboken, NJ: John Wiley.
Habermas, J. (1971), *Knowledge and Human Interests*, trans. J. J. Shapiro, Boston, MA: Beacon Press.
Habermas, J. (1973), *Theory and Practice*, trans. J. Viertel, Boston, MA: Beacon Press.
Horkheimer, M. ([1972] 2002), *Critical Theory: Selected Essays*, trans. M. J. O'Connell, London: Continuum.
Horkheimer, M., and T. Adorno (2002), *Dialectic of Enlightenment: Philosophical Fragments*, trans. E. Jephcott, Stanford, CA: Stanford University Press.
Kellner, D. (2003), "Toward a Critical Theory of Education," *Democracy & Nature* 9 (1): 51–64.
Schattschneider, E. E. (2003), *Party Government: American Government in Action*, London: Routledge.
Stanley, J. (2018), *How Fascism Works: The Politics of Us and Them*, New York: Random House.
Stromquist, N. P. (2014), "Critical Theory: Its Meaning and Its Application to Social Action through Education," paper presented at the Comparative Education Society in Europe, Freiburg, Germany, June 10–13.
Thompson, M. J. (ed.) (2017), *The Palgrave Handbook of Critical Theory*, London: Palgrave.

Part 1

Critical Educational Leadership for Understanding School and Society through the Theoretical and Reflective Lenses

Chetanath Gautam, Robert White, and Michael E. Hess
with insights from contributors

Introduction

Chetanath Gautam initiates this project, embracing an eastern modality for questioning that echoes the thoughtful style of question inherent to critical inquiry. With a discussion of the fundamental focus that critical theory offers on change in the system, he considers ways that school leaders using critical theory can think about dismantling oppressive structures. These structures subordinate or marginalize particular groups of people. Critical educational leaders have a role of critiquing the propositions and practices of broader social, educational, economic, and political structures. In fact, as Gautam argues, this is a *moral* responsibility for educators and educational leaders exploring and exposing inequalities in society. For these individuals, true education does not create wider gaps among students as humans. Instead, critical educators focus on closing gaps by equipping and empowering the marginalized groups or individuals through a just and equitable cycle of curriculum and pedagogy. How should they act to equip and empower them? How do they engage in this? Are the present physical, social, cultural, economic, and moral infrastructures suitable for this change? Gautam argues that these questions warrant a more in-depth reflection about the notion of education itself and educational leadership. Critical theory demands a critical review, deconstruction, and reconstruction of the entire tangible and intangible approaches of seeing and leading education. This chapter unfolds based on the necessary democratic theoretical framework of Habermas. Gautam poses Habermasian questions to model how educational leaders can reflectively and reflexively explore their perceptions and practice. These questions offer opportunities to make subtle yet distinct differences in creating democratic dialogues and serve as a starting point to initiate the exploration of critical narratives for educational leadership. As Habermas suggested, using narrative research, this chapter attempts to uncover the narratives of leaders' stories and lived dilemmas.

Robert White further situates our understanding of school leadership within a framework of critical theory that emphasizes the importance of the liberated mind for emancipatory leadership. The year 2020 will undoubtedly be front and center in future history books and remain embedded in the psyche of societies around the world for years to come. A year of uncertainty, chaos, and failed leadership during a pandemic resulting in growing political divisiveness, social unrest, and calls for equity and social justice in the growing inequities of modernity. However, those calls for social justice remain embedded in our history of oppression and seek to replace one set of oppressive structures with other, but just as oppressive structures. This chapter interrogates the role education, and more specifically educational leadership and school transformation, plays in establishing and maintaining inclusion, equity, and social justice. The chapter culminates in recommendations for schools and curricula developed and designed with all for all within a democratic and participatory approach to educational leadership. Education leadership committed to empowerment, inclusion, equity, social justice, and liberation for all. White discusses how educational leadership can be informed by the work of Frankfurt School of Critical Theorists, understood in terms of the French philosopher Michel Foucault and ultimately be embedded in David Hume's "is/ought" question. He argues for critical theory research that goes beyond the descriptive "what is," even beyond "what should be" and focuses on "what ought to be": school leadership as the catalyst for emancipation, transformation, and liberation. At the center of this chapter is the responsibility that educational leaders have in moving beyond the notion of equality to embrace concepts of equity and social justice reform that liberate all members of our society from the structural and systemic foundations of the enslavement of body, mind, and soul. A liberation of person and personhood based on transformative leadership that empowers both teachers and learners to engage in impactful, facilitated learning. That is, providing an education that breaks down the barriers of our biases and bigotries—barriers that trap us all in the perpetuation of the power structures that oppress our minds, our souls, and our bodies. This discussion argues that educational leadership must break the shackles of current curricula and embrace a curriculum that focuses on the liberation of the learners' thought processes if we are to achieve the liberation of all learners and free our societies from oppression. The very way we see the world is deeply rooted in the structural inequities within our schools that are mostly designed as institutions of oppression and indoctrination. The schools we send our children to are built around the very curricula that are produced by those in power for the maintenance of that power. Educational leadership informed by critical theory can provide the pathway to empower and liberate our school leaders so that they in turn become the liberators of our teachers, learners, and societies. True liberation comes from leadership committed to equity, social justice, and the building of cultures of peace. Liberation begins with throwing off the shackles of current oppressive school structures and curricula. The journey begins with liberated educational leaders.

Richard Niesche examines educational leadership through the lens of Adorno's idea of the culture industry (Adorno 1991; Horkheimer and Adorno 1979). Niesche offers the concept of the culture industry as a critical forebear to Stiegler's more recent conceptualization of a hyper-capitalist consumer industry. He initiates the discussion by looking at the notion of culture industry and its continued importance for an understanding of educational leadership today. He then turns to a more contemporary discussion of Stiegler's work on *psychopower* (2010)—one that considers yet moves beyond Foucault's notion of *biopower* (1990)—to show how educational leadership as a consumerist industry is failing to engage with more critical and socially critical work and scholarship to its detriment. As a result, the field is beset by fads, seductive rhetoric, hero discourses, and prepackaged products marketed and purchased to solve educational concerns of the day. As educational leadership researchers and scholars, Niesche asserts, it is our responsibility to maintain a voice for authentic approaches that are theoretically informed and continue to trouble and disrupt these instrumentalist and *edupreneurial* approaches to educational leadership and administration.

Transformational leadership is a long-accepted theory in the discussion around educational leadership. Kirsch highlights transformational leadership theory's focus on individual acts of heroism and yeoman effort to transform organizations, making it a highly appealing theory (Wilson 2017). However, in recent years, leadership literature has levied critique against the theory of transformational leadership, most commonly represented by the work of Bernard M. Bass (1985). These critiques vary, but are centered around notions of it being too individualistic, being synonymous with stale management practices, and that the characteristics of transformational leaders, such as charisma, often find perverse outlets that come with attendant deleterious effects (Berkovich 2016; Currie and Lockett 2007; Price 2003). This chapter adds a critical theory lens to this critique through the work of Frankfurt School critical theorist Herbert Marcuse and his theory of one-dimensionality. Kirsch lays out the stakes of Marcuse's seminal text, *One-Dimensional Man* (1964), to foreground an intervention in education administration. Marcuse presents here how concepts become reified in a "society without opposition" as ways to only reinforce the hegemony and status quo of the existing order. According to Marcuse, this reinforcement occurs culturally, politically, and linguistically by shaping all discourse to be in service of the established order. If concepts or language become too commonsensical or taken as a given, then that one-dimensionality is all the stronger. This will pose a uniquely ironical problem for transformational leadership since it purports to upend the established way of doing things.

Following up and elaborating on Kirsh's introduction to Marcuse, Patrick Jenlink explores the importance and relevance of Marcuse's work to educational leadership. Jenlink presents Marcuse as a central figure in the Frankfurt School of critical theorists that maintained language as one of the most powerful weapons in the armory of the establishment. Marcuse argued that Orwellian language represents hegemonic thought as a mixture of brutality and sweetness that, to borrow from Kellner, stifles consciousness, obscures possibilities, and grafts itself into the needs of the status quo into the thinking and doing of individuals. This has important implications for the education system with a goal to serve society in that the education system is a system that is most often created and controlled by the dominant political and economic ideologies in the world. As such, educational leaders can consider ways to cultivate new cultures in schools and confront the challenges they face to take responsibility for championing freedom.

Finally, to conclude this more theoretical section, Chris Brown posits the idea of "optimal rationality," which is a concept that stems from a critical engagement of notions of rationality based in Aristotle, Kant, and Habermas. In Brown's analysis, optimal rationality acknowledges that, although people are often motivated by a short-term and self-serving focus, individuals and groups of individuals behave in ways consistent with actions that will also benefit both society and self in the long term. Leadership and educational decision-making benefits from this analysis in that this notion of balance and optimality requires an understanding of decision-making grounded in a society's notion of reason. As well, it requires education systems to provide incentive for this work. Therefore, educational leaders must work to create disincentives to deter individuals—for example, teachers—from pursuing their intuitive decisioning too often, as well as incentives for optimal decisioning by encouraging engagement with research and evidence in practice.

References

Adorno, T. W. (1991), *The Culture Industry: Selected Essays on Mass Culture*, ed. J. M. Bernstein, London: Routledge.

Bass, B. M. (1985), *Leadership and Performance beyond Expectations*, New York: Free Press.

Berkovich, I. (2016), "School Leaders and Transformational Leadership Theory: Time to Part Ways?" *Journal of Educational Administration* 54 (5): 609–22.

Currie, G., and A. Lockett (2007), "A Critique of Transformational Leadership: Moral, Professional and Contingent Dimensions of Leadership within Public Services Organizations," *Human Relations* 60 (2): 341–70.

Foucault, M. (1990), *The History of Sexuality: An Introduction*, trans. R. Hurley, New York: Vintage.

Horkheimer, M., and T. W. Adorno (1979), *Dialectic of Enlightenment*, London: Verso.

Marcuse, H. (1964), *One-Dimensional Man: The Ideology of Industrial Society*, Boston, MA: Beacon Press.

Price, T. L. (2003), "The Ethics of Authentic Transformational Leadership," *Leadership Quarterly* 14 (1), 67–81.

Stiegler, B. (2010), *Taking Care of Youth and the Generations*, Stanford, CA: Stanford University Press.

Wilson, S. (2017), *Thinking Differently about Leadership: A Critical History of Leadership Studies*, Cheltenham: Edward Elgar.

Educational Leadership through the Lens of Critical Theory

Chetanath Gautam

Pakistani education activist and Nobel Peace Prize laureate Malala Yousafzai once shared the following words in a speech delivered to the United Nations:

> I speak not for myself but for those without voice … those who have fought for their rights … their right to live in peace, their right to be treated with dignity, their right to equality of opportunity, their right to be educated.

As I reflect on the words of Malala Yousafzai, I see the value of fighting against injustices in education and society. As a university professor who frequently engages with educational leaders or aspiring leaders, I find many opportunities to listen, share, critique, and imagine the educational world around us. I teach both research and theories. Whenever critical theory is introduced in the graduate classroom, I see my students excited, frustrated, or lost in deep thinking. We identify many injustices that are perpetuated in educational practices, systems, and resources. We imagine a more just and equal educational world. My students develop reflective papers critiquing the practices that continue to marginalize some. Most importantly, we try to install a new way of learning through critique. They further start to critique various unjust practices. We turn toward profound observation and thinking. We additionally continue a dialogic way of critiquing the injustices, unpacking the pains of less powerful individuals in school systems, and meeting their needs to give an equal playing field. I strongly believe, and hope, that such a critical approach of learning helps to grow and nurture critically conscious leaders (Jemal 2017).

Critical theory has a fundamental focus on change in any system. The typical "change that is intended with critical theory is to dismantle oppressive structures that subordinate or marginalize particular groups of people" (Winkle-Wagner et al. 2019: 5) is the goal. Critical educators/leaders have the role of critiquing the propositions and practices of broader social, educational, economic, and political structures. Educators' and educational leaders' moral responsibility is to explore and expose societal inequalities. For them, education should not be the vehicle for creating wider gaps among humans. Instead, they should focus on closing these gaps by equipping and empowering marginalized groups or individuals. How should/do they act to equip and empower them? Are the present physical, social, cultural, economic, and moral infrastructures suitable for this change? These questions warrant a more in-depth reflection on the notion of education itself and educational leadership.

Critical theory demands a critical review, deconstruction, and reconstruction of the entire tangible and intangible approaches to seeing and leading education. It interrogates the power structures of schooling. It critically examines "the knowledge production and intellectual resources used to understand and promote leadership and a concern for social justice" (Niesche and Gowlett 2019: 23). This chapter unfolds around the necessary democratic theoretical framework of Habermas. Habermas's questions—"Why do you say that?" or "Why did you do this?"—help us explore educational leaders' perceptions and practices. These simple questions make every difference in creating democratic dialogue and offer us a starting point for the critical narrative exploration of educational leadership.

Fleming and Murphy (2010) discussed the role education ought to play. Education "involves not only handing on skills, information, leadership abilities, the understanding of the dangers to democracy, but also the creation of classrooms that provide an experience of democratic investigation, critique, and collaborative action planning and implementation" (201). As Habermas suggested, written in a narrative approach of questioning educational leadership practice, this chapter attempts to uncover leadership stories, dilemmas, and critical leadership preparation practices. Therefore, this chapter provides a critical democratic framework of K-12 leadership and discusses practice scenarios in schools. The chapter begins with an introduction to critical theory, gradually unfolds into a different aspect of school leadership in relation to a critical theoretical perspective, and then concludes with a discussion on critical pedagogy, which inspires a framework for critical educational leadership practice.

Critical Theory in Education

Critical theory is a social theory that focuses on critiquing society and its institutions. It was initially developed by Marxist scholars such as Antonio Gramsci and Max

Horkheimer, but has since been adapted by other scholars to apply to different contexts. Clarifying the critical role of critical theory, Fay (1987) summarized that critical theory is "a theory which will simultaneously explain the social world, criticize it, and empower its audience to overthrow it" (23). Kincheloe and McLaren (2005) expressed that "critical social theory is concerned in particular with issues of power, justice and the ways that the economy; matters of race, class, and gender; ideologies; discourses; education; religion and other social institutions; and cultural dynamics interact to construct social system" (90). As well, Kincheloe and McLaren (2005) discussed critical *enlightenment*, which analyzes competing power interests between different social groups. On the same ground, Kincheloe and Steinberg (1997) commented on the shortcomings of liberal multicultural approaches, noting that those approaches fail "to see the power-grounded relationships among identity construction, cultural representations and struggles over resources" (17). The cause, as Kincheloe and Steinberg (1997) suggested, was the overlooked powerlessness, violence, and poverty outside the dominant group in the so-called celebration of differences.

Hogg (2010), speaking about influence and leadership, expanded this idea, stating, "Minorities are at an influence disadvantage relative to majorities. Often, they are less numerous, and in the eyes of the majority, they have less legitimate power and are less worthy of serious consideration" (1185). He demonstrated the need for a critical theoretical lens of questioning. How many of these propositions exist in our present educational leadership landscape? Have we made notable progress in creating meaningfully equitable and just schools? I dare ask the readers to reflect on the two fundamental *and critical* questions: "Why do you say that?" and "Why did you do this?"

Critical Theory and School Leaders

For a school leader, it is important to be aware of critical theory and its potential implications for a school's climate and culture, the leadership visions, and general educational practice. Broadly speaking, for school systems, critical theory provides a focus on the structures of power in school and society and offers a means of understanding how those structures can oppress, marginalize, and silence certain groups of students and adults associated with the school system. Critical theory-informed leaders and stakeholders find a lens to examine ways to strengthen their commitment to social change, and critical theory-informed leaders advocate for a dialectical approach to knowledge creation in schools.

Let's reflect upon some questions: As a school leader, how often have we used critical theory to examine our own schools? Have we looked at the structures and systems in place, evaluated them, and made genuine efforts to make it more equitable and just? If our answer is "Yes," congratulations. We are leading our school system through a critical theory-based framework already. If our answer is "somehow," it is time for us to strengthen our theoretical, social, and practical engagement. A huge commitment is needed. A relentless strength and determination may be required. If we find our answer is "No," we probably may need to rethink our identity as a leader for all. Critical theory can influence the day-to-day operations of school administration, and furthermore it could be translated as *praxis* in the classroom. Critical theory-guided schools advocate for student engagement in critical thinking about social issues. Critical theory-influenced leaders support teachers in becoming critical pedagogues (Freire 1970).

Critical Theoretical Lens for Social Justice in Schools

The management-oriented factory model, or traditional production-oriented role, of a school leader is to administer educational leadership and coordinate support for teachers and students. There is nothing wrong with this on the surface. Leaders are responsible for compliance with state and national standards in implementing the required curriculum. Leaders are viewed as key individuals when they play an essential role in creating a positive school culture and climate, building strong relationships with families and the community, engaging in budgeting and financial decision-making, and implementing school improvement efforts. These umbrella roles have multiple roles embedded in them. Then what is wrong with it? The question is pertinent because all can agree upon these roles. Why do we need a particular lens to analyze these roles? Leaders who are inspired or guided by critical theory advocate and act for social justice in schools (Furman 2012). Educational equity needs a nonthreatening and inclusive environment (Causton and Theoharis 2014).

School should be a place to teach and practice justice and fairness (Aiken 1997). We try to think about schools from the good side of it. I wish that were always the case. However, places like schools can cause injustice in several ways or, in some cases, function as a breeding ground for injustice (Yeager et al. 2017). Schools may perpetuate systemic inequalities by providing unequal access to resources or opportunities for some, or by tracking students into lower-level courses based on their race or socioeconomic status.

Additionally, schools can become hostile and unwelcoming environments for certain students, such as students of color, or LGBTQIA+ students (Russell et al. 2010; Truong et al. 2020). Then the obvious question arises: is it worth fighting for justice in schools? My easy answer to this question is the affirmative. The reality is a bit complicated. The fight is not easy. Schools are systems where historically competition is always preferred. Some of the schools in history were created for the chosen one—the elite few. That DNA may still carry in it the genetics of this type of school culture—the status quo. Social justice and equity-driven critical educational leaders believe it is essential to fight for justice in schools (Wang 2018), even if the odds are not in their favor. This is necessary to make progress toward a more equitable and just society. We know school is where we shape our identity (Erentaitė et al. 2018).

Vaillant (2015), in *Education for All Global Monitoring Report*, called for equality in access and learning and said it must stand at the heart of future education goals. However, more frequently we see news about the challenges school leaders are constantly navigating. Year after year, budget cuts, standardized testing, and increasing accountability are a few of the challenges. The race of the nations and states to be the top ranked adds some interesting dynamics (Holzer 2018). Teachers and students are forced to engage with the materials designed for increasing test scores only. Do test scores represent a holistic view of human potential? If so, why? A simple truth to consider is that perhaps leaders should initiate ways of supporting teachers and students in a rapidly changing educational landscape. Are they able to ask other pertinent questions? They should constantly ask questions like these: How do I advocate for equity in regard to minority students? How do I recruit educators and staff who can make a meaningful contribution to the school and the diverse body of students? How do I achieve at least proportional representations of adults in the school so that students from diverse backgrounds feel connected? How do I build trust with the students' parents and their communities? How do I allocate resources so that the needs of each child are met? What am I going to do about these questions?

A leader with critical orientation, as Dantley and Tillman (2010) stated, "interrogates the policies and procedures that shape schools and at the same time perpetuate social inequalities and marginalization due to race, class, gender, and other markers of difference" (31). Let's take an example of a middle school child coming from a minority and/or low SES background, who always seems to be withdrawn in class, on the playground, and in the cafeteria. They hardly complete their assignments. What could be the reason? This child is, let's say, one among a thousand students studying at this school. There are so many other so-called more significant problems there in this school. Should the school leader go to this individual unit of need? What could be the real story of the child beyond the school? How often do leaders reflect upon such individual cases? How often do they make arbitrary assumptions about a child such as this? How can leaders indeed be advocates for little persons like this child?

The questions I asked here are inspired by one of my actual school visits. When I asked the leader about this child, the leader mentioned that there was something wrong with the school culture. I was glad the leader was aware. I asked, "What are you doing about it?" I did not get a definite answer. In my informal conversation, the middle school minority male student affirmed, "The teacher never tries to understand me." How many such voices go unheard in our schools following so-called meritocracy policies—codes loaded with and developed to uphold the powerful groups' cultural, economic, philosophical, and social norms? Are school leaders advocating for fair and just practices, or remaining silent, or doing business as usual? Do their actions result in differing levels of justice and injustice? Critical theory suggests we work to understand that schools operate under the rules and structures created by the powerful and privileged—policies that are often historically initiated and socially perpetuated. Leaders should also know that they can use their power for advocacy and to practice real justice.

In one of my school leadership classes, I posed a question to my students: how do you support minority students in your school? One of my students, a practicing school leader, mentioned multiple reasonable strategies. The leader shared with the class:

> As a school leader, I can support minority students by creating inclusive and culturally responsive schools by initiating cultural representation and dialogues. I have programs like targeted interventions and support systems to help reduce the achievement gaps. I stand up in board meetings and other forums and advocate for policies and practices that benefit all students. All means each student in the school despite of their race, gender, sexual orientation, family's economic status, linguistic background, physical, psychological, and intellectual conditions.

It was an impressive answer. Well, have we thought about it? Why do we do that? As school leaders, have we ever asked ourselves if our efforts bring about real change? Could we dismantle the cultural, social, and physical barriers that hinder bringing about a notable change? I believe finding answers to these questions and doing something about them is one of the most important tasks a critical theory-oriented leader does. We may need to overhaul our entire way of thinking about achievement. What is an achievement gap? What does the concept of academic achievement really mean? Is it producing a factory worker and leveling them as A, B, C with grading tools? Is it merely to ensure they can contribute to the monetary gains of organizations? Or, is it looking into the development of a whole person—a citizen with the potential to have autonomy in their own lives and contribute to society holistically?

Critical Leaders for Closing Achievement Gap in Schools

What causes the *achievement gap* in schools? This question demands an in-depth reflection. Do educational leaders recalibrate the causes of the achievement gap? Do they ask a few questions to themselves, that is, do they reflect? Reflective critical questions could be as simple as these: What is the root cause of an issue? Who is responsible? Have I as a leader, and we as a school, community, or government, done enough? The theoretical answer to the question is: the achievement gap is the outcome of inequities in the education system. Students from less affluent homes and zip codes may face one type of need. Children from new immigrants' households and English language learners may have other requirements. Children who come from households of historically, racially, and culturally marginalized families could have multiple specific needs. Without accepting these differences, leaders cannot consider closing the achievement gap.

Take, for instance, the impact of the pandemic. Covid-19 exposed the global education system to a fundamental truth. Schools are not prepared to address unique needs. This particularly nuanced and instantaneous crisis was revealing. In the United States, we noticed a prominent picture of disparities in funding, resources, and support. The same controversial and divisive forms of interactions revealed during the pandemic carried over into other forms of contest and conflict. The hostile environment created by political discourses has fomented and now led to the banning of books/texts that question cultural hegemony. Educators are being publicly challenged to not question any form of discrimination based on race, class, gender, or origin. Any perceived antiracist discussion, even including the historical facts of slavery, can convert schools into hostile places, hinder learning, and increase the gap in the achievement of truth. What do leaders say about different forms of discrimination in schools? What are the sources of bias? What do they do about it? These causes could be as simple as possessing some unequal power. Discrimination has many reasons, including historical, social, and individual. It is critical for society and progress that educators and educational leaders challenge these reasons and teach students to do the same.

Do leaders see discrimination perpetuated by institutional policies and practices? Research shows that institutional racism (i.e., racist policy) is real in America and is one of the deep-rooted problems that has devastating impacts on students of color (Kohli 2017). How to fight against institutional racism is another question one leader must meditate upon. The typical approach to fight against institutional racism is advocacy. Being part of the grassroots and having a voice in the correct forum is desired. Revisiting schools' policies and practices is crucial. That means a leader must be a real advocate for the child and the communities who are historically, socially, and economically marginalized. Without accepting the fundamental need for equity in school, one leader may not even see a starting point. The classroom may be a place to begin. A leader who truly wants to close the achievement gap starts with the root cause of the achievement. The root cause is the issues and challenges related to educational equity. They advocate for critical or transformative pedagogy "to perceive social, political, and economic contradictions, and to take action against the oppressive elements of reality" (Freire 1970: 17).

What Does an Equitable Classroom Look Like?

I already discussed that an equitable classroom is one where all students can succeed. Providing additional resources and support to address the need of each learner is the first step. Additionally, an equitable classroom is one where all students feel safe, respected, and valued. Let's think about feeling safe. Schools should be physically, socially, and psychologically safe spaces. One could argue that utopian safety in dynamic human-created systems is impossible. However, the leaders should think about what they are doing about it to get there. Ensuring physical safety is the starting point. We read every day about the crumbling physical infrastructures of schools. Most of these schools have utmost students coming from a minority background (Filardo 2019). Are the schools well lit and well maintained? Do they have security mechanisms and well-practiced and clear emergency procedures?

The second but maybe the most important step could be *social safety*. The common buzzword concepts like "fostering a positive and supportive school culture" cannot be created if students do not feel they belong, are valued, and are connected. Unfortunately, a sense of belonging does not appear to be present among many students in schools today. What can I as a leader do about fostering a sense of community and belonging? Can I engage students in critical reflexive/reflective activities? Have I created policies and infrastructures that demand the inclusion of all students in activities and discussions? Are classrooms, cafeterias, playgrounds, and other common areas considered spaces that foster a democratic culture and sense of community and belonging? Are adults in the school capable of ensuring students feel comfortable and accepted everywhere in the school?

The third aspect, but equally important, could be meeting intellectual and psychological needs of individuals. Each student is unique, and each has a different learning need. Are leaders capable of creating urgency in meeting each student's needs that permeates the school culture? Can the entire school work to connect with the child's situation, to encounter them where they are as a person both personally and emotionally? Additional services like accommodations, individualized curriculum, and assistive technology (Durocher 2019), as well as support and guidance to families and educators, are crucial to meet this goal. How to develop equitable schools remains a subject of reflection for school leaders.

Critical Pedagogy as a Vehicle for Applying Critical Theory in Schools

Critical theory is a philosophy that critiques societal practices and demands fairness and justice. In educational practices, critical pedagogy is a teaching methodology that uses critical theory to empower students and disrupt traditional teaching and learning practices. Critical pedagogy is an educational approach that challenges students to think critically about the world around them. It is based on the belief that education should be used as a tool for social change. Critical pedagogy has its roots in critical theory, and its goal is to empower students to question and challenge oppressive structures. Critical consciousness is the ability to see the world through a critical lens and understand the social, political, and economic forces that shape our lives. Critically conscious school leaders are those who are aware of the ways in which schools reproduce inequality and hence work to disrupt and change these patterns using critical pedagogy as a catalyst—a critical theory-oriented pedagogical vehicle.

Nussbaum (2011) indicated a paradoxical role of education, explaining that education produces both justice and injustice, equity and inequity, advantage and disadvantages. She showed a requirement of critical pedagogical questioning about educational process and product. Dewey (1916) created a foundation for moving away from the traditional process of knowing when he said, "Education is not the process of 'telling' and 'being told,' but rather an active and constructive process involving both the teacher and the student" (38), advocating for the reconstruction and reorganization of experiences by adding new experiences. Freire and Macedo (1987) urged for contextualizing or localizing the pedagogies. In doing so, they stated, "Reading does not consist merely of decoding the written word or language; rather, it is preceded by and intertwined with knowledge of the world" (29), and "Reading the world always precedes reading the word, and reading the word implies continually reading the world" (29). In this pedagogical practice, the teacher supports the student to become creative and be responsible for constructing and understanding their own language of learning (Freire and Macedo 1987), which is "essentially democratic and for that very reason anti-authoritarian" (Freire and Faundez 1989: 45). A critical leader provides opportunities for teachers to be able to use critical pedagogies.

Cole (2005) argued for a transformative role of education and firmly reminded the educators that their role was to foster critical reflection with courage because "challenging the current climate requires courage, imagination and will power" (17). Scherr (2005) claimed, "Education is a socially existed praxis" (148), meaning how people interact with each other and with their environment daily. It includes both the individual and the collective aspects of human acts, the way we think, speak, work, and live. Critical pedagogy and critical inquiry form the "socially existed" bridge that connects the social situation to the feelings and reflections of individuals (Scherr 2005).

Hence, the aim and mission of critical pedagogy, as Scherr (2005) viewed, is to create a safe situation for experiential dialogue. For Scherr, "Recognizing individuals as subjects, as persons capable of self-awareness and self-determination is, then, both an aim and method of critical pedagogy" (152). This pedagogical approach is a well-established and well-discussed critical component of creating antioppressive schools. It is fair to argue for critical theory-oriented leaders to be well-versed in and able to use critical pedagogy as an essential aspect of becoming a leader for equity and justice.

Critical Theory-Inspired Practices on Promoting Equity in Schools

Problem-posing is the central teaching vehicle of the educational leadership prep program I engage with daily. One of the questions used in that process is, how to promote equity in schools? The very first answer I hear is, "Look at your hiring practice." "Hiring a diverse staff member that reflects the student population is the starting point," one of the practicing assistant principals, who was also my student, said. "To do just that, removing systemic barriers for possible applicants is important. Demonstrating true respect and value for them is not optional. They are not simply there to fill a quota," another added.

In this discussion scenario, the class continued. Conversations moved toward meeting students' needs. Providing targeted support and resources to underserved groups of students was another act that leaders said they do to ensure equity in school. Implementing culturally responsive curriculum and instruction and creating safe and welcoming learning environments for all students' needs represent a tireless investment of critical love. "A tough but unwavering love all soaked in care," a third student voiced. For me, this was noteworthy. As a class, we saw a further need to build true and authentic school–community partnerships. This "true" partnership implies partnerships with traditionally marginalized communities, not only with a particular interest group. Building partnerships with families and communities of traditionally neglected minoritized members of society demands a transcended understanding and respect for those communities.

For example, the needs of families from low SES differ depending on a specific situation. Leaders may look for financial resources to assist with school-related expenses; they should create impactful mentorship programs and provide mentors and role models. Likewise, children from disadvantaged families may need social and emotional support. They might not feel safe, confident, or welcomed in sociocultural activities organized at schools. Leaders should always be vigilant to identify the challenges and break those barriers by encouraging students to get involved in extracurricular activities. Students may have specific needs to participate in those activities. Leaders should go beyond to act to provide the necessary support. Most importantly, leaders could play an essential role in the life of students. Intentional social justice or equity-driven acts of leaders help to create and further develop a positive self-image among learners who need some support.

A critical theory-guided leader will genuinely accept that there are inequities in schools. They know that these inequities are on funding, access to resources, access to quality teachers, and access to quality curriculum and instruction. Disproportionate discipline rates and achievement gaps between students of color and other marginalized students exist in schools (Belser et al. 2016). Accepting and acknowledging that the problem exists is a significant first step to addressing the problem. A question arises then, "Who is responsible?" Different parties like the government, school leaders, teachers, parents, and students may pass the blame to one another. However, the greater responsibility falls upon the shoulders of the leader. The leader is the middle person. They could take the side of the powerful, or advocate for those at the lower end of the power pyramid. Without having a more profound conviction and clear critical theoretical orientation, a leader may struggle with how to advocate for minority families and communities. Promoting cultural competence, building relationships with minority families and communities, and providing resources and support are again common words for that narrative. Building real trust with all stakeholders is the entry point.

Equity does not mean lowering the rigor of learning. Equity-focused leaders encourage all students to learn. They genuinely believe in the capacity of every student and set high expectations. They achieve them by providing a variety of engaging and challenging learning opportunities, differentiating instruction to meet the needs of all students, and using both qualitative and quantitative assessment data to drive instruction. Critical theory-oriented leaders know and acknowledge the need of a teaching environment characterized by strong relationships between teachers, students, school administration, and parents. Additionally, the school culture puts emphasis on an antioppressive learning culture (Galloway et al. 2019) focused on each student. As we know, school culture has values, beliefs, and norms that define a school community. A positive equity-focused school culture is created and maintained by everyone in the school community. However, the leaders' proactive and critical steps toward that will help to set a tone. Discriminatory practices inside the schoolhouse and in the community cause a toxic culture that lacks trust or respect between members of the school community. These schools have a 100 percent focus on competition rather than cooperation and a lack of support from school leaders.

Educational equity refers to the principle that all students should have access to a high-quality education regardless of their background or circumstance. This takes into account the different levels of education and spectrum of access that people have to them. In many countries, compulsory education is provided to varying degrees, and it is often free—to everyone. However, postcompulsory education is highly selective and often inequitable in availability and access. Research shows that educational equity improves academic engagement and outcomes for all students, including students from minority backgrounds, resulting in reduced achievement gaps. Educational equity is important since it increases social and economic mobility. Some see the concept of educational equity as controversial. The reason being that achieving true educational equity demands enormous changes to the education system, which can be disruptive and costly. There are few stakeholders out there who think educational equity is impossible to achieve or the concept itself is unfair to students who have worked hard to achieve academic success. The same group of individuals may oppose the concept of diversity and inclusion in the name of meritocracy or individualism. These competition-driven narratives were always there and will remain. The critically minded social justice leader continues to develop policies and procedures that support educational equity, diversity, and inclusion. They create and organize effective professional development opportunities for teachers and staff on equity, diversity, and inclusion (Harrison-Bernard et al. 2020) and opportunities for students to learn in a diverse and safe environment (Tomlinson 2017).

Conclusion and Way Forward

The model in Figure 1.1 is created as a comprehensive summary of this chapter. It depicts an integrated relationship between envisioning antioppressive leadership, student-oriented acts or action, the essential elements of creating a positive learning environment through respectful and democratic cultural awareness, and finally the ever-emerging and ongoing work of leaders to develop their critical habits. For me, these are fundamental to critical school leadership. However, readers are welcome to add other components and further explore. Expansion and discussion of the model will follow in the future work.

In conclusion, critical theory-inspired leadership has been used to promote equity and social justice in education. Additionally, critical theory has been used to examine and challenge the traditional education system by providing opportunities for all students to participate in and contribute to the life of the school. This type of leadership will develop a strong sense of identity and belonging among students and other stakeholders. This type of leadership—a critical educational leadership—promotes a genuine respect for diversity and

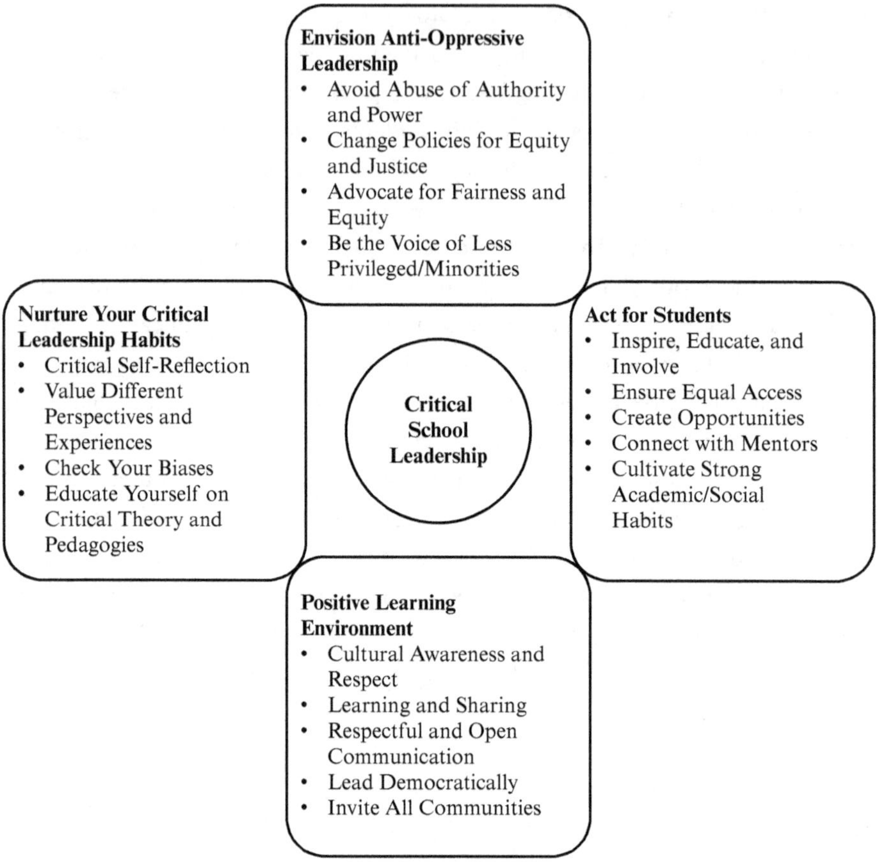

Envision Anti-Oppressive Leadership
- Avoid Abuse of Authority and Power
- Change Policies for Equity and Justice
- Advocate for Fairness and Equity
- Be the Voice of Less Privileged/Minorities

Nurture Your Critical Leadership Habits
- Critical Self-Reflection
- Value Different Perspectives and Experiences
- Check Your Biases
- Educate Yourself on Critical Theory and Pedagogies

Critical School Leadership

Act for Students
- Inspire, Educate, and Involve
- Ensure Equal Access
- Create Opportunities
- Connect with Mentors
- Cultivate Strong Academic/Social Habits

Positive Learning Environment
- Cultural Awareness and Respect
- Learning and Sharing
- Respectful and Open Communication
- Lead Democratically
- Invite All Communities

Figure 1.1 Critical school leadership framework.

difference. It strongly challenges unjust social norms and practices in and out of the school, eventually supporting students to become active and engaged citizens.

References

Aiken, J. H. (1997), "Striving to Teach Justice, Fairness, and Morality," *Clinical Law Review* 4 (1): 1–64.

Belser, C. T., M. Shillingford, and J. Richelle (2016), "The ASCA Model and a Multi-Tiered System of Supports: A Framework to Support Students of Color with Problem Behavior," *Professional Counselor* 6 (3): 251–62.

Causton, J., and G. Theoharis (2014), *The Principal's Handbook for Leading Inclusive Schools*, Baltimore, MD: Paul H. Brookes.

Cole, M. (2005), "New Labour, Globalization, and Social Justice: The Role," in G. Fischman, P. McLaren, H. Sunker, and C. Lankshear (eds.), *Critical Theories, Radical Pedagogies, and Global Conflicts*, 3–22, Lanham, MD: Rowman & Littlefield.

Dantley, M. E., and L. C. Tillman (2010), "Social Justice and Moral Transformative Leadership," in C. Marshall and M. Oliva (eds.), *Leadership for Social Justice: Making Revolutions in Education*, 19–34, Boston, MA: Allyn & Bacon.

Dewey, J. (1916), *Democracy and Education*, New York: Free Press.

Durocher, E., R. H. Wang, J. Bickenbach, D. Schreiber, and M. G. Wilson (2019), "'Just Access'? Questions of Equity in Access and Funding for Assistive Technology," *Ethics & Behavior* 29 (3): 172–91.

Erentaitė, R., R. Vosylis, I. Gabrialavičiūtė, and S. Raižienė (2018), "How Does School Experience Relate to Adolescent Identity Formation over Time? Cross-Lagged Associations between School Engagement, School Burnout and Identity Processing Styles," *Journal of Youth and Adolescence* 47 (4): 760–74.

Fay, B. (1987), *Critical Social Science: Liberation and Its Limits*, Ithaca, NY: Cornell University Press.

Filardo, M., J. M. Vincent, and K. Sullivan (2019), "How Crumbling School Facilities Perpetuate Inequality," *Phi Delta Kappan* 100 (8): 27–31.

Fleming, T., and M. Murphy (2010), "Taking Aim at the Heart of Education: Critical Theory and the Future of Learning," in M. Murphy and T. Fleming (eds.), *Habermas, Critical Theory and Education*, 209–15, New York: Routledge.

Freire, P. (1970), *Pedagogy of the Oppressed*, rev. ed., New York: Continuum.

Freire, P., and A. Faundez (1989), *Learning to Question: A Pedagogy of Liberation*, New York: Continuum.

Freire, P., and D. Macedo (1987), *Literacy: Reading the Word and the World*, South Hadley, MA: Bergin & Garvey.

Furman, G. (2012), "Social Justice Leadership as Praxis: Developing Capacities through Preparation Programs," *Educational Administration Quarterly* 48 (2): 191–229.

Galloway, M. K., P. Callin, S. James, H. Vimegnon, and L. McCall (2019), "Culturally Responsive, Antiracist, or Anti-oppressive? How Language Matters for School Change Efforts," *Equity & Excellence in Education* 52 (4): 485–501.

Harrison-Bernard, L. M., A. C. Augustus-Wallace, F. M. Souza-Smith, F. Tsien, G. P. Casey, and T. P. Gunaldo (2020), "Knowledge Gains in a Professional Development Workshop on Diversity, Equity, Inclusion, and Implicit Bias in Academia," *Advances in Physiology Education* 44 (3): 286–94.

Hogg, M. A. (2010), "Influence and Leadership," in S. T. Fiske, D. T. Gilbert, and G. Lindzey (eds.), *Handbook of Social Psychology*, 5th ed., vol. 2, 1166–207, New York: Wiley.

Holzer, H. J. (2018), "A 'Race to the Top' in Public Higher Education to Improve Education and Employment among the Poor," *RSF: The Russell Sage Foundation Journal of the Social Sciences* 4 (3): 84–99.

Jemal, A. (2017), "Critical Consciousness: A Critique and Critical Analysis of the Literature," *Urban Review* 49 (4): 602–26.

Kincheloe, J. L., and P. McLaren (2005), "Rethinking Critical Theory and Qualitative Research," in N. K. Denzin and Y. S. Lincoln (eds.), *The Sage Handbook of Qualitative Research*, 303–42, Thousand Oaks, CA: Sage.

Kincheloe, J. L., P. McLaren, and S. R. Steinberg (2011), "Critical Pedagogy and Qualitative Research," in N. K. Denzin and Y. S. Lincoln (eds.), *Handbook of Qualitative Methods in Health Research*, 4th ed., 163–78, Thousand Oaks, CA: Sage.

Kincheloe, J. L., and S. R. Steinberg (1997), *Changing Multiculturalism*, Philadelphia, PA: Open University Press.

Kohli, R., M. Pizarro, and A. Nevárez (2017), "The 'New Racism' of K-12 Schools: Centering Critical Research on Racism," *Review of Research in Education* 41 (1): 182–202.

Niesche, R., and C. Gowlett (2019), *Social, Critical and Political Theories for Educational Leadership*, Singapore: Springer.

Nussbaum, M. C. (2011), *Creating Capabilities: The Human Development Approach*, Cambridge, MA: Harvard University Press.

Russell, S. T., S. Horn, J. Kosciw, and E. Saewyc (2010), "Safe Schools Policy for LGBTQ Students and Commentaries," *Social Policy Report* 24 (4): 1–25.

Scherr, A. (2005), "Social Subjectivity and Mutual Recognition as Basic Terms of a Critical Theory of Education," in G. Fischman, P. McLaren, H. Sunker, and C. Lankshear (eds.), *Critical Theories, Radical Pedagogies, and Global Conflicts*, 145–53, Lanham, MD: Rowman & Littlefield.

Tomlinson, C. A. (2017), *How to Differentiate Instruction in Academically Diverse Classrooms*, Alexandria, VA: ASCD.

Truong, N. L., A. D. Zongrone, and J. G. Kosciw (2020), *Erasure and Resilience: The Experiences of LGBTQ Students of Color. Black LGBTQ Youth in US Schools*, New York: Gay, Lesbian and Straight Education Network.

Vaillant, D. (2015), *Education for All Global Monitoring Report 2015: School Leadership, Trends in Policies and Practices, and Improvement in the Quality of Education*, Paris: UNESCO.

Wadhwa, A. (2015), *Restorative Justice in Urban Schools: Disrupting the School-to-Prison Pipeline*, New York: Routledge.

Wang, F. (2018), "Social Justice Leadership: Theory and Practice. A Case of Ontario," *Educational Administration Quarterly* 54 (3): 470–98.

Winkle-Wagner, R., J. Lee-Johnson, and A. N. Gaskew (2019), *Critical Theory and Qualitative Data Analysis in Education*, New York: Routledge.

Yeager, D. S., V. Purdie-Vaughns, S. Y. Hooper, and G. L. Cohen (2017), "Loss of Institutional Trust among Racial and Ethnic Minority Adolescents: A Consequence of Procedural Injustice and a Cause of Life-Span Outcomes," *Child Development* 88 (2): 658–76.

2

Understanding the Role of Education in Emancipation, Liberation, and True Democracy

Robert White

Introduction

The early years of the second decade of the twenty-first century will undoubtedly be front and center in future history books and remain embedded in the psyche of societies around the world for years to come. Years of uncertainty, chaos, and failed leadership has resulted in growing political divisiveness, volatility, and social unrest juxtaposed with calls for equity and social justice in the face of the growing inequities of postmodernity. However, those calls for social justice remain embedded in our history of oppression and seek to replace one set of oppressive power-knowledge structures/discourses with others that remain just as embedded in the same dominance-oppression mindsets and just as unliberated and hegemonically repressive. An unliberated mind can only see power based on dominance and oppression, and therefore the quest for inclusion, equity, social justice, and true democracy remains elusive.

The argument for emancipatory educational leadership is informed by the work of Max Horkheimer (1895–1973) and Herbert Marcuse (1898–1979) of the Frankfurt School of Critical Theory, along with the philosophy of Max Scheler (1874–1928) and John Dewey (1859–1952), the philosophical anthropology of Jurgen Habermas (1929–present), and the sociology of Pierre Bourdieu (1930–2002) embedded in David Hume's (1711–1776) "is/ought" question, Immanuel Kant's (1724–1804) philosophical works on reason, power, and education, Émile Durkheim's (1858–1917) moral solidarity, and Karl Marx's (1818–1883) critique of political economy. The discussion will focus on the application of critical theory for transforming education—education grounded in learning as an act of discovery and seen as a catalyst for emancipation, transformation, and liberation through the development of democratic dispositions. The chapter discusses how critical theory-informed educational leadership can move the system beyond the current model of school for reproduction through learning as an act of construction and embrace ethical education that liberates all members of our society from the hegemonic bureaucratic structural and systemic power-knowledge ideologies of dominance and oppression through learning as an act of discovery.

A new paradigm for educational leadership will be offered and the discourse will provide the argument for leaders becoming not only advocates but also activists for justice, emancipation, and liberation of both the oppressed and the oppressors. The foundation to the argument is the perspective that current and historical social discourse, cultural conversations, and lenses of ideology trap us in dominance-oppression economic, social, and political reproduction. To overcome the cycle of endemic crises we continue to experience through this reproduction of dominance and oppression, a way forward is offered through the implementation of emancipatory education—education that embraces solidarity and focuses on the liberation required to engage in true democracy. Democracy not merely as a form of government but seen and known as a way of being that embraces moral individualism and moral solidarity simultaneously. Or, as Habermas (2015) might highlight, a way of being in which the emancipatory interest of reason can overcome the oppressive acts of dogmatism, compulsion, and domination. Education that is committed to the liberation of person and personhood based on school leadership that empowers all actors to engage in impactful "learning as an act of discovery" through ethical and rational problem-solving learning. An approach to education seen here as providing the bulwark required for the promise of inclusion, equity, and justice to be fully realized within true democracy.

A Brief Synthesis of Critical Philosophy and Critical Theory

Critical theorists argue for a union of philosophy and the social sciences to fully comprehend true human reality for the purpose of alleviating human suffering. This perspective is crucial as critical theory's primary aim is to change society through the process of continually critiquing society in its entirety. The purpose being to find and expose the underlying assumptions in social life that perpetuate human suffering, undermine solidarity, and impede personal freedom. Therefore, critical theorists assert that the social sciences must integrate philosophy into their methods to make its findings practical and advance the moral imperative of freeing humans from domination and oppression.

Habermas asserted that by combining social science and philosophical analysis, the results could be simultaneously explanatory, practical, and normative. Critical theory therefore accepts that social inquiry that does not effectively combine social science and philosophy analytically leads to impoverished thinking and inadequate conclusions for overcoming suffering perpetrated by the power-knowledge superstructures of dominance and oppression. The main argument for this claim is that it provides a path for inquiry to be distinctively practical within a moral sense rather than a merely instrumental manner. Therefore, to begin a synthesis of critical theory for education, we need to compare the two most influential critical moral philosophers of modernity, David Hume and Immanuel Kant. I would argue their thinking provides the foundation for not only critical theory-informed social inquiry but even more so for our purpose of engaging with emancipatory educational leadership within current structures of dominance and oppression.

Moral Philosophy and Education

Kant and Hume agreed on a couple of fundamental aspects of the foundations of morality: (1) the foundation of morality is not located in religion, and (2) it can only be found in mind-dependent facts. Both espousing the belief that it is the role of philosophy to dig beneath the surface of all things and provide a foundation for all human endeavors. However, their shared understanding of morality ends there. Hume's instrumentalist argument was grounded in the view that "personal merit" lies at the heart of morality (Beauchamp 2006). On the other hand, Kant sees morality more as "moral systems" and embedded in an inescapable obligation to duty and laws (Williams 1985). Within Hume's instrumentalism, the driving question about morality is, what motives are virtuous? Hume believed this can only be answered by the responses of others and the approval of those character traits and motives that are agreeable and useful, thereby not requiring a priori knowledge of what is right and what is wrong (Beauchamp 2006). However, for Kant the driving question is: if we are to live a virtuous life, what duties are commanded by law that demand the obligation of a uniquely moral necessity? For Kant, this question can only be answered by reason. In other words, determining the "virtuous will" comes through a priori knowledge of what is good (virtuous) and what is evil (nonvirtuous) and therefore not reliant on agreeableness or usefulness to others (Kant 2002).

For Kant, morality itself is unique, special, and above all other aspects of human life; it is what elevates us to be "persons" (Kant 2002: 46) and is the foundation of our autonomous rational will. In short, it is about respecting the unique rational autonomy of a person as the source of virtue. Hume, on the other hand, does not see morality as particularly pure or special. He believed that morality is no more or no less than any other aspect of life. And although moral virtue is often held in the highest regard, it need not be seen as unique, special, or above other aspects of life. For Hume ([1740] 2002), virtue arises from the same passions that drive all other human behavior. Therefore, Hume grounds morality in human nature, in particular the emotional response our behavior evokes in others. Kant and Wood ([1785] 1996) however grounds morality in the rational nature we share with all other rational beings. For Kant, the will of the moral agent is autonomous in that through reason it gives itself moral law (self-legislating) and follows moral law (self-regulating) without the need for extrinsic constraints, motivators, or authorities. Kant rebuts Hume by emphasizing that the source of morality is not found in the moral agents' feelings, natural tendencies, urges, or impulses, but is the rational will of one's true self that is both self-legislating and self-regulating. It is only through becoming emancipated from heteronomous will (i.e., the will governed by external forces) and embracing our rational will that we can discover our liberty within our autonomous self and live a truly liberated and virtuous life. Discovering the free will and thus the liberation to do what is right, not based on being watched by others but because it is the right thing to do, is what makes human morality special.

Through his writing on the role "rational will" plays in moral development, which is still pertinent today, Kant ([1803] 2007: 41) warned us 220 years ago, in the language of the day, that

> if you punish a child for being naughty, and reward him for being good, he will do right merely for the sake of the reward; and when he goes out into the world and finds that goodness is not always rewarded, nor wickedness always punished, he will grow into a man who only thinks about how he may get on in the world, and does right or wrong according as he finds advantage to himself [sic].

Kant ([1803] 2007) goes on to explain that morality helps us lead an autonomous and virtuous life and that the development of moral culture is best accomplished if based on "maxims" (39) that help us discover our rational will. In other words, while discipline through reward and punishment is reactionary and administered to prevent evil, morality is proactive and teaches us how to think virtuously and live an autonomous and virtuous life while thriving within the social solidarity of rational wills. Kant warns us, however, that even though the reasonableness of the maxims should be self-evident, it takes a great deal of insight from both parents and teachers to develop a moral culture. Therefore, "If we wish to establish morality, we must abolish punishment" (41). A key reflection if we are to move toward educational leadership that embraces emancipatory education based on self-legislating and self-regulating moral individualism within an inclusive and equitable democratic society of moral solidarity.

Critical Theory and Education

Building on the critical philosophy of Kant and Hume, scholars of the Frankfurt School of Critical Theory and others, such as the philosopher Max Scheler, the American pragmatist John Dewey, and the French sociologists Émile Durkheim and Pierre Bourdieu, along with the philosophical anthropologist Jurgen Habermas, enlivened the discourse associated with dominance, oppression, emancipation, and liberation. Although critical theory gives us the framework for exploring and challenging power-knowledge superstructures of dominance and oppression, we should first remind ourselves of Hume's (1740) assertion that we cannot simply make statements of "what ought to be" merely based on "what is."

Although this remains a common occurrence in value statements as much today as it was then, Hume states clearly there should be no "what ought to be" statements merely from "what is" statements if our goal is to engage in social inquiry and theorizing for the advancement of a moral society. It is paramount in our discussion of equitable education through emancipatory policies and practices that we realize that statements about "what ought to be" based on "what is/was" have the power to stifle innovation and transformation for the sake of maintaining the current power-knowledge superstructures and substructures of dominance and oppression. However, by employing critical theory in education, we gain the opportunity to bring our autonomous rational will to bear on the understanding of what is failing, who is being failed, what power-knowledge superstructures and substructures are perpetuating these failings, and what ought to be done to alleviate the suffering caused by these failings.

To gain a deeper understanding of the merging of philosophy and science for the purpose of emancipatory education, we can turn to Max Horkheimer's ([1939] 1982) assertion that the social scientists' main responsibility is to society. He goes on to highlight that sciences' responsibility to society can only be achieved if all its diversity of knowing is interwoven to provide a comprehensive framework that critiques what is of society and combines this with the improvement of society as its subject for inquiry. However, we should understand that all research begins from a socially situated perspective that often provides more insight into who we are in society instead of what is really happening in society.

Therefore, Horkheimer argues that if social science research loses sight of its social roots, it can lose sight of its purpose in society. This is also true in educational leadership; education is a social science and therefore if educational critique and inquiry does not combine philosophy and science in our understanding of "what could be" and only focus on "what ought to be" based on "what is/was," we run the risk of losing sight of our responsibility in achieving an equitable society based on "what ought to be" within a moral society. In short, if we remain enslaved to the reproduction of oppression and suffering inherent in the current organization of schooling, we miss the direction our work might have on transforming society into an equitable and just democracy. By utilizing Horkheimer's perspective for educational leadership, we can amalgamate links between education, economics, psychology, sociology, and cultural inquiry, such that these works can be leveraged to forge a critically informed picture of society, thereby providing the complexity of understanding required to inform emancipatory educational leadership committed to improving society by alleviating suffering through the liberated rational will of the self-legislating, self-regulating individual within a caring and loving community of solidarity.

Critical theory and the enactment of emancipatory education within this perspective rest on the basic recognition of human suffering and the consequent desire that all people have for happiness. Therefore, by engaging with critical theory to inform educational leadership, we can embrace Horkheimer's assertion that no social philosophy (or practice) that denies the singular importance of suffering, and the corresponding desire to overcome that suffering, can properly comprehend the dominance-oppression cycles of human reality and therefore lacks the power to achieve the social transformation required to establish equitable and just societies. Without educational leadership recognizing the dominance-oppression cycles that perpetuate human suffering within society, equitable education will remain elusive.

Why Critical Theory-Informed Emancipatory Education?

As Habermas stated in "Legitimation Crisis," endemic crises are one constant in the modern capitalist state; these arise from the fact that the state cannot meet the simultaneous demands for rational problem-solving, democracy, and cultural identity within the pluralistic nature of postmodernity (Miller 1975). Cycles of increasing crises continue unabated since Habermas' analysis; however, it may be possible that by transforming education we may transform society. However, Habermas warns us that if we are to achieve a stable society free of endemic crises, all members of society must perceive all aspects of society as legitimate. Therefore, Horkheimer asserts that society must be organized in accordance with what is self-evidently true, right, and good by all rational beings. A tall order in our current divisive reality of the twenty-first century.

Horkheimer however provides insight on ways to overcome the endemic suffering inherent in the divisiveness of postmodern society. Horkheimer asserts that human suffering results from a lack of rational social organization and proposes that any attempt to improve society must involve making it in some way more rational. Therefore, to meet this challenge I argue that education is uniquely situated to go beyond reproduction of repressive social organization and engage effectively with developing a more rational society through learning that paves the path for individuals to discover their rational will (the moral individual) while embracing moral solidarity (the moral collective). According to Durkheim (Durkheim and Bellah 1973), the moral individual is the foundation to the unity of a country. It is through unity that we can achieve an inclusive, equitable, and just society, which is crucial for a true democracy to thrive.

Crucial to our understanding for informing emancipatory educational leadership, Horkheimer's work can be organized into four key elements that can improve educational practices informed by critical theory and thus approaches to the improvement of society (i.e., the foundational purpose of education). He states that there must be an emphasis on the reality of human suffering, an understanding of the role rationality plays in emancipatory movements, a combining of the critiques of metaphysics and positivism, and an emphasis on the methodology of interdisciplinary research. By taking these four elements into account along with Durkheim's understanding of moral individualism when implementing emancipatory educational leadership, there needs to be recognition that it is possible to provide a more rational school organization for the purpose of alleviating suffering and enhancing happiness through policy and practice that liberates the rational will from pathological hegemonic power-knowledge structures of dominance and oppression.

If we adopt the perspective that critical theory-informed emancipatory education embodies the potential to liberate individuals and transform societies, we must also understand, however, that schooling is produced, reproduced, and enacted within society embedded in discourses of dominance and oppression. And, that society has powerful forces that seek to maintain domination through inequitable and divisive power imbalances. Therefore, by turning to Marcuse's (2001, 2005) work, we are reminded that within society the forces of liberation and the forces of domination do not develop in isolation. Instead, they develop in a dialectical relationship where one produces the conditions for the other (Farr 2008).

This does not mean that we cannot achieve liberation from forces of dominance-oppression, nor that a stable society is unattainable. But it does mean that those seeking liberation should clearly operate from an understanding of the realities of political division, social discord, and economic inequities. In other words, the power-knowledge superstructures of domination that maintain society's oppressive and unstable nature are deeply rooted in perpetuating human sufferings for the sole purpose of control through division and discord. Therefore, those seeking to engage in the rational analysis and critique of society for the purposes of informing schooling for liberation through emancipatory education need to reject any naivety and come to terms with how things "actually work" within society as a whole and more specifically within the social institutions (e.g., institutions of education) that reproduce the dominance-oppression of the power-knowledge structures of postmodernity that undermine loving solidarity, which for Scheler was at the heart of human beings' participation in community.

Emancipatory education is about providing inclusive and equitable spaces for learners to embrace their liberty as they decide their own future based not on what ought to be through the lens of what is but on their own liberated, ethical, and rational decisions. Therefore, within this call for emancipatory education through leadership as an act of deliberative solidarity, we must reconsider Scheler's rejection of the idea that knowledge is an act of construction, or coconstruction for that matter, and assert that knowledge must be seen as an act of discovery (Scheler et al. 2009). Scheler goes on to highlight that discovery requires the desire to go beyond oneself. We can take this further by understanding that to be inclusive, equitable, and just within our striving for solidarity, we need to be open not only to oneself but also to an ever-richer understanding of self in the complexity, challenges, and discord of the multicultural reality and globalizing nature of postmodern society. In other words, we should see the complexity of reality like a river with all its unique tributaries adding to its flow as it twists, turns, and churns its way toward an ocean of solidarity—an ocean full of complexity and diversity that is constantly moving, ebbing, and flowing as one.

However, for Scheler, the undermining of loving solidarity was directly related to the crisis of modernity that was the result of three central factors or mindsets: (1) the rise of late capitalism, (2) the mechanization of nature, and (3) liberal individualism (Scheler et al. 2009). For Scheler, these mindsets, as are all reductive mindsets, rooted in value reversal. Building from Scheler's perspective of modernity, I would suggest that the crisis of growing divisiveness and inequities in postmodernity and the receding of true democracy are the result of four central dispositions: (1) the rise of morally unmoored capitalism, (2) the mechanization of learning, (3) egoistic (individual or group) authoritarianism, and (4) dialogic incivility. Morally unmoored capitalism, the mechanization of learning, egoistic authoritarianism, and dialogic incivility are reductive deficit model mindsets. A reductive mindset is an uncritical way of viewing the world that devalues all other possible worldviews. A deficit model mindset is a perspective that attributes failure to a personal lack of effort or a deficiency in the individual. For example, the mechanization of learning through education embracing learning as an act of construction is enacted uncritically in the form of direct instruction, or mediated coconstruction through the simplification of seeing schooling merely for the purpose of test scores, and becomes the mantra for many as the only way in which schooling should be organized. As another example of value reversal of these reductive deficit model mindsets, if a learner fails to learn in school, it is seen as a lack of individual effort or a deficiency in the individual, and blame is often uncritically placed on the individual without a critical analysis of the whole. All four of these mindsets are tribalistic and enacted as a value reversal through egoistic authoritarianism emboldened by seeing all "others" (individual)/"outsiders" (collective) as deficient. The value reversal results in the shared promotion of utility of life over value of life. In other words, a person only has value if they are useful. Within postmodern society's embrace of morally unmoored capitalism, the utility of life is simply based on the wealth it can generate. The wealth generation potential a person has can now be calculated by capital through the control and commodification of assimilatory education and the subsequent reliance on standardized test scores as evidence of effective schooling.

Consequently, these mindsets and the utilitarian drive of education allow individuals/collectives to make crude representations of the "other" to justify their perceived superiority both in thought and in action. This justification is then used to perpetuate power-knowledge dominance over the "deficient other" and oppression of the "deficient outsiders" to the point of enacting institutional juridification within schools to achieve compliant assimilation for the standardization of acceptable thought and action for wealth production. Within a Marxist (Marx and Moore 2011) perspective, this can be seen as the calculability of the economic activity potential of the next generation of the proletariat for the wealth accumulation of the *bourgeoisie* (capitalist class).

Consequently, these mindsets continue to devalue all that is valuable (life, liberty, autonomy, solidarity) and value all that is valueless (material wealth, standardization, assimilation, compliance, division). Within these value reversals, morally unmoored capitalism has led to all things and all living beings only having value in so far as they are able to generate more production, more wealth, more power for the capital class who value only wealth and ceaseless irrational accumulation of more and more wealth. This in turn has led to the commodification of education and the rise of schooling for reproduction and uncritical thinking. Within these four mindsets, schooling, instead of being a space for resistance and liberation, has become the main bastion for the maintenance of status quo and a space of compliance for subjugation. The maintenance of power is ensured through the micromanagement of teaching and learning in which all thought and action must be homogenized, standardized, and reenacted under the guise of effective schooling through the receipt of certification.

Education as a Space of Resistance

Although Marcuse used art to highlight areas of resistance, we can use his work to inform our understanding of how schooling works and see the potential education holds as a space for resistance and liberation. Emancipatory education's potential for alleviating suffering, and for transforming schools into just and equitable spaces of solidarity, is suggested here to be the foundation for just and equitable society—a society that is resistant to the constant division and endemic instability that allows the structures of dominance-oppression to maintain their power. However, we must remain cognizant that the desire for autonomy, liberty, and solidarity develops in direct tension with the oppressive tendencies of the social order controlled by capital and the commodification of all things and all persons. Just as education embodies the potential for emancipation and liberation of the autonomous rational will, it remains susceptible to being taken over and subverted by systems of oppression and being used to expand and maintain dominance.

It can be argued that education became a target of acquisition by capital in mid- to late modernity as we turned away from education for enlightenment (Clifford-Vaughn 1963) toward education for the instrumentalism of the early industrial revolution (Carl 2009) and eventually embracing education for reproduction through coconstruction during the second half of the twentieth century. In the late twentieth and early twenty-first centuries, education for reproduction accelerated within postmodernity as capital saw the control of education (i.e., commodification of certification) as a direct route for moving beyond the early capitalists' control of the means of production to the very control of the means of mental production to produce compliant labor.

Moving beyond Coconstruction to Liberation

Although Scheler rejected the idea that knowledge is an act of construction and saw it as an act of discovery (Scheler et al. 2009), and Marcuse provided insight for resisting the control of means of mental production and commodification of education in postmodernity, educationalists have embraced learning as an act of construction and reproduction through overreliance on textbooks, accrediting bodies, and university marketization, in turn devaluing the intrinsic value of knowledge acquisition through learning for discovery and transformation. For example, observe the joy in learning of toddlers/young children as they explore and discover. Then compare this with school-aged children/young people's education activities and their engagement or lack thereof. By replacing the intrinsic value of learning for discovery and transformation with the extrinsic value of education for the exchange value of certification through coconstruction, learning has become impoverished. The natural state of learning (knowledge acquisition as an act of discovery) has been subverted by the unnatural state of schooling for reproduction (knowledge as an act of coconstruction).

Therefore, teaching has become overprescriptive, mechanistic, and homogenized through the micromanagement/scaffolding of knowledge construction for acquisition of favored knowledge (i.e., knowledge worthy only if it has the highest exchange value). Couple this with the market strategist Engelmann's (1980) direct instruction for retention, an approach overreliant on teacher-centered instruction and drill for skill acquisition; and schooling as a substructure of dominance and oppression has truly been entrenched within the social discourse of educators at all levels of education. In turn, these approaches are further entrenched through the neoliberal policies of standardized testing, merit pay based on test scores, and so on. These approaches to schooling are enacted for the purpose of reproduction of hegemonic knowledge, and therefore the emancipatory action of knowledge as discovery becomes lost through the indoctrination and the mediated coconstructed reproduction of the status quo. However, through a critical theory critique of schooling, we can see that the democratic values of emancipation, equality, liberty, and solidarity are needed to transcend the oppressive and divisive nature of the social reality of postmodernity's organization of schooling and the growing inequities of approaches to schooling that reproduce hegemonic knowledge, dominance, and oppression.

If we accept the emancipatory function of education and move beyond reproduction through coconstruction and direct instruction, we can regain learning as an act of discovery and embrace education as a space for resistance, thereby embracing the potential education embodies to liberate the autonomous rational will through learning as discovery and to engage with schooling for discovery, innovation, and transformation. This will develop the freedom required for learners to critically think and critically reflect on the inequities inherent in the current social order of postmodernity. This freedom can then empower each generation to discover the values, ideals, and democratic dispositions that can resist and overthrow the power-knowledge structures of dominance and oppression. A future with the potential to break the suffering inherent in oppressive social orders and reject hegemony in its entirety to achieve the promise of true democracy. Remembering Dewey's (1916) assertion that each generation must be free to decide their own future should resonate with educational leaders who embrace the joy of collaborating with learners.

An Emancipatory Paradigm for Transforming Educational Leadership

Education within an emancipatory and liberating paradigm therefore seeks to overcome the unpleasant, deceptive, objectionable, repressive approaches to knowledge as an act of construction employed in schools throughout the world. Specifically, if the goal of education is to be inclusive and equitable, educators at all levels must move beyond the societal need to restrict learning (i.e., by making it boring, dogmatic, uninspiring, repulsive, depressing, indoctrinational) and make it truly inclusive and equitable (i.e., inspiring, engaging, emancipatory, and liberating) through a sociocultural understanding of learning as an act of discovery. Emancipatory education must reject the behavioristic approaches of reward and punishment as is commonplace across uninspired bureaucratic juridification approaches to schooling if we are to achieve the promise of inclusive, equitable, and just schooling. By embracing the development of "rational will," we can engage in moral decision-making that goes beyond the reliance on extrinsic behavior management, and develop, nurture, and sustain inclusive and equitable engagement and cooperation through loving solidarity enhanced by holistic education and restorative praxis.

To enact emancipatory education and learning as an act of discovery through collegial problem-solving exploration, we can embrace teaching as both a science and an art. This will allow us to gain insight into the complexity of the profession. However, within the reductive deficit mindset of postmodernity, we must be aware that there has been an overemphasis on "scientification" (Weingart 1997: 610) of teaching and mechanization of learning to overcome underachievement for many years. This has resulted in the problematization of disaffection situated in the individual with often little critical interdisciplinary assessment of the systemic underachievement and oppressive nature of schooling for reproduction and learning as an act of coconstruction. This reductive deficit model approach misses the suffering caused by dysfunctional repressive school structures, leaving education both as a practice and as a social science complicit in the ongoing marginalization and oppression of so many.

The uncritical scientification, mechanization, bureaucratization, and subsequent juridification of education in conjunction with the problematization of the individual have led to the art of teaching—or what Biesta (2012) might classify as the pedagogy for publicness—becoming misunderstood, underappreciated, and suppressed, thus subverting the autonomy of the teacher and rejecting the interhuman artform of holistic teaching to develop moral individualism and solidarity through the inclusive and equitable approach inherent in learning as an act of discovery. This rejection of the art of teaching and the embrace of the science of teaching is embedded in the reductive deficit model mindset of dominance and oppression and facilitated through the assimilation processes inherent in standardization through learning as an act of coconstruction for the mechanization of knowledge acquisition and retention. This in turn has led to teacher education being degraded to teacher training, and teachers being relegated to instructors/technicians of uncritical policy, inequitable curriculum, and exclusionary practices that undermine both moral individualism and loving solidarity. In other words, if you focus too much on the science of teaching, you take the love and freedom out of learning and restrict access to education to only those who accept the role of the subjugated. Resistance to the outright unpleasantness of the standardization of education and mechanization of learning for indoctrination within the bureaucracy of schools leads to those who refuse to be subjugated being denigrated, marginalized, and excluded. Therefore, to overcome restriction to education inherent in schools based on subjugation of persons, emancipatory education seeks to engage in learning as an act of discovery for liberation.

Enacting Emancipatory Education through Deliberative Collective Leadership

Embracing learning as an act of discovery requires seeing emancipation as an inalienable freedom to enact our rational will to determine through critical analysis what our future ought to be. Freedom is being liberated not only from the oppressive policies and practices of institutions that enact reproduction for the purpose of maintaining the power-knowledge structures of dominance and oppression, but also from histocultural constructs of the heteronomous self. Emancipation is not about giving others freedom but becoming free through critical reasoning, autonomy, and self-actualization of the moral self. To be truly emancipated, we must first suppress and then reject the drive to control others and be controlled by others. Intrinsically embracing doing right because it is right.

Educational leaders committed to emancipatory education must realize that the space for others to achieve emancipation comes through the emancipation of self and the rejection of paternalism, colonialism, and hegemonic enslavement of the mind, body, and spirit. For educational leaders, this can be achieved through the communicative act of Deliberative Collective Leadership.

Deliberative Collective Leadership

Working from Habermas's *Theory of Communicative Action* (1981b), Deliberative Collective Leadership sees speakers (agents for change) coordinate their action and the pursuit of goals based on a shared vision and understanding that the goals are inherently reasonable (right) and thus worthy (virtuous) of pursuing. On the other hand, Hegemonic Leadership (egoistic authoritarianism) succeeds only to the extent the leader achieves their individual goals whether the vision or understanding is shared or not. Therefore, social coordination through Deliberative Collective Leadership rejects egoistic authoritarianism by embracing a cycle of communicative action for change and succeeds when all members of the community freely agree that their goal is reasonable, worthy, and merits collegial behavior and solidarity. Of course, we must realize that collegiality and solidarity is constantly challenged within postmodernity by Hegemonic Leadership (egoistic authoritarianism) that promotes dialectic incivility so that rational social organization and the stability of solidarity are thwarted by the ongoing rejection of metanarratives of deliberative solidarity. Therefore, it will take leaders who can undertake strong communicative action to overcome the hegemonic control imposed on education and schooling by postmodern power-knowledge structures of dominance and oppression.

To further understand leadership as an act of deliberative solidarity, we should understand that communicative action is inherently a consensual form of social coordination with the potential to achieve a more rational (i.e., inclusive, equitable, and just) organization of the social space. Therefore, emancipatory education enacted through Deliberative Collective Leadership requires strong communicative action (Habermas 1981a) that seeks rational change, which is seen to be reasonable and merits collegial action (dialectic inquiry and debate) and cooperation to achieve shared goals. Deliberative Collective Leadership in turn depends on communicative competence both at the speech act and at discourse level of engagement. Firstly, this requires the maturity (i.e., autonomous rational will) of the actors to first engage in the speech act with the understanding that all claims within the speech act must be open to criticism, revision, and justification. Secondly, it requires actors to have the patience (i.e., commitment to consensus through loving solidarity) to fully engage in the open and respectful nature of collegial discourse if we wish to throw off the chains of division and discord. The discourse level of the communicative acts is about fully engaging in critical dialectic inquiry to test, justify, and build consensus for the change under consideration. In the end, Deliberative Collective Leadership within emancipatory education can be seen as both deeply consensual and reasonable—being achieved through respectful and open dialogue. Consensus-building dialogue, although challenging, is when members of the community freely share their perspectives, criticisms, and questions without rancor. The goal being sincere agreement that the change can be pluralistically justified as just, equitable, and empirically supported/verifiable and merits action to deimplement current policy and/or practice and implement the agreed change.

To enhance our understanding of Deliberative Collective Leadership as an act of loving solidarity, we can turn to Scheler's analysis of the collective person. Scheler's most crucial understanding of the collective person is that of "loving solidarity." For the communicative act to achieve sincere consensus, we must reject division and seek solidarity. For Scheler, solidarity entails two distinct types of responsibility: a responsibility for one's own actions, and a coresponsibility for the actions of others. However, to reject division and discord, we must understand that coresponsibility does not compromise the autonomy and rational will of the individual; every person remains fully responsible for their actions. Scheler sees coresponsibility as a radical form of questioning. Questioning, and the freedom to question and be questioned, is paramount in a stable rationally organized society. Therefore, emancipation is the freedom to question, be questioned, and enact the moral self within the collective life of deliberative solidarity.

However, emancipation without liberty is void of the inalienable freedom of the rational will. Therefore, to fully understand emancipatory education, we must understand liberation as foundational for the rational organization of the social space. Liberation is the ability to live our lives based on the autonomy of our rational will within a deliberative and loving solidarity with others. Liberation sprouts from the freedom of emancipation to engage in critical and creative questioning, thinking, and problem-solving all aspects of society and social life—processes that provide us with the rational will to see the world for what it ought to be based on rational deliberation instead of what it is/was. Liberation in education begins with rejecting learning as an act of coconstruction for reproduction and accepting the emancipatory process of learning as an act of discovery for innovation and transformation. Liberation is the emancipation of thought unshackled from the dogma, prejudices, biases, and bigotries of hegemonic knowledge.

The liberated mind is the true freedom of emancipation if we are to fully realize Dewey's (1916) liberating argument that it is right for each generation to question society and determine the future they wish to inhabit—a future not based on what is but based on what ought to be as determined by the rational will of the moral self through the communicative act; a future based on the possibilities of transformation through discovery of a future unhindered by past and present power-knowledge structures of dominance and oppression.

Conclusion

To clarify, let me highlight that emancipation and liberation are not seen here as about the act of emancipating or liberating, nor are they about the need to have emancipators and liberators to become emancipated and liberated. To be clear, a discourse based on the need to free others or be freed by others remains embedded in the power-knowledge structures of oppression and hegemonic control of all things and all beings. To achieve higher-order thinking and reasoning within education, we must recognize that we begin free, and it is through psychosociocultural processes that subjugate us and undermine our liberties. When we are very young and before we enter formal schooling for standardization, we explore the world and develop knowledge through the act of discovery.

However, when we enter formal schooling, we quickly become subjugated to hegemonic knowledge through the act of learning as coconstruction. This is when liberty is lost and emancipation denied through the reproduction of the dominance-oppressive discourse of indoctrination maintained in the institutions of education as currently structured and enacted.

Emancipatory education is about setting the stage that returns human thought, endeavors, and desires to their natural state of freedom and autonomy so that learning can be an act of discovery that seeks the liberation of self and the freedom and stability of collective life. Freedom and the desire to be free are the natural state of human existence, and therefore emancipatory education is the liberation of the teaching and thinking processes that enable us to openly explore possibilities of our social existence beyond what ought to be based on what is. Emancipatory education is founded on developing the freedom, character, and dispositions required to engage in deliberative collective communication for the enactment of the rational self and the fulfillment of peace through the deliberative enactment of loving solidarity

Marx might even assert that postmodern schooling has become ruled by capital (e.g., education at all levels governed by market strategies and neoliberal policies for the sole purpose of the exchange value of certification). Capital's dominance, maintained through paternalistic bureaucracies of juridification that perpetuates capital's pathological desire to have control and power over all things, carries over into even the production of the mental processes of labor through the commodification of education. Not for the welfare of individuals, communities, or societies but only for the welfare of capital. These pathological forms of control maintain the capital-colonialist mindset of morally unmoored capitalism's desire for the endless accumulation of wealth and power by the few through the suffering of the many. Therefore, let us be reminded that power does not like to relinquish power and that transformation often requires revolution in times of egoistic authoritarianism, dialogic incivility, and excessive power balance inequities.

However, the argument here offers a peaceful revolution in the form of emancipatory education through educational leadership informed by critical theory that rejects postmodernity's pathological forms of control. Educational leadership provides a pathway to empower and liberate our schools so that they in turn can empower teachers and learners to enact their liberated rational self, thus gaining the rational will required to reject the subjugation of the many by the few.

Emancipatory education for liberation and a democratic way of being rest in leadership committed to learning as an act of discovery, equity, social justice, and the building of cultures of peace through deliberative and loving solidarity. Liberation requires throwing off the shackles of current oppressive school structures and hegemonic approaches and curriculum. Educational transformation begins with liberated educational leaders who can leverage critical theory methods to critique the whole of human society and offer learning focused on the alleviation of suffering and the attainment of happiness for all.

References

Beauchamp, T. L. (ed.) (2006), *David Hume: An Enquiry Concerning the Principles of Morals: A Critical Edition*, Oxford: Clarendon Press.

Biesta, G. (2012), "Becoming Public: Public Pedagogy, Citizenship and the Public Sphere," *Social & Cultural Geography* 13: 683–97.

Carl, J. (2009), "Industrialization and Public Education: Social Cohesion and Social Stratification," in R. Cowen and A. M. Kazamias (eds.), *International Handbook of Comparative Education*, Springer International Handbooks of Education, vol. 22, 503–18 Berlin: Springer. https://doi.org/10.1007/978-1-4020-6403-6_32.

Clifford-Vaughan, M. (1963), "Enlightenment and Education," *British Journal of Sociology* 14: 135.

Dewey, J. (1916), *Democracy and Education*, New York: Free Press.

Durkheim, E., and R. N. Bellah (1973), *On Morality and Society*, Chicago: University of Chicago Press.

Engelmann, S. (1980), *Direct Instruction*, vol. 22, Englewood Cliffs, NJ: Educational Technology.

Farr, A. L. (2008), *Critical Theory and Democratic Vision: Herbert Marcuse and Recent Liberation Philosophies*, Lanham, MD: Lexington Books.

Habermas, J. (1981a), *Theory of Communicative Action, Volume One: Reason and the Rationalization of Society*, trans. T. A. McCarthy, Boston, MA: Beacon Press.

Habermas, J. (1981b), *Theory of Communicative Action, Volume Two: Lifeworld and System: A Critique of Functionalist Reason*, trans. T. A. McCarthy, Boston, MA: Beacon Press.

Habermas, J. (2015), *Knowledge and Human Interest*, 1st ed., Kindle.

Horkheimer, M. ([1939] 1982), *Critical Theory: Selected Essays*, New York: Continuum.

Hume, D. ([1740] 2002), *A Treatise of Human Nature*, Kindle.

Kant, I. ([1803] 2007), "Lectures on Pedagogy," in *Anthropology, History, and Education*, New York: Cambridge University Press.

Kant, I., and J. B. Schneewind (2002), *Groundwork for the Metaphysics of Morals*, trans. A. W. Wood, New Haven, CT: Yale University Press.

Kant, I., and A. Wood ([1975] 1996), "Groundwork of the Metaphysics of Morals," in M. Gregor (ed.), *Practical Philosophy* (The Cambridge Edition of the Works of Immanuel Kant), 37–108, Cambridge: Cambridge University Press. https://doi.org/10.1017/CBO9780511813306.007.

Marcuse, H. (2001), *Towards a Critical Theory of Society: Collected Papers of Herbert Marcuse*, vol. 2, ed. Douglas Kellner, London: Routledge.

Marcuse, H. (2005), *The New Left and the 1960s: Collected Papers of Herbert Marcuse*, vol. 3, ed. Douglas Kellner, London: Routledge.

Marx, K., and S. Moore (2011), *Das Kapital: A Critique of Political Economy*, Scotts Valley, CA: CreateSpace.

Miller, J. (1975), "Legitimation Crisis," *Telos* 25: 210–20. https://doi.org/10.3817/0975025210.

Scheler, M., M. S. Frings, and E. Kelly (2009), *The Human Place in the Cosmos*, Evanston, IL: Northwestern University Press.

Weingart, P. (1997), "From 'Finalization' to 'Mode 2': Old Wine in New Bottles?" *Social Science Information* 36 (4): 591–613.

Williams B. (1985), *Ethics and the Limits of Philosophy*, Cambridge, MA: Harvard University Press.

3

Educational Leadership as a (Consumer) Culture Industry

Richard Niesche

Introduction

This chapter brings together into conversation the work of Theodor Adorno, Bernard Stiegler, and Michel Foucault to examine how educational leadership as a field has been seduced by a consumer capitalist industry in the pursuit of "best practice" approaches and "what works" discourses as answers to educational problems and issues. Specifically I explore the notion of the culture industry (Adorno 1991; Horkheimer and Adorno 1979) as an important precursor to what Bernard Stiegler more recently terms a hyper-capitalist consumer industry (Stiegler 2011, 2014), and think how this work can understand and interrogate many current approaches to educational leadership.[1] In addition, I also draw on the ideas of Foucault in concert with Stiegler through the notions of biopower (Foucault 1976) and psychopower (Stiegler 2010). In particular, I argue that there has been a consistent flow of writing in educational leadership that is increasingly designed for ongoing consumption, badged for the purposes of solving many problems in education around the world—with "leadership" as a key driver of such reforms and changes. Thomson et al. (2013) have previously referred to these kinds of discourses as a Transnational Leadership Package (TLP). I argue that these discourses have manifested largely through school effectiveness and improvement research that can also be linked to the rise of gurus, experts, and edupreneurs to form what Kellerman calls a "leadership industry" (2012) but in education.

It is important to note that while one could argue that Foucault and Stiegler are not seen as part of the formal Critical Theory school per se, nor is their work necessarily easily compatible, there is certainly some overlap and congruences between the ideas of these major thinkers (see Cook 2018). Here I am taking a wider view of Critical Theory to include more than just the Frankfurt School. I acknowledge the potential issues of doing so and the criticisms this may likely draw from some readers. However, Bernard Stiegler (2015) argues that we need to revisit the work of Critical Theory (among others, including a rereading of Hegel, Kant, and the poststructuralists such as Derrida, Foucault, Lyotard, and Deleuze) to understand our present condition. I am taking this argument from Stiegler as a starting point for my thinking in this chapter.

To begin, my focus is first on describing Adorno's work on what he terms the culture industry and how relevant these ideas are for understanding educational leadership discourse today. I then discuss Foucault's notion of biopower (1976) and its role in understanding power and the politics of leadership ideas in the governing of educators and educational leadership discourse. In the next section, I move to a discussion of Stiegler's more contemporary work on psychopower (2010)—that moves beyond Foucault's notion of biopower—to argue that educational leadership as a consumerist industry is failing to engage with more critical and socially critical scholarship to the field's detriment.

In the final section, I bring these conceptual ideas together to unpack and problematize the leadership fads, seductive rhetoric, hero discourses, and packaged products to be bought and sold as solutions for educational problems that are so prevalent as part of this consumerist industry. My overriding concern through the writing of this chapter is that, as educational leadership researchers and scholars, it is our responsibility to maintain theoretically informed work that continues to trouble and disrupt these narrow, self-serving, instrumentalist, and "edupreneurial" approaches to educational leadership and administration. I believe there is a need to think deeply and critically about work that will lead to those potential leadership practices that may prove more helpful for educators rather than serve the interests of the international gurus that beset the field and social media platforms (see Eacott 2017, 2018, 2020). The role of universities, academics, and researchers is examined as key spaces for contestation of these ideas rather than, say, at the school level. This chapter is not a criticism of leaders and educators in schools, but rather of the educational leadership industry for which educators are subsumed as consumers to their detriment. As busy professionals working hard in challenging circumstances, they deserve an alternate educational leadership discourse.

Adorno and the Culture Industry

Theodor Adorno is one of the most prominent scholars of the Critical Theory movement, or Frankfurt School, that came to prominence in the 1930s via the work of the Institute for Social Research. In the 1940s, Horkheimer and Adorno shifted to a new line of inquiry in their book *Dialectic of Enlightenment* (1979), analyzing history and culture to show how reason had turned into its opposite as a form of social domination (Best and Kellner 1991). In this work, they referred to the notion of mass culture and later the culture industry (see Adorno 1975 for an acknowledgment of this shift, also reprinted in Adorno 1991) in which advancing societies no longer automatically embody freedom and progress and instead demonstrate forms of social regression and societal administration. Horkheimer and Adorno focus on the role of art and culture in this mythical form of enlightenment progress. The break between high and low art, and the illusions of mass art and culture, reveals forms of domination. In their depiction of the culture industry, Horkheimer and Adorno (1979) outline a number of elements. In this section, I will attend to some of these main points and reflect on them in relation to educational leadership as an example of the culture industry at work. Where Horkheimer and Adorno refer to art and music as examples, here I refer to educational leadership discourse as a corresponding example:

- Sameness, standardized forms— "Culture today is infecting everything with sameness. Film, radio and magazines form a system" (Horkheimer and Adorno 1979: 41). "All mass culture under monopoly is identical" (42). Horkheimer and Adorno argue that film and radio call themselves industries, and that the reproduction process involved through these results in standardized forms that best serve those at the top of the hierarchy. What distinguishes difference then is diluted or done away with in the process of mass production and consumption. Similarly, leadership has become a vast industry (Kellerman 2012), and arguably educational leadership. The development of leadership standards for the purposes of articulating what counts as "good" leadership or "best" practice has resulted in thousands of adjectival leadership models that seek to provide utility across systems and contexts. By the very nature of this reductionist and instrumentalist work, leadership models tend to start to look the same and become decontextualized (I have previously argued this in relation to transformational and distributed leadership models drawing on the work of Derrida—see Niesche 2013a). The normalizing of these models into standards has taken hold in many countries around the world, to the point where they are even used for leadership training, development, and professional learning. Ideologies of leadership as an inherent good are promoted in the pursuit of these industries and consumer dollars. It is a mistake to see this development as serving the purposes of society; as Horkheimer and Adorno argue, "The relentless unity of the culture industry bears witness to the emergent unity of politics" (1979: 43), serving those most powerful and economically advantaged by such practices. They use the examples of Chrysler and General Motors in car manufacturing in the United States as a pretense to differentiate between cars and car manufacturers that serve an illusion of competition and choice for consumers. Educational leadership discourse similarly reports differences in a model or approach to leadership, but ultimately results in a kind of sameness whereby leadership models become largely interchangeable albeit with a different adjective as a rhetorical device. It is the adjectival naming that alludes to difference, but usually results in a similar assumption and hierarchy at work. Numerous scholars have been critical of these many approaches to leadership for decades (e.g., Lakomski et al. 2017; Niesche and Gowlett 2019; Smyth 1989).

- Detail, logic, and specialization of discourse is subsumed into the large economic machinery. That is, the idea, content, concept, or detailed work (research) is liquidated as it is subsumed into the economic and consumerist machinery. The construction of leadership into a consumable and quickly digestible phrase or quip destroys the detailed work and development of the idea. It becomes a consumer item. Leadership as a product becomes the target rather than deeply-thought-about critical, contextual, nuanced, or robust thinking. The producers of these phrases and feel-good assertions of leadership then become the experts; as Horkheimer and Adorno argue, "In the culture industry the subject matter itself, down to its smallest elements, springs from the same apparatus as the jargon into which it is absorbed" (1979: 47). There is arguably no other field than leadership that is more seduced by feel-good catchphrases in the pursuit of consumerist products over rigorous and deeply-thought-about research and content. The expert then becomes the one known for and in charge of the industrial product to be sold via the professional development package, keynote address, and having a turn on the lecturer/speaker circuit. Furthermore, to speak out against this economic and industrial complex, one risks becoming the pariah, the marginalized ivory tower academic out of touch with reality and what the public allegedly want. To truly question or be critical (even though many of the proponents and contributors to the leadership industry say they are critical, they are not) means the real criticalists are ignored, marginalized, or worse—they are subsumed into the industry itself. On this, Horkheimer and Adorno write, "Connoisseurship and expertise are proscribed as the arrogance of those who think themselves superior, whereas as culture distributed its privileges democratically to all" (1979: 50). Thus, what becomes important is the business of entertainment rather than scholarship.

- "The culture industry endlessly cheats its consumers out of what it endlessly promises" (Adorno and Horkheimer 1979: 53). Through the leadership industry, the notion of leadership becomes an empty signifier that promises much but delivers little to those who seek genuine solutions and alternatives. More disarmingly, those customers then become co-opted into promotion and contribution to the leadership industry via advertising on platforms such as Twitter or through professional organizations and networks, and so on. Ultimately, "The blindness and muteness of the data to which positivism reduces the world passes over into language itself, which is limited to registering those data" (70). And finally, as Horkheimer and Adorno argue, "That is the triumph of advertising in the culture industry: the compulsive imitation by consumers of cultural commodities which, at the same time, they recognize as false" (71).

In the "Culture Industry Re-considered," Adorno (1991) covers much similar terrain as the articulation of mass culture in *The Dialectic of Enlightenment* (Horkheimer and Adorno 1979). So, I will not cover the same points here but provide a few further reflections on these issues concerning the educational (culture) industry. While I have been deliberately critical and provocative here in comparing the educational leadership industry to the culture industry, there are other scholars who have done extensive work on education and education policy as a business (e.g., Ball 2012) and also examinations of the influence and role of particular companies such as Pearson (see Hogan et al. 2016), the corruption of schools and education (Thomson 2020), not to mention explicit critiques of educational leadership as a commodity (see English 2013; Gunter 1997). While it is not possible—nor my aim here—to provide a detailed review and history of this critical research into these aspects of educational leadership, it is important to note the longer history of the introduction of business efficiency into educational administration (Callahan 1960). Therefore, the work in this chapter drawing on the notion of culture industry, and next the work of Foucault and Stiegler, is a further theoretical development of this previous and important research. Adorno's descriptions of the culture industry are informative for an understanding of the educational leadership industry still underway.

Foucault and Biopower

Foucault made a point of saying that he found some resonances between his work and that of Adorno (Foucault 2000). While Adorno was situated more closely in the Marxist tradition that Foucault came to critique, it is worth noting that there are similarities as well as key differences in their work and development of ideas (see Cook 2018). It is not my aim to explore these in detail here, but more so for noting this when attempting to bring together their respective works for the stated purposes of this chapter.

Foucault's work has been used extensively in education (e.g., Ball 1990, 2013; Baker and Heyning 2004; Peters and Besley 2007) and more recently in educational leadership (Dolan 2020; Gillies 2013; Mifsud 2017; Niesche 2011, 2013a, 2013b, 2020, 2021). However, there has been less focus on the notion of biopower in relation to how populations are governed. Arguably the notion of biopolitics has been discussed extensively (Peters 2008; Simons 2013) and certainly the notion of governmentality in education (Gobby 2013; Niesche 2015, 2020; Peters et al. 2009), but in the latter part of his book, *The History of Sexuality: Vol. 1*, Foucault shifted his approach to an analysis of what he termed biopower. The conceptualization of this is worth exploring in more detail, especially as it relates to Adorno's culture industry (1991) and Stiegler's approach to hyper-industrial consumerism (2015).

Foucault was concerned with the proliferation of sexuality discourse and the role of power as a part of this in *The History of Sexuality: Vol. 1* (Foucault 1976). He developed this notion of biopower to designate both the individualizing forms of power and also power as exercised over the social body or whole populations. While this may seem to be a long way from the idea of educational leadership, there is a need to understand how educational leaders are spoken into discourse through various forms of governing and through educational leaders' own practices. This is where the notion of biopower has been and continues to be helpful for those interested in theorizing or thinking differently about the work of leaders in education both as individuals and as part of a larger population of educators within the formal schooling apparatus. In my own work, I have been particularly interested in this way of theorizing the principalship (Niesche 2011), but for the purposes of this chapter, I am thinking more generally across both principals and others practicing leadership at various levels in educational organizations rather than a narrow focus on the principalship itself.

Returning to Foucault's notion briefly, he designated biopower as a form of power being both centered on the body or individual (the individualizing power of disciplining as examined in *Discipline and Punish* (Foucault 1975) is one such example), and the organization of power over whole populations, or at the level of the social body. This might be manifest through education policy or leadership standards frameworks specific to educational leadership. For Foucault, this notion of biopower is an essential component in the development of capitalism. Foucault describes this development of power since the seventeenth century as being "centred on the body—through its disciplining, the optimizing of its capabilities and its integration into efficient and effective systems of economic and social control" (1976: 139); and the second "through the regulation of populations through levels of health, birth and mortality, life expectancies and so on" (139).

Foucault argues how the explosion of discourse around sexuality was one area in which these techniques of power were developed. He states when introducing the term: "Hence there was an explosion of numerous and diverse techniques for achieving the subjugation of bodies and the control of populations, marking the beginning of an era of 'biopower'" (1976: 141). As a result, there were a range of techniques of power at numerous levels in the development of the sexualized body. Biopower then becomes indispensable through the development of capitalism (Foucault 1976: 141).

As mentioned above, the proliferation of leadership standards documents and discourses is one example of how leadership as discourse is exercising power over and through individuals and populations of educators. In many parts of the world, school principals require some form of official accreditation to become a principal or head as this requires levels of policy discourse that target both populations and the individual in preparation for a leadership position. This is not to necessarily criticize these approaches but more so to highlight the exercise of power through leadership discourse via these accreditation frameworks and standards documents that articulate what a principal or educational leader should do as a part of their role or position.

Many of these documents are also used for ongoing monitoring and performance review of school principals, thus exercising forms of disciplinary power. It is beyond the scope of this chapter to detail how Foucault's concept of power works in educational leadership more broadly, but more to acknowledge the ongoing importance of biopower as an explanatory concept for how educational leaders are governed (see Anderson 2001; Anderson and Grinberg 1998; English 2003, 2006 for examples of these kinds of analysis and critiques). What is also important to note is that Foucault's work does have some limitations in its explanatory potential, as identified by Bernard Stiegler in his development of the idea of psychopower. It is to this concept that I now turn as Stiegler is influenced by the work of both Foucault and Adorno in his own conceptual development.

Stiegler and Psychopower

In his reflections on the work of Horkheimer and Adorno, Stiegler (2011) argues that their examination of the toxic, addictive, and self-becoming of consumerism has been an important contribution that we have failed to adequately reflect upon in describing contemporary society. He argues that the poststructuralists (e.g., Deleuze, Foucault, Derrida, Lyotard) have ignored this focus, or certainly a focus on political economy through their derision and critique of Marxism. Stiegler sees as problematic the influence of consumer capitalism as a part of hyper-industrial societies. While expanding his analysis and discussion to many aspects of society, Stiegler does also target education as a particular kind of example of these shifts. In *Taking Care of Youth* (2010), Stiegler examines how education contributes to forms of attention control via cultural and cognitive technologies. He focuses on the infantilization of adults and the early maturation of youth through these culture industries as a part of what he terms hyper-industrial society. In that book, Stiegler critically engages with Foucault's work to argue that it is necessary to move beyond what Foucault terms biopower to examine a psychotechnical apparatus of attention control and the politics of intelligence as witnessed through media and technology, and so on. Stiegler's emphasis is on the notion of psychopower through culture industries rather than what Foucault described as biopower through individuals and over populations. As Stiegler writes, "The question is no longer that of a bio-power over producers, but a psycho-power over consumers" (n.d.: 9).

What Stiegler means by psychopower is the consumerist or short-term drives that are no longer formed through desire but rather through techniques of attention control as a part of the culture industry. Also important for Stiegler is how the individual's attention is made of both the psychic and the collective through society—or a form of collective individuation. Stiegler is particularly critical of the development of globalist consumer culture emanating from the United States via social media platforms like Facebook, Twitter, and other forms of technologies such as DVDs, CDs, MP3s, and so on. What is significant in this development is the influence of these technologies in developing the consumerist drive to always be captured by and looking at multiple sites and forms of technologies. It is the attention-capturing technologies for the purposes of mass consumption—and not critical, sustained long-term engagement and reflectivity—that is changing people's behaviors and drives leading to the destruction of both attention and maturity. The conceptual development Stiegler engages in throughout his oeuvre is targeted at fighting these changes (through which reading and writing are important but also compromised too) and recapturing people's attention and intelligence to fight the stupidity (or "performative nihilism" as he describes (2010: 41)) that he argues is permeating society (Stiegler 2012).

Stiegler is also particularly critical of the role of universities in this malaise. He explains how knowledge that is created in universities is that which is also taught in schools throughout Western society and that the shift to consumerism is also developed through universities' research mechanisms and technologies. Stiegler argues that the university must nourish society, and yet it has been caught up in this development of a hyper-industrial consumerist society and that we are poorly armed conceptually to deal with and address these changes. In the following, Stiegler articulates both the problem and the potentiality of the university in its role:

> The *responsibility of the university* [Stiegler's emphasis throughout] is the subject of this book, which thus tries to follow up on the reflections of Adorno and Horkheimer, but by going back over the paths traced after them by the "French thought"—if it is true that, ultimately, the university and the school of tomorrow will be the institutions through which reason-on-potential, always accompanied by its shadow, unreason-in-potential, can and must become reason-in-actuality, that is, must struggle *with this shadow* against the passage to the act of stupidity or madness. But *with* this shadow means not only against it, but by reckoning with it, and by relying on it, and even on the *basis* of this shadow. (2012: 29)

This notion of stupidity comes up in relation to universities and the damage of attention through consumer culture. Stiegler reflects on this via the work of Derrida in describing the situation in which a state of shock can send people into a stupor. However, Stiegler does argue that he believes it is possible to struggle against this economic and political situation that is leading to this reign of stupidity—of which universities must play a key part in this fight rather than be co-opted with this state of shock (Stiegler 2012).

Knowledge along social and psychic lines is being destroyed, but stupidity and simplistic solutions and technologies can be struggled against and the invention of new educational models and concepts as forms of knowledge is important. This was the goal of Stiegler's work via revisiting the works of Adorno and Horkheimer and the poststructuralists. However, unfortunately, he did not live to see further development of this work with his untimely death in 2020.

Educational Leadership as a Form of Culture Industry/Consumerism

In this final section, I draw upon this potentiality of Stiegler as well as the earlier thoughts of Adorno and Foucault to examine how educational leadership functions and has been corrupted and seduced by the culture industry and consumerism. The rise of consultants and consultancy in education is an interesting example of how private industry has entered the education arena with the development of a new kind of policy actor via the education consultant (Gunter and Mills 2017). The leadership industry (Kellerman 2012) has been underway for several decades and is a multi-million-dollar industry in which leadership (and educational leadership) as a discourse is both constructed and promoted as a source of educational solution to the various crises in education in many countries. This rise of a leadership culture industry coincides with the rise of neoliberal approaches to education with the privatization of education provision and shifts to school-based management and school autonomy along with the promotion of choice and marketization in education.

These issues have been explored at length elsewhere, so it is not my aim to repeat these arguments and critiques here. However, what is important to note is the rise of the education expert, gurus, and the 4Cs according to Gunter and Mills (2017) —consultant, consulting, consultation, and consultancy. This has become a vast industry in the selling of services and products (see Ball 2007) with significant effects and consequences for notions of leadership, the role of public education, and the commercialization of research into products and services. Gunter and Mills (2017) distinguish between the education professional as consultant, the corporate consultant, and the researcher as consultant. Of particular note is this notion of researcher as consultant, or the academic as consultant, that I want to explore here.

The idea of the researcher as consultant indicates the shifting role of academics and/or academia in society whereby over recent decades there has been a notable shift towards an emphasis on public and societal impact and engagement as part of the individual academic's performance criteria and, more broadly, university key performance indicators. The increasing reliance on academics to bring in research grant dollars and funding and actively seek out consultancies to fund their research activities has led to a shift in the kind of knowledge that is being produced and the kinds of research that are being conducted. At face value it might be easy to say that this is necessary and important as it means academics can be seen to be solving "real-world problems" and conducting research into areas of great public need and interest. However, this is a form of governance of knowledge production and what counts as both knowledge itself and important knowledge. An example in education is the "what works" and "best practice" discourses for solving education problems, of which educational leadership has been constructed as an integral part of any solution (or, at least, certainly a particular kind of leadership).

It is necessary to state that I am not arguing that educational leadership (or rather the work of school and educational leaders) is not important. It is indeed important. However, what is constructed as "good leadership" and the kind of research that is being conducted can be limited by such instrumentalist approaches and research designs to serve government and private purposes and thus for wider consumption. This type of work often goes hand in hand with a failure to adequately consider the complexity and nuances of context. Approaches involving critical social theory, for example, are then seen as abstract academic pursuits that can get in the way of solving education's real-world problems via funded research projects that might become more about attracting research dollars and the selling of education products as an end in itself for some academics, universities, and professional organizations. Furthermore, theories informing understandings of society, culture, religion, politics, policy, economics, and so on, while being removed from grant applications and bids altogether, might also be approached as unproblematically described to become more palatable for media and popular consumption.

What can be seen in these changing research environments is the shifting of research into the impact and engagement discourse—thus changing the kinds of critical questions that can be asked about a particular issue, often at the whims of those providing the research dollars, rather than the conducting of independent, rigorous, and high-quality research. The impact and engagement agenda now seen as a core part of academic work has seen the rise of education gurus who cultivate followership rather than engaging in high-quality rigorous research (see Eacott 2018, 2020). Research becomes more about the popular dissemination and profit. The education celebrity or "expert" then sets out on a lucrative speaking circuit based on this high level of followership, likes, citations, and branding that can reach cult status in some settings (Eacott 2017), thereby selling their brand of solutions and creating an education (culture) industry. A form of hyper-industrial consumer industry is built, complicit in the creation of educators and practitioners as consumers for education products to be bought and sold. There are elements here of Adorno's culture industry, in addition to Foucault's notion of biopower and Stiegler's psychopower in the development and expansion of this phenomenon. One only needs to look at some of the publicization on Twitter for examples of this gratuitous self-promotion hidden under the guise of "sharing" or disseminating "research."

That is why I have brought together the ideas of these three thinkers even though there may be significant tensions between their work in many respects. However, bringing them together may help to better understand and critically interrogate the situation in education discourse whereby educators, and those in schools such as teachers and principals, are necessarily created as consumers to keep this industry functioning. In the aims of Stiegler, it also may provide a new set of tools or language with which to speak out against problematic actions and behaviors. This multi-million-dollar industry supports certain, but not all, academics as consultants to sell their solutions and products. It also sustains the universities that require this model of "researcher as celebrity" as it fosters the creation of forms of pursuits (and in some cases whole departments created) like "knowledge exchange." John Smyth (2017) has written about the toxic effects of zombie leadership and rising rock stars of academia as a damning critique of the modern university. Others such as Richard Hil and Raewyn Connell have also raised concerns about the shifts in universities in recent years toward neoliberal ideologies in managerialism and privatization (Connell 2010, 2013, 2015; Hil 2012, 2015).

Stiegler reflects on these developments in universities as forms of systemic stupidity in which theoretical and deep knowledge is proletarianized and liquidated in favor of forms of knowledge to be quickly consumed. In fact, knowledge can itself become stupid, according to Stiegler (2012). Alvesson and Spicer have written about the stupidity paradox with particular attention given to what they term "leadership-induced stupidity" (2016: 101). Here they describe a huge leadership industry whereby leaders develop and work with deluded ideas about leadership that rely on "flawed reasoning and pseudo-science" (103). In spite of this, leadership still emerges with models and approaches that overemphasize the importance of the agentic individual at the top (or in a position of authority) despite the needs and contexts that might warrant a different set of actions or practices. As Alvesson and Spicer write, "Continuing to believe in leadership when the circumstances don't warrant it may not be particularly wise" (110)—or certainly systemic stupidity in action. However, the consumerist drives and attention, as described by Stiegler, can also help explain this situation. This "big noting" or boasting, of leadership gives rise to the leadership industry that is so revered by its proponents and in many cases revered by professionals in schools crying out for help in their day-to-day work.

The current crises in education in Australia (and, in fact, in many Western countries) as described by crisis writers include issues around declining educational performance over the last two decades, a lack of trust in teachers, overwork and work intensification reported by teachers and principals, a shortage of people going into and staying in teaching, and the list goes on. It is disingenuous and problematic to promote solutions that rely on leadership gurus and the leadership industry (and the dollars to go with it) that have clearly had little impact so far. Preference is given to "research" that is "evidence-based" and often via meta-analyses as the tool of choice for the "best" evidence for a particular model or intervention to take hold (read: *bring in the income*). This then helps to elevate the promoter to guru status or expert as they can then do the rounds of keynote circuit, establish a consultancy business, or even obtain an academic title of professor for credibility.

Conclusion

As I already stated, this is a provocative charge against the educational leadership industry. I am not the first to write about this as demonstrated by other scholars referenced throughout this chapter. However, in this chapter, I have attempted to think critically via the work of Adorno, Foucault, and Stiegler to understand this phenomenon so that it is possible to continue to speak out against this deleterious situation. And, more theoretically informed and robust concepts and theories can be further developed to demonstrate the role of Critical Theory and critical perspectives as integral to the field of educational leadership, and not just from the outside looking in. My position as a researcher on educational leadership, while also being critical of the educational leadership industry, is a position of difficulty, tension, and potential marginalization. However, it is a necessary and important work.

I began this chapter with a brief examination of Adorno's and Horkheimer's writing on mass culture along with Adorno's further reflections on the culture industry. I then moved to look at Foucault's writing on biopower as a way of explaining how educational leadership discourse governs individual leaders and leadership discourse. In the third section, I explained the work of Stiegler on consumer capitalism and psychopower in his critical engagement with both Adorno and Foucault to develop new tools and concepts for critique of this culture industry. Finally, I reflected more deeply on issues specific to educational leadership discourse and the role of educational leadership industry in promoting its own generation of business entrepreneurs and various forms of consumerism in the development of this industry. The danger, of course, is that proponents of the educational leadership industry can simply ignore these reflections and theorizations via the claim that they simply disagree and that they do not see educational leadership as portrayed in this way. I have certainly experienced these critiques before. Therefore, the potential "siloing" of perspectives will continue (Lakomski et al. 2017), and the field will be compromised as a result. However, it is nonetheless necessary and important to continue to speak out against that which is intolerable, and it is a responsibility of us as scholars of educational leadership to create space and opportunities to develop critically informed, theoretically rich approaches to these issues—and to see them as valuable and not simply to be pushed aside for the latest fad and seductive short-term solution, for this does all of us a disservice in the pursuit of a stronger education system and society. Coming back to Adorno, one must note the importance of education (and educational leadership) as a critical practice, and to "disconnect commonsense learning from the narrow ideological impact of mass media" (Giroux 2004: 13). There is an opportunity for educational leadership researchers and scholars to become more critical, think more deeply, engage in debate and dialogue rather than vacuous and seductive slogans, and resist problematic discourses and approaches that simply serve the culture industry.

Note

1 The practice of educational leadership can be substantially different in primary/secondary schools than in universities and colleges. Concepts such as biopower and

psychopower are used in analyzing educational leadership, and it should be clarified that these concepts lend complex and nuanced depth to framing and critiquing these variations. However, this nuance neither fits within the scope of this chapter, nor is it the purpose of the work presented here.

References

Adorno, T. W. (1975), "Culture Industry Re-considered," *New German Critique* 6: 12–19.
Adorno, T. W. (1991), *The Culture Industry: Selected Essays on Mass Culture*, ed. J. M. Bernstein, London: Routledge.
Alvesson, M., and A. Spicer (2016), *The Stupidity Paradox: The Power and Pitfalls of Functional Stupidity at Work*, London: Profile Books.
Anderson, G. (2001), "Disciplining Leaders: A Critical Discourse Analysis of the ISLLC National Examination and Performance Standards in Educational Administration," *International Journal of Leadership in Education* 4 (3): 199–216.
Anderson, G., and J. Grinberg (1998), "Educational Administration as a Disciplinary Practice: Appropriating Foucault's View of Power, Discourse and Method," *Educational Administration Quarterly* 34 (3): 329–53.
Baker, B. M., and K. E. Heyning (eds.) (2004), *Dangerous Coagulations? The Uses of Foucault in the Study of Education*, New York: Peter Lang.
Ball, S. J. (ed.) (1990), *Foucault and Education: Disciplines and Knowledge*, London: Routledge.
Ball, S. J. (2007), *Education PLC*, London: Routledge.
Ball, S. J. (2012), *Global Education INC. New Policy Networks and the Neo-Liberal Imaginary*, London: Routledge.
Ball, S. J. (2013), *Foucault, Power and Education*, London: Routledge.
Best, S., and D. Kellner (1991), *Postmodern Theory: Critical Interrogations*, New York: Guilford Press.
Callahan, R. E. (1960), *The Cult of Efficiency*, Chicago: University of Chicago Press.
Connell, R. (2010), "Building the Neoliberal World: Managers as Intellectuals in a Peripheral Economy," *Critical Sociology* 36 (6): 777–92.
Connell, R. (2013), "The Neoliberal Cascade and Education: An Essay on the Market Agenda and Its Consequences," *Critical Studies in Education* 54 (2): 99–112.
Connell, R. (2015), "Markets All Around: Defending Education in a Neoliberal Time," in H. Proctor, P. Brownlee, and P. Freebody (eds.), *Controversies in Education: Orthodoxy and Heresy in Policy and Practice*, 181–97, Cham: Springer.
Cook, D. (2018), *Adorno, Foucault and the Critique of the West*, London: Verso.
Dolan, C. (2020), *Paradox and the School Leader: The Struggle for the Soul of the Principal in Neoliberal Times*, Singapore: Springer.

Eacott, S. (2017), "School Leadership and the Cult of the Guru: The Neo-Taylor-ism of Hattie," *School Leadership and Management* 37 (4): 413–26.

Eacott, S. (2018), "Educational Leadership Researchers, (Social) Scientific Credibility, and the Kardashian Index." https://ssrn.com/abstract=3248811 or http://dx.doi.org/10.2139/ssrn.3248811.

Eacott, S. (2020), "Educational Leadership Research, Twitter and the Curation of Followership," *Leadership, Education, Personality: An Interdisciplinary Journal* 2: 91–9.

English, F. W. (2003), "Cookie-Cutter Leaders for Cookie-Cutter Schools: The Teleology of Standardization and the De-legitimization of the University in Educational Leadership Preparation," *Leadership and Policy in Schools* 2 (1): 27–46.

English, F. W. (2006), "The Unintended Consequences of a Standardised Knowledge Base in Advancing Educational Leadership Preparation," *Educational Administration Quarterly* 42 (3): 461–72.

English, F. W. (2013), *Educational Leadership in the Age of Greed*, Ypsilanti, MI: NCPEA Publications.

Foucault, M. (1975), *Discipline and Punish: The Birth of the Prison*, Harmondsworth: Penguin.

Foucault, M. (1976), *The History of Sexuality: Vol. 1*, Harmondsworth: Penguin.

Foucault, M. (2000), *Essential Works of Foucault (1954–1984), Vol. 3: Power*, ed. J. D. Faubion, New York: New Press.

Gillies, D. (2013), *Educational Leadership and Michel Foucault*, London: Routledge.

Giroux, H. A. (2004), "What Might Education Mean after Abu Graib? Revisiting Adorno's Politics of Education," *Comparative Studies of South Asia, Africa and the Middle East* 24 (1): 5–24.

Gobby, B. (2013), "Principal Self-Government and Subjectification: The Exercise of Principal Autonomy in the Western Australian Independent Public Schools Programme," *Critical Studies in Education* 54: 273–85.

Gunter, H. (1997), *Rethinking Education: The Consequences of Jurassic Management*, London: Cassell.

Gunter, H. M., and C. Mills (2017), *Consultants and Consultancy: The Case of Education*, New York: Springer.

Hil, R. (2012), *Whackademia: An Insider's Account of the Troubled University*, Sydney: NewSouth.

Hil, R. (2015), *Selling Students Short: Why You Won't Get the University Education You Deserve*, Sydney: Allen & Unwin.

Hogan, A., S. Sellar, and R. Lingard (2016), "Commercialising Comparison: Pearson Puts the TLC in Soft Capitalism," *Journal of Education Policy* 31 (3): 243–58.

Horkheimer, M., and T. W. Adorno (1979), *Dialectic of Enlightenment*, London: Verso.

Kellerman, B. (2012), *The End of Leadership*, New York: HarperCollins.

Lakomski, G., S. Eacott, and C. W. Evers (eds.) (2017), *Questioning Leadership: New Directions for Educational Organisations*, London: Routledge.

Mifsud, D. (2017), *Foucault and School Leadership Research: Bridging Theory and Method*, London: Bloomsbury.

Niesche, R. (2011), *Foucault and Educational Leadership: Disciplining the Principal*, London: Routledge.

Niesche, R. (2013a), *Deconstructing Educational Leadership: Derrida and Lyotard*, London: Routledge.

Niesche, R. (2013b), "Foucault, Counter-Conduct and School leadership as a Form of Political Subjectivity," *Journal of Educational Administration and History* 45 (2): 144–58.

Niesche, R. (2015), "Governmentality and MySchool: School Principals in Societies of Control," *Educational Philosophy and Theory* 47 (2): 133–45.

Niesche, R. (2020), "Subjectivity and the School Principal: Governing at the Intersection of Power and Truth," in R. Niesche and A. Heffernan (eds.), *Theorising Identity and Subjectivity in Educational Leadership Research*, 140–53, London: Routledge.

Niesche, R. (2021), "The Archaeology of Educational Leadership as an Enunciative Field," in F. English (ed.), *The Palgrave Handbook of Educational Leadership and Management Discourse*, 1–14, London: Palgrave.

Niesche, R., and C. Gowlett (2019), "Critical Perspectives in Educational Leadership: A New 'Theory Turn'?," in *Social, Critical and Political Theories for Educational Leadership*, 17–34, Singapore: Springer.

Peters, M. (2008), "Foucault, Biopolitics and the Birth of Neoliberalism," *Critical Studies in Education* 48 (2): 165–78.

Peters, M. A., and T. Besley (2007), *Why Foucault? New Directions in Educational Research*, New York: Peter Lang.

Peters, M. A., T. Besley, M. Olssen, S. Maurer, and S. Weber (eds.) (2009), *Governmentality Studies in Education*, Rotterdam: Sense.

Simons, M. (2013), "Learning as Investment: Notes on Governmentality and Biopolitics," *Educational Philosophy and Theory* 38 (4): 523–40.

Smyth, J. (ed.) (1989), *Critical Perspectives on Educational Leadership*, London: Routledge Falmer.

Smyth, J. (2017), *The Toxic University: Zombie Leadership, Academic Rock Stars and Neoliberal Ideology*, London: Palgrave Macmillan.

Stiegler, B. (2010), *Taking Care of Youth and the Generations*, Stanford, CA: Stanford University Press.

Stiegler, B. (2011), *The Decadence of Industrial Democracies*, Cambridge: Polity Press.

Stiegler, B. (2014), *The Lost Spirit of Capitalism*, Cambridge: Polity Press.

Stiegler, B. (2015), *States of Shock: Stupidity and Knowledge in the 21st Century*, Cambridge, MA: Polity.

Stiegler, B. (n.d.), "Biopower, Psychopower and the Logic of the Scapegoat." http://arsindustrialis.org/node/2924.

Thomson, P. (2020), *School Scandals: Blowing the Whistle on the Corruption of Our Education System*, Bristol: Policy Press.

Thomson, P., H. M. Gunter, and J. Blackmore (2013). "Series Forward," in H. M. Gunter (ed.), *Educational Leadership and Hannah Arendt*, London: Routledge.

4

Is Transformational Leadership One-Dimensional?

Robert E. Kirsch

Introduction

Transformational leadership has proliferated across many areas of scholarship, but perhaps taking root most firmly in the realms of business and education. It is not hard to see why; the allure of transformational leadership is multivalent. By relying on one person to be able to instill vision and change followers' hearts and minds toward the bright future of an organization, it is an economical and totalizing attempt at changing the culture with high rewards. However, all is not well with transformational leadership. Though much is promised on the backs of one leader, transformational leadership is plagued with conceptual, empirical, and falsifiability problems. Yet, it enjoys pride of place among many leadership scholars, not least in the field of education research. This chapter seeks to analyze why this is the case and does so by adding an ideological critique of transformational leadership from the "Frankfurt School" critical theory of society, particularly Herbert Marcuse's contribution to this body of critical theory.

Specifically, it deploys the "one-dimensionality" thesis in Marcuse's 1964 *One-Dimensional Man*, as well as his methodology of "immanent critique," which emphasizes the gap between theory and lived reality to prod theory to build stronger positive formulations while avoiding simply reifying existing social relations. The promise of this intervention, then, is that it not only addresses the critiques of transformational leadership theory from empirical objections, about its falsifiability, validity, and so on, but also places it in broader social contexts to gain a critical vantage of the social forces shaping the discourse around the theory in question, which adds a layer of complexity about a given theory's usefulness.

The chapter investigates what kind of ideological work transformational theory performs, how the theory itself reifies existing social relations in the established order, and then offers what a critical conception of transformational leadership might look like that could break out of the one-dimensional view of currently existing transformational leadership that will lead scholarship in transformation leadership to become more, as Marcuse formulates as a central aim of critical theory, "adequate to its task."

The Promise of Transformational Leadership

Transformational leadership originated in James MacGregor Burns's book *Leadership*, and his conceptualization of transformational (Burns called it "transforming") leadership is rooted in historicopolitical change, and transformational leadership is one borne out of the turmoil of reform/revolutionary scenarios happening on a global scale (Burns 1978). In Burns's conception, transformational possibilities require that the leader focus on normative values like "liberty, justice, [and] equality" and "'raise' their followers up through levels of morality" (1978: 449). Burns also cautions that these levels of morality must remain uncorrupted, or bad outcomes may emerge. While this may seem innocuous, this is an important insertion of ideology into the notion of transformational leadership. The idea of corruption introduces a teleological notion that presumes a normative element of morally good or bad outcomes.

How those are to be adjudicated is not explained in Burns's text, and his use of world-historical dictators, war criminals, and practitioners of genocide might be instructive on the sweeping stage of historical development but says little about transformational leadership in its other scholarly—to say nothing of its everyday—applications. Still, these normative foundations set the stage for a notion of leadership where a leader builds a coalition of followers toward a morally righteous objective through reform or revolution. In other words, a transformational leader is definitionally a morally good leader, and these morals are agreed upon prior to the leader–follower relationship (Price 2003). Whether this formulation presents any problems or ambiguity regarding shared, ethical, charismatic, or authentic leadership is explored later in the chapter, but having a shared normative foundation is vital for transformational leadership to take hold.

It is easy to see how that relationship can translate to organizations. Rather than limiting its use to its genesis in theories and practices of statecraft, the level of analysis can be applied to organizations like businesses or education.

The logic remains the same—a leader who can raise the morality of their followers to achieve the vision of the organization more effectively. The seminal work of transformational leadership in its broader organizational contexts is Bernard Bass's *Leadership and Performance beyond Expectations* (1985). Here, Bass lays out the four basic psychological drives that prompt transformational organizational change: idealized influence, inspirational motivation, intellectual stimulation, and individualized consideration. These are broad concepts, but generally mean exhibiting the behaviors the leader wants followers to emulate, being able to charismatically articulate and invite others into a shared vision, inviting a variety of perspectives to overcome challenges, and making sure that followers have their needs individually attended to (Avolio et al. 1991). Others have formulated different operationalizations but tend to be related to these initial offerings from Bass. In any case, the emphasis is on the psychology of leadership behavior to engender organizational change.

This emphasis on psychology makes sense given how much of the effectiveness of transformational leadership is on the basis of the heroic efforts of individuals, at all levels of an organization, not just the rarified air of heads of state (Bass 1995). The theory purports to measure the behaviors of effective leaders in the same way Burns describes above; by pursuing these four "I"s, transformational leaders are able to raise the level of morality, turn followers into leaders, and pursue effective behaviors that meet organizational goals (Bass 1985). Bass insists that transformational leadership is both quantitative and qualitative and that the effectiveness of the transformational properties of the leader can be captured both objectively and subjectively by way of personality traits such as charisma (Bass 1995). Such a holistic approach is necessary to move the theory down from statecraft to organizational change and development.

The applied study of transformational leadership tries to capture these various strands of effectiveness, with an initial culmination in the Multifactor Leadership Questionnaire (MLQ) (Bass and Avolio 1990). While revised and tweaked since, the MLQ remains the standard for measuring transformational effectiveness and provides metrics for just how transformational a given leader is. However, a tension emerges here. If the MLQ can measure indicia of transformational effectiveness, then how transformational can the leadership—which, again, purports to overhaul an organizational culture through bold efforts—really be? A genuinely revolutionary change seems difficult to measure piecemeal as discrete variable relationships. Still, the MLQ is the central basis for those researchers who begin from a base of logical positivism and the subsequent need to measure the phenomena in question (Bass and Avolio 1990).

In business organizations, scholars have analyzed the effects of transformational leadership on organizational behaviors, such as employee creativity (Cheung and Wong 2011), how it enhances organizational innovation (Charbonnier-Voirin et al. 2010; Jung et al. 2003, 2008), its effects on team performance (Schaubroeck et al. 2007), its relationship to organizational trust (Podsakoff et al. 1990), and how it might help achieve diversity, equity, and inclusion initiatives in organizations (Chun and Evans 2015; Velasco and Sansone 2019). There are two key insights to take from this use of transformational leadership. First, it generally follows the trajectory presented in the MLQ, namely that these various operationalized behaviors, outcomes, and attitudes can be measured against organizational goals to gauge the effectiveness of a leader as transformational. Second, and perhaps more interesting, is the underlying normative assumptions that guide these questions. As established above, transformational leadership always already has normative assumptions baked into its conceptual framework. In this case, the idea is that concepts like team trust are necessarily geared toward broader, measurable, organizational goals, or at least that they can never have divergent purposes. Thus, to be operationalized and measurable, these phenomena are reduced to a function of the broader organizational aim. This may be appropriate, but it forecloses other conceptions of these behaviors, attitudes, and personality traits. Many of the critiques of logical positivism apply here, about the supposedly neutral positional vacuum of research and how these lead to reifying existing social relations (Popper 2002), which will be explored further below. Still, the result of transformational leadership and its organizational deployment in broader areas of social life remains alluring for many researchers because it promises big change with relatively little organizational disruption and promises to give people a quantitative indicator of just how transformational their leadership practices are within various organizational contexts.

Transformational Leadership in Education Research

Education research might be uniquely disposed to the promises of transformational leadership because the field of education itself is focused on high-impact restructuring and transformation, and there is an expectation that school teachers and administrators should be a part of that (Berkovich 2016; Bush 2014; Hallinger 2003). The emphasis on how leaders go about achieving the goals of increasing educational outcomes seems like ripe ground for the large gains offered by transformational leadership theory, especially given that increasingly educational institutions are prompted to act more like businesses (Anderson 2017). This is especially true given the context where educational leaders are asked to do a lot with a little, and overcoming resource gaps is part of the job (Berkovich 2016). Indeed, transformational leadership is the most researched kind of leadership in education, comprising more than all other leadership theories combined (Anderson 2017).

In many ways, transformational leadership in education research has almost alchemical properties. The application of transformational leadership by principals in terms of being able to articulate and share their ideas during critical transitions of school change can apparently make or break the effort, especially given that teachers want to see transformational leadership from principals and other administrators to make a sustainable, positive institutional change (Hauserman and Stick 2013; Yang 2014). Furthermore, there are empirical studies that demonstrate that high-performing schools have principals who use transformational leadership to achieve culture change, improve or sustain academic achievement, and manage stakeholders, whereas low-performing schools have principals who do not employ such a leadership style (Knab 2009; Quin et al. 2015; Turan and Bektaş 2013). There emerges the idea of a heroic leader, who, given the proper training and exhibiting the proper characteristics of the four "I"s of transformational leadership, can almost single-handedly manage an overhauled culture change in schools that is sustainable, brings teachers along via a shared vision, and increases students' academic outcomes. It is small wonder then that transformational leadership enjoys such a pride of place among education scholars.

Perhaps this seems like an open and shut case; that is, the key to changing schools overnight is to get principals and administrators to ramp up their transformational leadership. Students will achieve, culture will change, and all from the yeoman efforts of the awesome transformational power wielded by the principal or administrator. This is an alluring narrative, as stated above, because it promises to achieve a lot with few resources and even fewer moving parts. Yet, some cracks begin to emerge. What follows are some initial points of critique that might be held onto as the chapter moves into the empirical objections to transformational leadership as well as the role of critical theory in assessing not only the role of transformational leadership but also the very context in which such a theory has found such purchase.

First, the literature seems to acquiesce all too quickly to the idea that educational institutions are businesses. Not only that, but transformational leadership is a compelling theory of change for that very reason (Anderson

2017). It might make sense to take pause and question whether schools ought to be run like businesses in terms of the historical purpose of educational institutions (Collini 2017). It might further be wise to interrogate what is lost in the neoliberal paradigm,[1] which pushes everything into logics of marketization and makes vanishingly small space for the public realm that cultivates things like civic virtues outside of market rationality (Brown 2019; Giroux 2013). In other words, it is wise to ask the question of whether education researchers should so easily adapt to the neoliberal shift in education, or if a role in education research is to critically assess such trends.

Second, the relationship between the variables of high-performing schools and principals exhibiting high levels of transformational leadership is ripe for a critical analysis. The relationship itself is methodologically sound, but it still calls for an investigation into why it is that high-performing schools have the luxury of transformational leaders. Part of that is questioning to what extent resource equity matters in school performance; can schools that are adequately resourced from high socioeconomic indicators "afford" transformational leaders, or at least create the conditions (less scarcity, better home life for students, more institutional stability, etc.) in which transformational initiatives can take hold?

Third, it is worth asking the foundational question of whether transformational leadership, with the above questions taken into account, is really all that transformative. That is, there seems to be a distance between the low-performing schools that ostensibly would benefit the most from transformational leaders and the schools where transformational leaders seem to be flourishing, but who are perhaps less in need of it. That raises the question of the impact of transformational leadership more broadly speaking. If it is most observed where it is least needed, does it really achieve all that it promises? Finally, there is a question of impact. If transformational leadership promises maximal impact, albeit with minimal overhead, then there is reason to question the uneven distribution of transformational leadership. There should be transformational leaders in the worst performing schools to get the maximum benefit from the charismatic, transformational leaders who embody the four "I"s. This lacuna between the promises of transformational leadership and its uneven deployment sets the stage for questioning some of the fundamental qualities of transformational leadership, and for integrating those questions with Marcuse's critical theory that asks how much adaptation to the existing order can be tolerable, or to what extent the underlying social facts must change for conditions in education to be different.

Objections to Transformational Leadership Theory

Transformational leadership's path from a historicopolitical analysis of "great men" who turn the world on revolutionary campaigns to a method of achieving business success to the heroic personality of the school principal or administrator has been a winding road. Making the pieces of a theory "fit" to different circumstances understandably comes with conceptual slippages, and transformational leadership is no exception. As a result, there have been objections to transformational leadership. This chapter will divide them into empirical objections as well as ideological objections. In both cases, the objections are not meant to reject transformational leadership wholecloth, but rather to refine it so it is more practical to the lived world of educators.

The first line of objections is empirical and takes two related vectors: that transformational leadership has conceptual ambiguity, and that it often lacks falsifiability. Van Knippenberg and Sitkin (2013) provide the most comprehensive overview of these empirical problems. They lay out four that are related and cumulative. First, they note that transformational leadership lacks a coherent conceptual definition (evidenced by the fact that Knippenberg and Sitkin refer to the theory as "charismatic-transformational" because they find no compelling reason to treat them as different styles of leadership), instead relying on "a listing of behaviors ... presumed to cohere simply because it has a label" (10). While surely cataloging behaviors can help sharpen a theoretical construction, without first defining the theory itself, the behaviors have little analytical value beyond simply being grouped together and their relationships under the aegis of a broader theory simply insisted upon. They also note that transformational leadership does not have clear indicators for what kinds of behaviors should be included or excluded in the analysis. Transformational leadership often lacks a complete picture of stakeholders such as community members not part of the leadership team (Yukl 1999).

The second objection, there is no clear delineation between transformational leadership behaviors, such as trust, from other behaviors in other leadership theories like fairness in leader–member exchange (van Knippenberg and Sitkin 2013). Second, the theoretical models built to capture the causal relationships between these behaviors cannot explain moderating behaviors (van Knippenberg and Sitkin 2013). This means that a lot of work in transformational leadership theory takes the given a priori assumptions and then does additive analysis to flesh out the theory. The problem with such an approach is that this does not justify the underlying theory by merely adding to it, thus eliding the conceptual problems in the first objection, and the theory should be definable independent of its effects or the specific types of behavior under consideration. Third, they find that transformational leadership, in concept and in operationalization, confuses the effects of transformational leadership with the concept itself (van Knippenberg and Sitkin 2013). This essentially displaces the analysis from the content of the theory to analyze its consequences. Rather than theorizing what transformational leadership itself looks like and then testing it, much research instead focuses on finding certain behaviors (see the second objection, previous paragraph), proclaiming that these are what transformational leaders do, and thus anybody who exhibits these behaviors is a transformational leader.

Finally, as a result of all these conceptual and empirical problems, transformational leadership research often has a difficult time building valid instruments to measure transformational leadership as a separate and distinct kind of leadership from other theories (van Knippenberg and Sitkin 2013). This difficulty in measuring stems from the previous objections, and the result is that it is difficult to pair transformational leadership with the effects that one wishes to see. For instance, while there is some evidence that transformational leadership has a positive correlation with teacher job satisfaction, there is little evidence that it has any effect on student achievement (Anderson 2017). It may be that teachers who are more fulfilled in their work may generate increased student achievement in a roundabout way, but the theory as such is not able to capture that, even if it may be reasonably assumed.

Related to these problems is an issue of falsifiability in transformational leadership. Of course, if the concept under investigation is slippery and not easily measured, then it is difficult to attain validity through falsifiability. Given the finding of Anderson (2017) that transformational leadership has not yet shown a relationship between that leadership style and student achievement, and that there are difficulties in measuring transformational leadership as distinct from other forms of leadership, it is difficult to devise a falsifiability test using experimental measures to show the capacity of the theory to be wrong (Berkovich 2016; Popper 2002). In educational leadership, the practical impact of this lack of falsifiability is to treat transformational leadership as a panacea; every good thing that happens is a result of transformational leadership, and every failure is a lack of sufficient transformational leadership (Berkovich 2016; van Knippenberg and Sitkin 2013). The theory, in other words, can never be imprecise, impractical, or otherwise wrong; one can only fail to live up to it.

These empirical shortcomings of transformational leadership are vital for education researchers who wish to develop the field. It is possible that these shortcomings of transformational leadership theory are so fundamental that the theory needs to be scrapped and something else built in its stead to better capture the interesting concepts the theory tries to capture (van Knippenberg and Sitkin 2013). It is also possible that educational research needs to adapt the theory to make it more appropriate for education as opposed to business by building its own instruments or phasing out parts of the four "I"s of transformational leadership (Berkovich 2016). In any event, addressing these empirical objections would be an important part of building a reliable and valid theory of transformational leadership for education.

Building a Critical Theory Framework

If the objections were only methodological, empirical, or otherwise a matter of tightening up the logical positivist foundations, the task would seem easy enough. Educational leadership scholars would either simply avoid transformational leadership altogether, or at least take care to chart out what behaviors count as transformational, and build testable models that are falsifiable and then get a sense of what role the transformational leader plays. However, there are substantive critiques that question the fundamental premises of the notion of transformational leadership by levying an ideological critique. This section takes some of these ideological critiques into consideration in order to set the stage for Herbert Marcuse's specific variant of critical theory to be applied to transformational leadership.

Before that, however, it is worth establishing what makes "critical" a worthy category of objection apart from normative or empirical, as set forth above. Highlighting the difference between critical thinking and critical theory will help set critical theory apart from procedural objections. Critical thinking is a pedagogical tool that builds up the skills of individuals to ask good questions about an object or phenomenon; it is often a disciplinary practice that mostly serves to reinforce the commonsense findings of what the field is already confident that it knows (Hayes 2015; Mulnix 2012; Papastephanou and Angeli 2007; Yanchar et al. 2008). Critical theory, on the other hand, is centered around the idea of a crisis, which is derived from the Greek *krisis*, a medical term meaning a rupture wherein something is so wrong with the patient that decisive, corrective action must be taken and where prior normal operating procedures cannot restore the patient back to health (Brown 2005). Critical theory makes this case at the social level, where social relations are so degraded that there emerges a gap between how a given theory purports to explain the world (such as transformational leadership theory and its high marks in high-performing schools) and the actual lived reality of the world that it is trying to explain (such as low student achievement, chronic underfunding, crumbling infrastructure). Analyzing this gap should be part of a good critical leadership approach (Chandler and Kirsch 2018). What makes an approach critical theory as opposed to critical thinking are these gaps—in the difference between peoples' lived experiences and the way the world is "supposed" to work and how such a difference emerges.

There have been some inroads into building a critical theory approach to leadership. Two strands in particular show promise for building a critical theory perspective into education research. First is a historicization approach to leadership. Using discourse analysis informed by a Foucauldian perspective, there is a strong case to be made that virtually all contemporary leadership theories have a historical hangover from their Taylorist roots (Wilson 2017). That is, even as leadership theories evolved from their "great man" theories that emphasized the special traits that a blessed few had, and into more socially or organizationally determined styles of leadership, the basis of trait-based theories of leadership is smuggled through, and so even the more supposedly relationally determined theories of leadership, like transformational leadership, still carry with them a germ that assumes that it takes a certain kind of person, with certain special qualities, to lead (Wilson 2017). For Wilson, the discursive structure of leadership studies itself has been shaped by this Taylorist great man basis, and leadership studies must confront that to build a new basis for studying leadership as opposed to trying to fix theories while retaining their basis.[2] Studying these discourses of leadership through a critical lens applies not only to the grand sweeping view of the field itself, but looking at the discursive realities that are cocreated in a variety of leadership settings also can show where leadership theories depart from the lived experiences of people (Alvesson and Karreman 2000). In the case of educational leadership research, the same questions are apt regarding transformational leadership. What kinds of discursive structures produce transformational opportunities? Much in the same way asked above, discourses around what counts as "high-performing" and "low-performing" schools and how those are measured indicate where transformational leadership is needed and where it may actually be enacted. Even so, from where does this discourse of "performing" come, who sets it, and to what end? To what extent does transformational leadership in education still boil down to capturing the "right" kind of person? Investigating these discursive elements can help explain the current context. Second, critical theory maps out patterns of power and domination, such that they might be overcome (Alvesson and Spicer 2014; Carroll et al. 2015). Relations of leadership never happen in a vacuum, and leadership may well be a uniquely rife place for inequity, domination, and subjugation to happen. Critical approaches make use of feminist theory to show how organizational structures can sneak in gender-based bias through leadership hierarchies, for instance (Ford 2005). This is especially important for critically analyzing transformational leadership theory because so much of the "great man" hangover does indeed center on men, supposedly "masculine" traits and therefore the (perhaps unconscious) subjugation of women in the leader–follower dynamic (Ford 2005). Specifically, transformational leadership has been critiqued through the lens of critical race theory, finding that the language deployed by transformational leadership also reifies power relations of white domination. As an example, Bass's blithe parroting of now discredited tropes about lower mean rates of African American intelligence has been challenged as an explanation for the lack of leadership from that marginalized group (Ladkin and Patrick 2022). This othering builds an architecture of leadership that centers whiteness as the normative core of the phenomenon, to which other groups may be additive but are nevertheless not part of the core idea itself (Ospina and Foldy 2009).

As education researchers engage in transformational leadership, a critical theory perspective compels a perspective that engages these underlying assumptions and the power inequities that either result or are sustained by them. In the case of transformational leadership, education researchers should not merely investigate whether the theory is empirically sound, valid, and reliable but also question the socially constructed underpinnings through which the theory enjoys its academic place, to see where it falls short or sustains patterns of inequity and domination. To wit, an apt question for an education researcher critically analyzing transformational leadership theory is to what extent transformational theory is built around assumptions that a charismatic white male is the default avatar of transformational leadership, and to what extent that (at least in part) explains why high-performing schools have transformational leaders, who transformational leadership benefits, and why it has little relationship to student achievement. It can unfairly center charisma and the striving of individuals with little concern for ethical content, so the question for education researchers must go beyond enhancing transformational qualities in leaders as an inexorable good (Tourish 2013). To reiterate, a critical engagement requires more than objecting to empirical blemishes, but insists on inspecting the fundamental assumptions about social relations that are embedded in a given theoretical practice.

What Can Marcusean Critical Theory Teach Us?

It is beyond the scope of this essay to delve deeply into the history of the *Institut für Sozialforschung* (known colloquially as the Frankfurt School) and its contributions to building a unique version of the critical theory of society, but it is enough to say that this group of German émigrés built the foundation for a comprehensive theorization of society by systematically investigating the underlying ideologies of contemporary society (Arato and Gebhardt 1982). At risk of oversimplifying, a central project of the Frankfurt School's critical theory of society is to critique "normal" theory, which is quantitative, assumes an empirical view from nowhere, and accepts the established facts as an unchangeable given with a "critical" theory that shows how the established facts do not produce the society they aspire to and that a liberated, qualitatively different world is possible (Horkheimer 1975). Herbert Marcuse was part of this group, and this section argues that in a complementary way to the critical interventions above, his contributions to critical theory help theorize the vectors of domination and why established theories, such as transformational leadership, might inadvertently sustain them. Marcuse's scholarly contributions were vast, but this section focuses on two particular Marcusean interventions: his one-dimensionality thesis, and his methodological approach of immanent critique.

Marcuse's best-known work is his *One-Dimensional Man*. In it, he argues that advanced industrial society has foreclosed alternatives to itself. This manifests in the realms of politics, where parties are treated like political teams and the quantitative results are more important than the policies pursued; in culture, where consumer choices and purchasing power say more about the makeup of an individual than an aesthetic development aimed at personal fulfillment; and in language, where the only discourses taken seriously are the ones that are feasible in that they reify the existing social order (Marcuse 1968). Such a flattening, Marcuse argues, makes society one-dimensional, with alternative dimensions being excluded from consideration not out of some sinister design but as a result of "a society without opposition," because the productive forces of society deliver enough of the goods, enough of the time, to enough people (Box 2011). Instead, new forms of social control and managed resistance limited the chance of meaningful alternatives. All this means is that the existing social order generates its own faux opposition through consumer choices, but they all end up reinforcing the established reality and diminishing the ability of people to engage in "critical thinking and oppositional behavior" (Kellner 2006: 2). One-dimensional society thus stifles awareness of alternative forms of life and personal development and fulfillment (Kellner et al. 2008). A prerequisite for human flourishing, in Marcuse's theory, is the generation of negativity, which is not merely refusing the existing order but formulating an alternative centered on human liberation. These two insights—that qualitatively different ways of living are stifled at the level of politics, culture, and language itself; and that what gets presented as opposition only serves to reinforce the existing order—give Marcuse an urgent valence in the current context.

Transformational leadership is ripe for this kind of Marcusean critical engagement, because of its purported promise of bringing a holistic change in organizational culture. If Marcuse's thesis holds, then the transformations promised by transformational leadership, even though they promise a qualitatively different and better result, end up reinforcing the established order. Further, transformational leadership would be meted out in highly specified quantified metrics that did more to obscure the thrust of the theory—wholescale organizational culture change—with incremental, piecemeal metrics that mean little in lived experience. What does it mean, after all, to increase transformational leadership by, say, 10 percent? As well, even leadership scholars who intend to deliver on the radical promise of transformational leadership merely end up offering strategies for adapting or coping with broader social forces, not seriously attempting to change them (Sharma 2017). Finally, transformational leadership still accepts the hierarchy of the leader/follower dynamic, where a charismatic (often white, male) leader is given the power to change things, even if presumably for the better. This model for change does not upset the unequal hierarchies or strive for equity. Putting this all together, transformational leadership looks one-dimensional in that it accepts discourses of leadership as individuals vested with the power to make organizational changes to the exclusion of marginalized or othered groups; fetishizes metrics to the point of obscuring any liberatory potential of an alternative mode of organization; and indeed contributes to making those alternatives unthinkable. Marcusean critical theory, through making these critiques, not only questions the effectiveness of transformational theory but also, through his one-dimensionality thesis, argues that these uphold a nonliberatory social relations that are embedded in the leadership practice.

It might be easy to suggest that everything is one-dimensional, given a one-dimensional society would make everything so, even vectors of supposed opposition. More on that below, but Marcuse also provides a methodology by which to critique a theory or practice of falling short—immanent critique. Immanent critique "is a means of detecting the societal contradictions which offer the most determinate possibilities for emancipatory social change" (Antonio 1981: 332). The point of critiquing a theory as one-dimensional is not thus to add to a catalog of one-dimensional life, but to show how there is liberatory potential in a given vector of one-dimensional thought, if one "starts from the theoretical premises" of a given theory and "develops their ideological and sociological consequences, and reexamines the premises in light of these consequences" (Marcuse 1958: 1). It methodologically takes a given theory to its logical endpoints to see if it delivers what it purports to. What makes this an immanent critique is that it is based on the internal logic of the phenomenon under investigation to see if the theory is adequate to its task and promise. It is also worth pointing out that it prohibits judging a theory by an external logic because that does not say anything meaningful about the premises of the theory under investigation.

What this means for transformational leadership is additive to the one-dimensional critique above. One starts by taking its premise (holistic and wide-ranging organizational culture change), and then looking at its consequences (charismatic leaders who do better in more well-funded organizations, or an incremental quantified improvement of transformational potential), to find that the theory is unable to deliver what it purports to deliver on its own merits. What immanent critique adds, however, is the insight that under different circumstances and with different social relations, the theory could live up to its potential. The idea of people building a collective vision for organizational culture change and then working collaboratively to that goal is a potentially liberatory one, but in the dictates of the one-dimensional version of transformational leadership, it cannot meet its own lofty goals. Immanent critique complements the one-dimensionality hypothesis in that it takes the inference of the needful lack of negativity from social theory and provides it with a methodology to think through how that one-dimensionality could be overcome to make a social theory more liberatory. This is what Marcuse means when he says that negativity in critical theory is the first step to making a social theory "adequate to its task" (Marcuse 1973: 4). Transformational leadership theory has a liberatory potential in education research, but cannot achieve it through the overly quantified, prescribed application of the theory; it must be reformulated to meet the mark it sets for itself for transformed schools.

Building a Multidimensional Transformational Leader in Education

Resisting one-dimensionality is not a one-time task. In fact, it is exceedingly difficult given the overall state of society and requires an ongoing self-reflexive critique to resist it as best as researchers can. Still, the promise of transformational leadership in education is promising because of what it might achieve. Marcuse argues that education is uniquely positioned as a force for negativity and social change, and that explains why it is so stratified by class, with high barriers to access; a holistic liberal education with a critical perspective can yield students who are able to better articulate alternatives to the existing order (Marcuse 2008). Changing educational structure to achieve those goals means far more than increasing principals' scores on the four "I"s by a few percentage points. For this reason, educational leadership scholars should resist importing wholesale the version of transformational leadership theory from management and business. Accepting this framework smuggles in the problems laid out above with its gender, racial, and socioeconomic inequities. Education scholars should consider instead starting with the question from the method of immanent critique, namely, what would it take for transformational leadership to produce the kind of schools that one wishes to see, and what are the broader social forces preventing that? It would mean recasting leadership in a novel way relevant to education, based on the needs and goals of educators and students.

Part of the critical perspective of education research could be engendering negativity. Again, that does not mean simply denying everything about an existing theory, but investigating the ideological underpinnings of a theory or course of action could uncover the gap between what a given theory purports to accomplish and what kind of life it actually produces for people. In education that means critically investigating why schools that are high-performing have better transformational outcomes than schools that are low-performing. It goes further, even still. It leads to questions about what "school performance" means anyway. Who sets those metrics? In whose interests are they set? How do school funding patterns establish discourses of education that reify the existing social order? What does "transformational" mean? Should it be related to student achievement, and if so, how? What is "student achievement" and who sets those parameters? Are the neoliberal trends of submitting formerly public institutions like schools to market forces helping or hurting students? This kind of critical questioning can go on and on, but is geared toward thinking through the needs of educators and students that builds a theory of transformational leadership generatively from these needs. This is not merely nitpicking at the level of vocabulary but an attempt to loosen the one-dimensional grip on the concept of transformational leadership by putting it in its broader social context, with a critical emphasis on how investigating its underpinnings can lead to researchers and practitioners building a better structure that can better achieve the task of transformation.

To be clear, it is probably safer to simply port over the theory from another discipline, try to apply it in schools, and see how transformational school leaders are, rank their improvement, and try to find some correlation between job satisfaction and transformational leadership. The question leadership scholars are confronted with, however, is whether that approach actually has anything to do with transforming education, valuing student success, or making a more inclusive educational culture. Indeed, education research scholars are further confronted with racism, sexism, and unequal power dynamics embedded in the version of transformational leadership inherited from these other disciplines. It is a much more arduous process to build the critical foundations upon a transformational leadership approach that is adequate to the task for education, but perhaps all the more vital because of it.

Conclusion

The criticisms leveled against transformational leadership in the realm of business and management should be enough to make educational leadership scholars pause. With myriad empirical problems and fundamental critical interventions, it is worth considering the extent to which transformational leadership can articulate anything important about the current context, even as it enjoys a pride of place among many leadership scholars from different disciplinary perspectives. This chapter encourages education leadership scholars to consider foregoing the hyper-quantitative and overly prescriptive iteration of transformational leadership from business and management. Instead, educational leadership researchers might find a compelling critique of that version of transformational leadership theory to be the basis upon which to articulate a qualitatively different and more liberatory version of transformational leadership more suited to the needs and goals of educators, students, and administrators.

Critical theory is sometimes lampooned for being overly dour and unwilling to be optimistic about virtually anything. Hopefully, this chapter has overcome such a stereotype by establishing how negative thinking, via overcoming one-dimensional thought, can set the stage for accessing the liberatory potential of a given theory. Transformational leadership theory and education have a good deal of such potential. For education to live up to its promise, and for transformation to be as complete as the theory suggests, provides a tantalizing vision for an education system not based merely on testing competency, or administration that is not based solely on stringent metrics, but instead having an eye toward a pedagogy that values democratic citizenry, a critical engagement with the world, and a hope of transformation. Herbert Marcuse's seemingly pessimistic critical theory is not a cry of resignation, but an articulation of hope that alternatives can still be articulated and that humans can meet the goals they put in front of themselves.

Notes

1 The neoliberal push within the field of education, and by extension educational leadership, is substantial. This push often manifests as a global educational reform movement that adds pressure on educators and guides educational research toward certain directions, such as school effectiveness and school improvement research. However, one should also acknowledge that resistance from educational leadership scholars and educators exists. The privatization of education and marketization of curriculum has been long criticized in the literature (perhaps since the early 2000s or earlier) and therefore is not presented here as a new idea but one that is nonetheless critical.

2 This work recognizes that Carlyle's "Great Man Theory of Leadership" long preceded Taylor's "Scientific Management." These are in fact distinct concepts. However, Suze Wilson's work addresses the fact that these theories, although distinct, are nonetheless related and have a common influence on how we think of leadership today.

References

Alvesson, M., and D. Karreman (2000), "Varieties of Discourse: On the Study of Organizations through Discourse Analysis," *Human Relations* 53 (9): 1125–49.

Alvesson, M., and A. Spicer (2014), "Critical Perspectives on Leadership," in D. V. Day (ed.), *The Oxford Handbook of Leadership and Organizations*, 40–57, Oxford: Oxford University Press.

Anderson, M. (2017), "Transformational Leadership in Education: A Review of Existing Literature," *International Social Science Review* 93 (1): 1–13.

Antonio, R. J. (1981), "Immanent Critique as the Core of Critical Theory: Its Origins and Developments in Hegel, Marx and Contemporary Thought," *British Journal of Sociology* 32 (3): 330–45.

Arato, A., and E. Gebhardt (eds.) (1982), *The Essential Frankfurt School Reader*, London: Continuum.

Avolio, B. J., D. A. Waldman, and F. J. Yammarino (1991), "Leading in the 1990s: The Four I's of Transformational Leadership," *Journal of European Industrial Training* 15 (4): 9–16.

Bass, B. M. (1985), *Leadership and Performance Beyond Expectations*, New York: Free Press.

Bass, B. M. (1995), "Theory of Transformational Leadership Redux," *Leadership Quarterly* 6 (4): 463–78.

Bass, B. M., and B. J. Avolio (1990), *Transformational Leadership Development: Manual for the Multifactor Leadership Questionnaire*, Palo Alto, CA: Consulting Psychologists Press.

Berkovich, I. (2016), "School Leaders and Transformational Leadership Theory: Time to Part Ways?," *Journal of Educational Administration* 54 (5): 609–22.

Box, R. C. (2011), "Marcuse Was Right," *Administrative Theory & Praxis* 33 (2): 169–91.

Brown, W. (2005), *Edgework: Critical Essays on Knowledge and Politics*, Princeton, NJ: Princeton University Press.

Brown, W. (2019), *In the Ruins of Neoliberalism: The Rise of Antidemocratic Politics in the West*, New York: Columbia University Press.

Burns, J. M. (1978), *Leadership*, New York: Harper Perennial Modern Classics.

Bush, T. (2014), "Instructional and Transformational Leadership: Alternative and Complementary Models?" *Educational Management, Administration & Leadership* 42 (4): 443–4.

Carroll, B., J. Ford, and S. Taylor (eds.) (2015), *Leadership: Contemporary Critical Perspectives*, Thousand Oaks, CA: Sage.

Chandler, J. L. S., and R. E. Kirsch (2018), *Critical Leadership Theory: Integrating Transdisciplinary Perspectives*, London: Palgrave Macmillan.

Charbonnier-Voirin, A., A. E. Akremi, and C. Vandenberghe (2010), "A Multilevel Model of Transformational Leadership and Adaptive Performance and the Moderating Role of Climate for Innovation," *Group & Organization Management* 35 (6): 699–726.

Cheung, M. F. Y., and C.-S. Wong (2011), "Transformational Leadership, Leader Support, and Employee Creativity," *Leadership & Organization Development Journal* 32 (7): 656–72.

Chun, E., and A. Evans (2015), *The Department Chair as Transformative Diversity Leader: Building Inclusive Learning Environments in Higher Education*, Sterling, VA: Stylus.

Collini, S. (2017), *Speaking of Universities*, New York: Verso.
Ford, J. (2005), "Examining Leadership through Critical Feminist Readings," *Journal of Health Organization and Management* 19 (3): 236–51.
Giroux, H. A. (2013), "Beyond Dystopian Education in a Neoliberal Society," *Fast Capitalism* 10 (1): 109–20.
Hallinger, P. (2003), "Leading Educational Change: Reflections on the Practice of Instructional and Transformational Leadership," *Cambridge Journal of Education* 33 (3): 329–52.
Hauserman, C. P., and S. L. Stick (2013), "The Leadership Teachers Want from Principals: Transformational," *Canadian Journal of Education* 36 (3): 184–203.
Hayes, D. (2015), "Against Critical Thinking Pedagogy," *Arts and Humanities in Higher Education* 14 (4): 318–28.
Horkheimer, M. (1975), *Critical Theory: Selected Essays*, trans. M. J. O'Connell, London: Continuum.
Jung, D., A. Wu, and C. W. Chow (2008), "Towards Understanding the Direct and Indirect Effects of CEOs' Transformational Leadership on Firm Innovation," *Leadership Quarterly* 19 (5): 582–94.
Jung, D. I., C. Chow, and A. Wu (2003), "The Role of Transformational Leadership in Enhancing Organizational Innovation: Hypotheses and Some Preliminary Findings," *Leadership Quarterly* 14 (4): 525–44.
Kellner, D. (2006), "Marcuse's Challenges to Education," *Policy Futures in Education* 4 (1): 1–5.
Kellner, D., T. Lewis, and C. Pierce (2008), *Marcuse's Challenge to Education*, Lanham, MD: Rowman & Littlefield.
Knab, D. (2009), "A Comparison of the Leadership Practices of Principals of Making Middle Grades Work Schools as Measured by the Leadership Practices Inventory," *Academic Leadership* 7 (3): 1–16.
Ladkin, D., and C. B. Patrick (2022), "Whiteness in Leadership Theorizing: A Critical Analysis of Race in Bass' Transformational Leadership Theory," *Leadership* 18 (2): 205–23.
Marcuse, H. (1958), *Soviet Marxism*, New York: Columbia University Press.
Marcuse, H. (1968), *One-Dimensional Man*, Boston, MA: Beacon Press.
Marcuse, H. (1973), *Studies in Critical Philosophy*, Boston, MA: Beacon Press.
Marcuse, H. (2008), "Lecture on Education, Brooklyn College, 1968," in D. Kellner, T. Lewis, and C. Pierce (eds.), *Marcuse's Challenge to Education*, 33–8, Lanham, MD: Rowman & Littlefield.
Mulnix, J. W. (2012), "Thinking Critically about Critical Thinking," *Educational Philosophy & Theory* 44 (5): 464–79.
Ospina, S., and E. Foldy (2009), "A Critical Review of Race and Ethnicity in the Leadership Literature: Surfacing Context, Power and the Collective Dimensions of Leadership," *Leadership Quarterly* 20 (6): 876–96.

Papastephanou, M., and C. Angeli (2007), "Critical Thinking beyond Skill," *Educational Philosophy & Theory* 39 (6): 604–21.

Podsakoff, P. M., S. B. MacKenzie, R. H. Moorman, and R. Fetter (1990), "Transformational Leader Behaviors and Their Effects on Followers' Trust in Leader, Satisfaction, and Organizational Citizenship Behaviors," *Leadership Quarterly* 1 (2): 107–42.

Popper, K. (2002), *The Logic of Scientific Discovery*, 2nd ed., Oxfordshire: Routledge.

Price, T. L. (2003), "The Ethics of Authentic Transformational Leadership," *Leadership Quarterly* 14 (1): 67–81.

Quin, J., A. Deris, G. Bischoff, and J. T. Johnson (2015), "Comparison of Transformational Leadership Practices: Implications for School Districts and Principal Preparation Programs," *Journal of Leadership Education* 14 (3): 72–85.

Schaubroeck, J., S. S. K. Lam, and S. E. Cha (2007), "Embracing Transformational Leadership: Team Values and the Impact of Leader Behavior on Team Performance," *Journal of Applied Psychology* 92 (4): 1020–30.

Sharma, M. (2017), *Radical Transformational Leadership: Strategic Action for Change Agents*, Berkeley, CA: North Atlantic Books.

Tourish, D. (2013), *The Dark Side of Transformational Leadership: A Critical Perspective*, London: Routledge.

Turan, S., and F. Bektaş (2013), "The Relationship between School Culture and Leadership Practices," *Eurasian Journal of Educational Research* 13 (52): 155–68.

van Knippenberg, D., and S. B. Sitkin (2013), "A Critical Assessment of Charismatic-Transformational Leadership Research: Back to the Drawing Board?," *Academy of Management Annals* 7 (1): 1–60.

Velasco, M., and C. Sansone (2019), "Resistance to Diversity and Inclusion Change Initiatives: Strategies for Transformational Leaders," *Organization Development Journal* 37 (3): 9–20.

Wilson, S. (2017), *Thinking Differently about Leadership: A Critical History of Leadership Studies*, Cheltenham: Edward Elgar.

Yanchar, S. C., B. D. Slife, and R. Warne (2008), "Critical Thinking as Disciplinary Practice," *Review of General Psychology* 12 (3): 265–81.

Yang, Y. (2014), "Principals' Transformational Leadership in School Improvement," *International Journal of Educational Management* 28 (3): 279–88.

Yukl, G. (1999), "An Evaluation of Conceptual Weaknesses in Transformational and Charismatic Leadership Theories," *Leadership Quarterly* 10 (2): 285–305.

5

Cultivating Relations of Freedom through Education Leadership by Drawing from the Critical Theory of Herbert Marcuse

Patrick M. Jenlink

Introduction

The educational leader, guided by critical theory and thought[1] and by a concern for education and the well-being of the individual, group, and society, faces ideological and political domination that seeks to restrict freedom. The educational leader today confronts many of the same concerns that fostered the intellect and criticism Karl Marx brought to bear on modern society. The language and dialectic of controlling political ideologies that were prominent during the nineteenth and twentieth centuries remain equally, if not more so, dominant in society and its education systems in the twenty-first century. Reitz (2000), in his critical engagement with Herbert Marcuse's work, asked the question, "What are the intellectual, moral, and political qualities of life and thought that can make theory *critical*, society *democratic*, and education *liberating?*" (1, original emphasis). This question throws light on the quintessential philosophical issues of our time. Reitz further stated, "Marcuse's continuing merit and appeal stems precisely from his work on the problems of knowledge and on the political impact of education" (2000, 7).

As one of the twentieth century's visionary and a central figure in the Frankfurt School of critical theorists,[2] German philosopher Herbert Marcuse[3] (1898–1979) theorized the real possibility education could act against political alienation and oppression. Marcuse's theorizing of the importance of education was drawn in small part from his early analysis of education and his belief in the importance of critical thought. Marcuse was concerned that "the *dialectic of education* in this society involved an increasing dependence on education, unrestricted knowledge in the competitive economic process, and in the steering of the political process" (2009, 34, original emphasis).

At the same time, Marcuse noted the increasing need in society to restrict "knowledge and reason within the conceptual a value universe of the established society and its improvement and growth in order to protect this society against radical change" (2009a, 34). This restriction of knowledge and reason, in particular in and through education, placed "an emphasis on professional, vocational training, and a decline of the 'humanities,' transcendent, critical thought" (34).[4] The decline in critical thought—and, by extension, critical praxis—gave way to domination. Marcuse's critical examination focusing on education as the dominant mode of enculturation to one-dimensionality,[5] "unfreedom," and alienation is ever more relevant in today's society.

Keniston (1968), writing in *Young Radicals* in the 1960s, provides perhaps an appropriate metaphor for conceiving of critical educational leaders today, speaking of the young radicals of that era. Their aim was to critically search out the "problems of [a] changing, affluent, and violent society, a society that [had] barely begun to catch up with the dilemmas it [had] created ... problems [that] lie deeper than a particular election result or a particular war" (289). Today's society is emblematic of the 1960s in many ways; the fight for freedom from domination of society by the political and ideological barons of control continues, in particular for education.

In today's educative spaces, critical educators face no less a daunting challenge, no less social responsibility to the public. Education and the leading, learning, and teaching processes that define the work within schools and universities as educative spaces, at its best, must be seen as connected with the obligation of social responsibility and political agency (Giroux 2003). The following sections bring into specific relief Marcuse's influence on education and society, providing a foundation for a critical perspective of educational leadership, praxis, and the work needed to ensure societal freedoms and the future of education.

Liberating Education and the Need for Critical Theory

Revolutionary critical educators—critical educational leaders—having a responsibility for bringing a critical praxis to offset the domination and "unfreedom"[6] that Marcuse believed was offsetting the advancement of education and society have been a factor in the liberation[7] of society. Concerning "unfreedom," Cunningham elaborates on Marcuse's concern for the ideology of industrial society and the narrowing to a logic of one-dimensionality:

> One dimensionality is the negation of the critical theory. At times a disciplinary mechanism, at times a compulsory mind-set focused primarily on consumption, it is a condition through which a society relinquishes the difficulties of proper criticism in favour of general agreement with the tides of capitalism. (2013: 541)

The control of education and society, the narrowing of hegemonic ideology to "one dimensionality," was the central concern Marcuse focused on and has been the basis for his belief in essential need for critical theory.[8] Importantly, in today's society, one-dimensionality "has proven itself to be a relevant basic concept of critical theory that first of all critically analyzes society as it is, by revealing the forces that sustain, legitimize, and stabilize the existing structures" (Winter 2017: 71) of society and, more specifically, its influence on education. "However, critical theory is primarily interested in those forces that can negate and subversively circumvent the system and can contribute to emancipation" (71).

Liberating education, and therein instruction and learning, requires that critical educational leadership focus on a critical theoretical perspective[9] and understanding that activates critical leadership praxis. As Kellner emphasizes, this can have a real emancipatory impact:

> Critical social theories conceptualize the structures of domination and resistance. They point to forms of oppression and domination contrasted to forces of resistance that can serve as instruments of change .... Thus, critical social theories are weapons of critique and instruments of practice as well as cognitive maps .... If a theory illuminates a phenomenon ... and produces altered reception of it (or perhaps rejection), or inspires the production of oppositional ... practices, then the theory turns out to be valuable both in its theoretical and practical effects. (1995: 25–7)

Critical leadership in education is concerned with the evolution of human intelligence that works to offset the negative effects of domination. For Kellner (1995), in alignment with Marcuse's work, this evolution is emergent from the need to overcome material, historical, and cultural oppression through liberating education, in both the school and university.

Critical Theorizing of Educational Leadership

Drawing from Reitz's (2019) discussion of the relevance of Marcuse's critical theory today, the argument is made for the importance of critical theorizing and the necessity of emancipatory action and learning in order to understand the existing dominant dialectic overshadowing education and the social conditions within society. Educational leaders responsible for enacting a liberation from the "unfreedom" exacted on society and its domination require an understanding of how to grasp the theoretical and possess the political acumen necessary to secure freedom from economic processes that today divest society and its educational endeavors of creative work and communal power (Reitz 2019). Importantly Cunningham stated the "central tenets of Marcuse's philosophy of education, which stands as both a promise and challenge to traditional concepts of education, moving it away from basic instruction to a model for liberation" (2013: 542).

A critical theorizing of educational leadership that seeks liberation of education from historical domination has importance to the advancement of freedom and the success of liberation in school and university classrooms. As Marcuse (2009a) explained, "By its own inner dynamic, education thus *leads beyond the classroom*, beyond the university, *into the political dimension*, and into *the moral*, instinctual dimension" (35, original emphasis). This necessitates the need for a critical theoretical approach to educational leadership and the liberation of educators who instruct students as future generations moving forward with the liberation from "unfreedom" ideologies. In simpler terms, the critical perspective embodied in critical theory enables the education leader and others within the educative process to become aware of the societal ideological restraints placed upon them and, through critical reflection and praxis, to become liberated from the ideological controls (Peca 2000).[10]

As Cunningham (2013) explained in his discussion of Marcuse's *One-Dimensional Man* (1964), "Ultimately, what marks *One-Dimensional Man* as a canonical work in critical theory is its ability to blend a variety of critical frameworks and implications into a single work and apply them so readily to numerous situations" (541). Importantly, this canon of critical theory as denoted has significant merit today for educational leaders as they confront the continued threat of domination and "unfreedom" in education and society.

Critical Theory of/in/for Education

The value of and continuing "appeal for Marcuse's writings stems especially from his work on the nature of learning and the political implications of different types of knowledge, particularly his critique of the alienating effects of the prevailing modes of education" (Reitz 2009a: 1). Marcuse's social and critical theorization holds importance for education and society today, in particular for advancing a critical educational leadership for today's education system, in order to recapture dialectically a dimension of the emancipatory theory and enact political and educational freedom.[11] Marcuse, in a speech given in 1975 at Berkeley to students and faculty, set forth the basis for his critical theory of education.

It is true that we cannot change the goals of education without changing the society that sets these goals. But it is also true that we cannot wait for the revolution in order to become human beings, to eradicate sexism and racism in ourselves, to learn solidarity with the victims, and to free ourselves from the cynicism and hypocrisy of the established morality. In other words, the radical consciousness and the vital need for radical change must emerge within the existing society and its institutions—there is no without! (Marcuse 2009b: 39).

Importantly, as Pierce (2013) acknowledged, "Marcuse's critical theory of education figures into his liberatory project oriented toward emancipating humans from the 'open-air prison' of one-dimensional society and culture" (605). Concerning society and culture, Gitlin (2005) is instructive in understanding the importance of, as well as the power of, culture in education and society. As a critical educational leader, "what one needs to be cautious of is the norms, traditions, a priori commitments, images, and so forth, that in one sense limit our ability to be human and to imagine" (18). The cultural artifacts of a society and its education, born out of economic and political domination and control, work in opposition to change and advancement toward something new, imagination is quelled, and the paradigm remains the same one generation to the next.

Marcuse on Language and Dialectic: Contemplative Praxis

The greater obligation of critical educators and leaders today is to foster a kind of critical discourse that makes transparent and then sets about to change the existing order. This critical discourse moves the educative experience (or miseducative as is often the case) toward one that is concerned with preparing new generations of those who Keniston (1968) characterized as *young radicals*. These "radicals" are equipped to address the current tensions in our society. Therein, the focus on language and dialectic[12] is in keeping with the position of Marcuse who maintained that language is one of the most powerful weapons in the armory of the establishment. In his writings, Marcuse argued that the language that represents hegemonic thought is a mixture of unprecedented brutality and sweetness (Kellner 2001).

Marcuse refers to this hegemonic thought as an Orwellian language, which monopolizes communication and "stifles the consciousness, obscures and defames the alternative possibilities of existence, implants the needs of the status quo in the mind and body of men and makes them all but immune against the need for change" (Kellner 2001: 118). The threshold of societal dominance and change lies in the education system that serves society, a system that is too often controlled by the dominant political and economic ideologies. Marcuse (1968) advanced the position that "engagement with education involves radical critique of the existing systems of education and the search for emancipatory alternatives" (Kellner 2006: 2), an emancipatory exercise with freedom as the critical outcome.[13] The uncertainty that the individual, group, and society experience with respect to dominance and the role of education in effecting freedom is at the forefront of driving a need to cultivate relations of freedom—a cultivation of a new culture that educational leadership in schools and universities is challenged to take responsibility if freedom is to be recognized. The critical educational leader and educator is motivated by the contradiction between existence and possibility, between "the is" and "the ought" (Marcuse 1965) in ensuring freedom in schools and universities. The source of knowledge that is free from domination and control is "engagement itself" (Papson 2014: 383),the active engagement in seeking to know and understand.

However, this freedom, as Marcuse recognizes, requires that society cannot be indiscriminate where freedom and happiness are at stake. Freedom requires negation against established social order that works to control education and the larger culture wherein education exists. As Marcuse argued concerning freedom, "certain things cannot be said, certain ideas cannot be expressed, certain policies cannot be proposed, certain behavior cannot be permitted without making tolerance[14] an instrument for the continuation of servitude" (1965: 88).

Almost the sum total of Marcuse's educational thought is devoted to purely contemplative praxis[15] on the university level, relationships with educational leadership, and preparation. As Marcuse recognized, education in *abstracto* can serve as an immensely important critical device in potential social change:

> If "education" is more and other than training, learning, preparing for the existing society, it means not only enabling [educational leaders] to know and understand the facts which make up reality but also to know and understand

the facts that establish the facts so that [educational leaders] can change their inhuman reality. (1965: 122)[16]

While living with uncertainty appears to be the antithesis of progress in our modern world, where all advancements are defined in terms of measurable goals and outcomes, educational leadership guided by critical theory and "imagination"[17] views uncertainty as the genesis of progress, for this is where "imagination" finds its own freedom. And it is through imagination that one becomes able to "form notions of what should be and is not yet, [and] at the same time, remain in touch with what presumably is" (Greene 1995: 19). And it is through an emancipatory education, as Marcuse explained, that society is able to see new generations of citizens take responsibility for the future amidst a predatory culture (Reitz 2009b).

Responsibility to Ensure Education for a Free Society

Critical educational leaders have a responsibility to ensure education's role for a free society. As Marcuse stated, in a lecture at Brooklyn College in 1968 titled "Education and Social Change":

> To create the subjective conditions for a free society [it is] no longer sufficient to educate individuals to perform more or less happily the functions they are supposed to perform ... [We must also] educate men and women who are incapable of tolerating what is going on, who have really learned what *is* going on, has always been going on, and why, and who are education to resist and to fight for a new way of life. (Marcuse 1968)

There is a pressing need for critical educational leader, through critical praxis, to necessarily understand the importance of imagining alternative possible futures, recognizing, as Marcuse noted, that the purpose is to move toward relations of freedom. Critical educational leaders and educators, in schools and universities, seeking an understanding for future generations of the relations of freedom must necessarily continue to take risks and struggle to infuse the curriculum, instruction, and learning experiences with analysis and recognition of the "critical, radical movements and theories in history, literature, philosophy" (Marcuse 2009a: 37).[18]

Importantly, what is required is that the critical educational leader, guided by Marcuse's thoughts on political socialization, engage in "the negation of 'false consciousness' and the realization of the necessity of change must accompany any growth in objective material conditions. The [critical educational leader] must take it upon himself to free men who do not know that they are not free" (DeVitis 1974: 260). In turn, this requires that the critical educational leader be educated in critical theory that enables a critical praxis in the day-to-day responsibilities of leading in education, in both the school and the university, that fosters an understanding of and concern for liberation.[19] Also required of critical educational leaders is an understanding, as Giroux has argued, that the concept of critical theory "refers to the nature of self-conscious critique and to the need to develop a discourse of social transformation and emancipation that does not cling dogmatically to its own doctrinal assumptions" (1983: 8); rather, it "refers to both a 'school of thought' and a process of critique" (8).

Hope and the Focus on Freedom

Throughout his career Marcuse focused on freedom, a focus that required a vision of liberation in the otherwise controlled social fabric of society. Liberation, and therein freedom as it relates to critical educational leadership, is concerned with the full development of the individual in a nonrepressive society, which distinguishes Marcuse's work along with a sharp critique of existing forms of domination and oppression. In an era of hegemonic neoliberalism,[20] Marcuse's critical perspectives are necessary to ensure that critical educational leadership prevails. Included is the interrogations of the power structures of education and society, critical examinations of knowledge production and intellectual resources used to understand and promote a criticality in leadership, and a concern for liberation from domination by the political mechanizations of a hegemonic state ideology (Niesche and Gowlett 2019).

These critical perspectives are more needed now than ever before and provide educational leaders clarity of the importance for critique and alternative vision concerning education necessary "to keep hope alive and envisage a different and better future" (Kellner 2006: 5). Marcuse's emblematic role in the transformation of education and society was/is the embodiment of hope. While recognizing the increasing effectiveness of technological rationality and social control in contemporary society, Marcuse did not give up. As Van Heertum noted, "Marcuse knew that hope was essential in planting the seeds for change. So while there were moments in his intellectual career when he was among the most deterministic of thinkers, he always embraced all efforts at transforming society" (1992: 50).[21]

Kellner, writing on critical theory and the future of society and education, emphasized the importance of a critical praxis bound to new critical theory and the understanding it can have on a real emancipatory impact:

> Critical social theories conceptualize the structures of domination and resistance. They point to forms of oppression and domination contrasted to forces of resistance that can serve as instruments of change .... Thus, critical social theories are weapons of critique and instruments of practice as well as cognitive maps .... If a theory illuminates a phenomenon ... and produces altered reception of it (or perhaps rejection), or inspires the production of oppositional ... practices, then the theory turns out to be valuable both in its theoretical and practical effects. (1995: 25–7)

Critical educational leaders, who understand and commit to the belief in and use of critical praxis, guided by new critical theory, can make a commitment to ensuring that education in schools and universities seeks freedom from political and ideological domination.

Final Thoughts

The most important recurring debate confronting education today centers squarely on the tension between remaining neutral or having the courage to challenge and change the existing social order. Here the early work of Marcuse is instructive. We are at a time in our history that requires us to move beyond acknowledgment and take action upon the tension. This means as critical educational leaders and educators we must make a decision between the preparation of a new generation of critical educators along ideological lines that reify and perpetuate schools and universities as they exist in American society, and which contribute to the dedemocratizing of our education systems. Or, conversely, should the focus be on the preparation of educators along lines of a social imaginary of freedom and nondomination by political ideologies that work to transform schools and universities into critical social spaces, which serve as agencies to reinvigorate society and its education through inculcating new ideals, taking direction from Marcuse and critical theories that work to benefit all? While there are perhaps some exceptions sparsely located across the country, educator (leader and teacher) preparation programs more often than not serve the hegemonic role of assimilating students of teaching and leading into public schools and classrooms hallmarked by forms of power and domination, overshadowed by ongoing political fervor.

Against these ways of thinking, universities and therein faculty members who prepare educators and educational leaders must seek to open up the debate regarding the ends and purposes of education, to expand and render more democratic, and at the same time more inclusive, the spaces where individuals begin the process of becoming the counternarratives necessary to Marcuse's belief in liberation from "unfreedom" in society. As well, universities and therein those who prepare educators and educational leaders must recognize the diversity of human perspective and beliefs that comprises those spaces. What universities and therein those responsible for preparing future educators can do—are obligated to do—is focus on political drama playing out in society. Such drama leads to ideological and political domination and then takes a direct action to forge a critical public language—a liberating dialectic—and the necessary critical pedagogical conventions and critical praxis that have the capacity to affirm and create an educated citizenry and, most importantly, populate schools and universities with critical educators committed to ensuring the freedom of society and its citizenry. Unarguably, at present the dominant language and pedagogical conventions currently at our disposal are emphatically *not* directed toward such ends and purposes. Our obligation as critical educational leaders and guardians of society begins here.

A closing reflection on the legacy of Marcuse, and the importance of education and the society it serves, is that the school and university should not serve as political battle grounds suffering from the political and ideological undercurrents of neoliberalism or the far right. Nor should schools and universities fall victim to "unfreedom" and domination of select political ideologies that seek to control our education and its work to liberate out society and its people. Critical educational leaders who are committed to the project of fighting political and ideological domination and putting into practice[22] an emancipatory praxis to transform "education in real institutions and real communities, defending it against the predictable rightist and neo-liberal attacks that he faced for years" (Apple 2003: 116) need to be observant of the current political movements that are redefining our nation and our education systems. As Paulo Freire (2004) argued, "Tomorrow is neither a necessary repetition of today, as the dominant would like it to be, nor something predetermined. Tomorrow is a possibility we need to work out, and, above all, one we must fight to build" (75). Simply stated, this is the work of critical educational leaders.

Notes

1. For the purposes of the discussion on critical theory and thought presented in this chapter, the author draws from the work of Herbert Marcuse and Henry Giroux. Drawing on a 1937 essay by Herbert Marcuse for the journal *Zeitschrift für Sozialforschung* (*Journal for Social Research*) titled "Philosophy and Critical Theory," Marcuse outlined critical theory, noting that critical thought

   > compels theory anew to a sharper emphasis on its concern with the potentialities of man and with the individual's freedom, happiness, and rights... For the [critical] theory, these are exclusively potentialities of the concrete social situation ... human freedom is no phantom or arbitrary inwardness that leaves everything in the external world as it was. Rather, freedom here means a real potentiality, a social relationship on whose realization human destiny depends. (105)

   Concerning critical theory, Giroux (1983) notes:

   > The concept of critical theory refers to the nature of self-conscious critique and to the need to develop a discourse of social transformation and emancipation that does not cling dogmatically to its own doctrinal assumptions. In other words, critical theory refers to both a "school of thought" and a process of critique. It points to a body of thought that is, in my view, invaluable for educational theorists.

2. Hebert Marcuse's philosophy is foundational to subsequent work in critical theory that has also developed on the basis of the general philosophical innovations of the Frankfurt School and Western Marxism (Albrecht Wellmer, Douglas Kellner, Ben Agger, Paulo Freire, Henry A. Giroux, Max Horkheimer, Leo Löwenthal, Theodor W. Adorno, Walter Benjamin, and others). Herbert Marcuse and the Frankfurt School members proposed the task of a critical theory of society, one in which education was grounded in culture, in the tradition of *Bildung* (education as culture) in German intellectual thought. Important it is to note that Max Horkheimer, Theodor W. Adorno, and Herbert Marcuse pioneered an interdisciplinary approach to humanities and social sciences that informed a new generation of critical theory (Višić 2019: 660).

3. The Frankfurt School took as one of its central values a commitment to penetrate the world of objectified appearances and expose the underlying social relationships they often conceal. In adopting such a perspective, the Frankfurt School not only broke with forms of rationality that wedded science and technology into new forms of domination; it also rejected all forms of rationality that subordinated human consciousness and action to the imperatives of universal laws.

4 Marcuse's concern focused on the absence of critical thought, and by extension critical praxis, on the part of those responsible for questioning the unfreedom of education. He noted that positioning of the "establishment" in relation to the control of education.

> Education today takes place in a society which intensifies the social ambivalence of education to the breaking point. On the one hand, their mutual dependence: society depends on education, education on financial support from the government, Foundations, etc. Its value: education for the Establishment. On the other hand, the transcendent force of knowledge beyond the Establishment. Its value: education for a better, different society against the Establishment. ([1968] 2009: 35)

5 Kellner, based on his research of Marcuse's work, explains that "one-dimensional society is a social order that lacks negativity, critique, and transformative practice" (2009: 8). See also Herbert Marcuse (1964).
6 The term "unfreedom" draws from Marcuse's concern for a "one-dimension" logic that permeates society and takes away freedom. See Herbert Marcuse (1964).
7 Marcuse, in *Eros and Civilization* (1955), *Soviet Marxism* (1958), and various texts in his later work, speaks to his vision of a truly liberated society in a very broad sense. Reflected in his view of liberation, Marcuse envisioned a total break from the values and ethos of both capitalism and Soviet-style socialism, two political forces that are a part of the dialectic of Marcuse's critical theory concerning domination. It would entail a complete rejection of technological rationality and the ethos of domination and control, both of human beings and of nature.
8 Henry Giroux notes:

> Critical theorists from Herbert Marcuse to Theodor Adorno have always recognized that the most important forms of domination are not simply economic but also cultural and that the pedagogical force of the culture with its emphasis on belief and persuasion is a crucial element of how we both think about politics and enact forms of resistance and social transformation. (2004: 32)

9 Theoretically, the foundation of critical theory and critical educational leadership involves "knowledge, intelligence, reason as catalysts of social change—projection of the possibilities of a 'better' order; violation of socially useful taboos, illusions" (Marcuse [1968] 2009: 33–4).
10 A mere understanding of the oppressive ideologies affecting the culture and those within the culture is insufficient from a critical perspective. As Hoy (1994) explains: "Critical theory attempts to raise the [leader's and educator's] consciousness about their living and working condition through logic and debate, but in the process it relies on the generation and analysis of ideologies" (183–4).

11 In examining the work of Herbert Marcuse, Višić (2019) notes:

> Marcuse's complete oeuvre is defined by the consistency of dialectical thinking (through negation, preservation and elevation), refuting of any positivism favorable to reality, by the care for an individual and by the overcoming of reified relations and creation of a more humane world in which human being (re)discovers oneself and sees the world as one's own doing, as a stage in which one, in a peaceful and libidinal coexistence with others, can develop one's all-around being. (661)

12 Marcuse, in speaking on the power of dialectic, acknowledges that

> the power of facts over the world, and to speak the language of those who establish, enforce and benefit from the facts [is difficult]. As the power of the given facts tend to become totalitarian, to absorb all opposition, and to define the entire universe of discourse, the effort to speak the language of contradiction appears increasingly irrational, obscure, and artificial. (1960: x)

13 Herbert Marcuse, in many of his works including *Eros and Civilization* (1955) and *One-Dimensional Man: Studies in the Ideology of Advanced Industrial Society* (1964), provided both a forceful critique of modern industrial society and a path to collective liberation. His project was largely influenced by Friedrich Hegel, Karl Marx, and Sigmund Freud and was adopted by parts of the New Left and the counterculture of 1960s America. He felt, by and large, he articulated what they perceived—even if many did not fully grasp his ideas.

14 Reitz, in considering the political positioning of "tolerance" and the utmost significance for the present situation in terms of liberation versus domination, posits:

> If we all have a de jure right to express any opinion in public, the de facto condition is that left opinions are usually marginalized and often suppressed, while right-wing ones, which benefit the ruling class, are given free play. (2013: 18)

15 Regarding Marcuse's concern for praxis, Aronowitz (1999) notes:

> Marcuse was a philosopher of praxis; he was forever searching for the openings for revolution and believed that theory was intimately linked to action. (139)

16 Marcuse thus recommends a course of study consisting in critical analysis of contemporary societies and a general survey of the "great nonconformist movements in civilization"—for example, speculative philosophy and theoretical sociology, psychology, and political science (Marcuse 1965: 61).

17 Herbert Marcuse (1955: 172) explained the importance of imagination. Educational leaders must necessarily understand that

> imagination sustains the claim of the whole individual, in union with the genius with the archaic past .... Like imagination, which is its constitutive mental faculty, the realm of aesthetics is essentially "unrealistic"; it has retained its freedom from the reality principle at the price of being ineffective in the reality .... Before the court of theoretical and practical reason, which has shaped the world of the performance principle, the aesthetic existence stands condemned.

18 Aronowitz and Giroux (1986) are instructive in their critical examination in *Education under Siege*, acknowledging the necessity of empowering students and of confirming their histories and possibilities. The critical analysis presented has relevance equally for school and university:

> Schools [and universities] should be regarded as sites around which a struggle should be waged in the name of developing a qualitatively better life for all. Teachers would have to develop forms of knowledge and classroom social practices that validate the experiences students bring to school. This means confirming such experiences so as to give students an active voice in institutional settings that traditionally try to silence them by ignoring their cultural capital. (155–6)

19 Marcuse's *An Essay on Liberation* (1969) and *Repressive Tolerance* (1967) provide an inferential basis for assessing the ends and means of Marcuse's plan of action.
20 In contemporary twenty-first-century society, the political imperatives of neoliberalism are more openly aggressive than the "comfortable, smooth, reasonable, democratic unfreedom" society that Marcuse condemned in the 1960s (see Marcuse 1964: 1).
21 Importantly, as Van Heertum notes:

> Marcuse lived the change he wanted to see in the world, rather than sequestering himself in the comfort of the academy. Critical teachers and researchers must also embody the change they are advocating, showing students an alternative through their actions together with their words. This requires more than critique, activism and alluding to the Great Refusal; it also most include a positive dream that can inspire others to follow, embracing their creativity and beliefs. (1992: 50)

22 In considering the importance of critical theory in practice, Marcuse posited:

> Theory accompanies the practice at every moment, analysing the changing situation and formulating its concepts accordingly. The concrete conditions

for realizing the truth may vary, but the truth remains the same and theory remains its ultimate guardian. Theory will preserve the truth even if revolutionary practice deviates from its proper path. ([1941] 1970: 322)

References

Apple, M. (2003), "Freire and the Politics of Race in Education," *International Journal of Leadership in Education* 6 (2): 107–18.

Aronowitz, S. (1999), "The Unknown Herbert Marcuse," *Social Text* 58: 133–54.

Aronowitz, S., and H. Giroux (1991), *Postmodern Education: Politics, Culture and Social Criticism*, Minneapolis: University of Minnesota Press.

Cunningham, J. (2013), "Praxis Exiled: Herbert Marcuse and the One Dimensional University," *Journal of Philosophy of Education* 47 (4): 537–47.

DeVitis, J. L. (1974), "Marcuse on Education: Social Critique and Social Control," *Educational Theory* 24 (3): 259–68. https://doi.org/10.1111/j.1741-5446.1974.tb00642.x

Freire, P. (2004), *Pedagogy of Indignation*, Boulder, CO: Paradigm.

Giroux, H. (1983), *Critical Theory and Educational Practice*, Victoria: Deakin University.

Giroux, H. A. (2003), "Youth, Higher Education, and the Crisis of Public Time: Educated Hope and the Possibility of a Democratic Future," *Social Identities* 9 (2): 141–68.

Giroux, H. A. (2004), "Critical Pedagogy and the Postmodern/Modern Divide: Towards a Pedagogy of Democratization," *Teacher Education Quarterly* 31 (1): 31–47.

Gitlin, A. (2005), "Inquiry, Imagination, and the Search for a Deep Politic," *Educational Researcher* 34 (3): 15–24. https://doi.org/10.3102/0013189X034003015.

Greene, M. (1995), *Releasing the Imagination: Essays on Education, the Arts and Social Change*, San Francisco, CA: Jossey-Bass.

Hoy, W. K. (1994), "Foundations of Educational Administration: Traditional and Emerging Perspectives," *Educational Administration Quarterly* 30: 178–98.

Kellner, D. (1995), *Media Culture: Cultural Studies, Identity and Politics between the Modern and the Postmodern*, London: Routledge.

Kellner, D. (ed.) (2001), *Towards a Critical Theory Society: Herbert Marcuse*, London: Routledge.

Kellner, D. (2006), "Marcuse's Challenge to Education," *Policy Futures in Education* 4 (1): 1–5.

Keniston, K. (1968), *Young Radicals*, New York: Harcourt, Brace and World.

Marcuse, H. (1937), "Philosophy and Critical Theory," *Zeitschrift für Sozialforschung/Journal for Social Research* 6 (1): 54–94. https://doi.org/10.5840/zfs193761135.

Marcuse, H. (1941), *Reason and Revolution: Hegel and the Rise of Social Theory*, New York: Oxford University Press.

Marcuse, H. (1955), *Eros and Civilization: A Philosophical Inquiry into Freud*, New York: Vintage Books.

Marcuse, H. (1958), *Soviet Marxism: A Critical Analysis*, New York: Columbia University Press.

Marcuse, H. (1960), "A Note on the Dialectic (Preface)," in *Reason and Revolution*, vii–xvi, Boston, MA: Beacon Press.

Marcuse, H. (1964), *One-Dimensional Man: The Ideology of Industrial Society*, Boston, MA: Beacon Press.

Marcuse, H. (1965), "Remarks on a Redefinition of Culture," *Daedalus* 94 (1): 190–207.

Marcuse, H. (1967), "Repressive Tolerance," in K. H. Wolff and B. H. Moore, Jr. (eds.), *A Critique of Pure Tolerance*, 81–118, Boston, MA: Beacon Press.

Marcuse, H. (1968), "Education and Social Change," lecture given at Brooklyn College, Frankfurt Marcuse Archive (Stadt-und Universitätsbibliothek), manuscript number 0343.01. www.ub.uni-frankfurt.de/archive/marcuse.html.

Marcuse, H. (1969), *An Essay on Liberation*, Boston, MA: Beacon Press.

Marcuse, H. (2009a), "Lecture on Education, Brooklyn College, 1968," in D. Kellner, T. Lewis and C. Pierce (eds.), *Marcuse's Challenge to Education*, 33–8, Lanham, MD: Rowman & Littlefield.

Marcuse, H. (2009b), "Lecture on Higher Education and Politics, Berkeley, 1975," in D. Kellner, T. Lewis, C. Pierce, and D. K. Cho (eds.), *Marcuse's Challenge to Education*, 39–43, Lanham, MD: Rowman & Littlefield.

Niesche, R., and C. Gowlett (2019), "Critical Perspectives in Educational Leadership: A New 'Theory Turn'?" in R. Niesche and C. Gowlett (eds.), *Social, Critical and Political Theories for Educational Leadership*, 17–34, Singapore: Springer.

Papson, S. (2014), "Scholars, Intellectuals, and Bricoleurs," *Arts and Humanities in Higher Education* 13 (4): 377–94. https://doi.org/10.1177/1474022213487951.

Peca, K. (2000), *Critical Theory in Education: Philosophical, Research, Socio-behavioral, and Organizational Assumptions*, Educational Resources Information Center, US Department of Education.

Pierce, C. (2013), "Educational Life and Death: Reassessing Marcuse's Critical Theory of Education in the Neoliberal Age," *Radical Philosophy Review* 16 (2): 603–24. https://doi.org/10.5840/radphilrev201316245.

Reitz, C. (2000), *Art, Alienation, and the Humanities: A Critical Engagement with Herbert Marcuse*, Albany: State University of New York Press.

Reitz, C. (2009a), "A New Marcuse: Educational Theorist for a New Generation." https://sites.google.com/site/marcusesociety/past-conferences/2009-conference-marcuse-and-the-frankfurt-school-for-a-new-generation/charles-reitz-2009-conference-paper.

Reitz, C. (2009b), "Herbert Marcuse and the Humanities: Emancipatory Education and Predatory Culture," in D. Kellner, T. Lewis, C. Pierce, and D. Cho (eds.), *Marcuse's Challenge to Education*, 213–28, Lanham, MD: Rowman & Littlefield.

Reitz, C. (2018), *Ecology and Revolution: Herbert Marcuse and the Challenge of a New World System Today*, New York: Routledge.

Reitz, C. (2019, August 23), "Marcuse's Relevance Today: Violence, Racism, and the Critique of Purse Tolerance," Radical Philosophy Association. https://www.rpamag.org/2019/08/marcuses-relevance-today-violence-racism-and-the-critique-of-pure-tolerance.

Van Heertum, R. (1992), "Marcuse, Bloch and Freire: Reinvigorating a Pedagogy of Hope," *Capitalism, Nature, Socialism* 3 (3): 45–51. https://doi.org/10.2304/pfie.2006.4.

Višić, M. (2019), "Renaissance of Herbert Marcuse: A Study on Present Interest in Marcus's Interdisciplinary Critical Theory," *Interdisciplinary Description of Complex Systems* 17 (3b): 659–83. https://doi.org/10.7906/indecs.17.3.19.

Winter, R. (2017), "Resistance as a Way Out of One-Dimensionality: The Contribution of Herbert Marcuse to a Critical Analysis of the Present," in M. Butler, P. Mecheril, and L. Brenningmeyer (eds.), *Resistance: Subjects, Representations, Contexts*, 71–86, Buchanan, NY: Transcript Verlag.

Wolf, K. P., B. Moore, Jr., and H. Marcuse (1965), *A Critique of Pure Tolerance*, Boston, MA: Beacon Press.

6

How Educational Leaders Make Better Decisions through a Frankfurt School Understanding of Rational Decision-Making

Chris Brown

Evidence-Informed Decision-Making in Education

Although it is true that the notion of using evidence to aid policy or practice-related decisions is not without controversy or debate (Hammersley 2013), it can also be strongly argued that engaging with evidence is socially beneficial for educationalists. This is because policy decisions or teaching practice grounded in an understanding of what is or could be effective, or even simply an understanding of what is currently known, are likely to be more successful than those based on experience or intuition alone (Coldwell et al. 2017; Cain et al. 2019). For instance, correlational evidence suggests that when research and evidence are used effectively as part of high-quality initial teacher education and continuing professional development, with a focus on addressing improvement priorities, it is linked to a positive difference in terms of teacher, school, and system performance (Mincu 2014; Cordingley 2013; Godfrey 2014, 2016). Bell et al. (2012), meanwhile, lists a range of positive teacher outcomes that emerge from evidence-informed practice, including improvements in pedagogic knowledge and skills and greater teacher confidence. Furthermore, the experience of "research-engaged" schools that take a strategic and concerted approach in this area appear to be positive, with studies suggesting that research engagement can shift school behaviors from a superficial "hints and tips" model of improvement to a learning culture in which the staff work together to understand what appears to work, when and why (Handscomb and MacBeath 2003; Godfrey 2016; Greany 2015).

Rationality and Evidence Use

At the same time, the notion of using evidence is one steeped in what is commonly understood as "rationality." By this I mean that, since the premise behind evidence use is that acting in this way can enhance the efficiency, equity, and value for money of policy or practice decisions (Oxman et al. 2009), it would seem sensible for policymakers and practitioners, when they are able, to use available quality evidence. This notion of underpinning rationality is perhaps best reflected in the number of initiatives and signifying activity that have been established to better ensure evidence use (Gough et al. 2011; Brown 2013; Coldwell et al. 2017; Cain et al. 2019). Therefore, why, in a post-Covid age of austerity, would governments invest time and money encouraging a specific activity if there is no benefit from doing so?

As is widely acknowledged elsewhere, however, evidence use is not widespread in educational policy or practice (Malin et al. 2020). Likewise, it is widely understood that evidence used by educators is often a form of discursive defense rather than meaningful input. A key question then for any analysis of evidence use concerns what we know and understand about rational behavior and whether current conceptions should be revised in line with actual observed behaviors (i.e., the nonuse of evidence). This question also leads me to consider how, as social researchers, we might engage in enhancing the optimality of rational behavior: in other words, how to encourage more instances of educational decision-making that is deemed to be rational.

With this chapter I seek to address such considerations. I begin by examining and critiquing Aristotelian and Kantian notions of rationality. I then illustrate how a revisioning of Aristotelian rationality—in light of understanding provided by Habermas and others—can result in an understanding of rationality as the actual actions we engage in as they relate to maximizing our well-being: correspondingly, how optimal rational behavior represents the extent to which our actions are congruent with more culturally contextualized and widely promulgated notions of what rational behavior might entail.

Aristotelian Ethics

My examination of rationality starts with Aristotle, who, like Socrates, was concerned with how people might best live virtuously: how people might acquire and come to act through excellent and well-chosen habits, a situation regarded as synonymous with a state of happiness or "human flourishing." Aristotle asserted, at the time of his writing, that popular accounts concerning what might comprise a happy life seemed to divide most easily into one of three common types: a life dedicated to vulgar pleasure; a life dedicated to fame and honor; or a life dedicated to contemplation.

To judge these, Aristotle employed the concept of *reason* to define the "natural" function of a human in action: the ability to use reason or *logos*, he argued, serves to act as the essential attribute characterizing what it is to be human. At the same time, Aristotle opined that reason may be exercised in two ways: theoretically and practically (i.e., both in thoughts and in deeds). Happiness, therefore, can emerge only through *rationality*—the appropriate exercise of practical reason and emotional control to ensure our actions are congruent with human nature (theoretical reason), rather than work against it. Although actions and thought can be married in all three typologies of human flourishing, Aristotle however also argued that the question of how one *maximizes* happiness equates to a question of which activities of the human soul represent the "highest" excellence in using reason. Correspondingly, the Aristotelian solution for a virtuous happy life is to live the life of philosophy and contemplation, since this truly realizes man's purpose or nature as found in the reasoned soul.

Aristotle's notions of rationality and ethics remained broadly accepted until the time of the enlightenment. In part this may have been due to the compatibility of the broader Aristotelian position (for instance, Aristotle's study of the "fundamentals" or first causes), and his contribution to the process of deductive inference and reasoning (see *The Metaphysics*) with a number of Christian philosophical traditions that emerged during this time. These include St Anselm's "ontological argument" for the proof of god and, to an extent related to this, Descartes's own system of reasoning, based on the idea that self-evident truths should form the basis of all scientific argument.

This was a position also held, albeit in a modified form, by Spinoza, who argued for the existence of *a priori truths*: in other words, that the fundamental premises of human knowledge can only be established using reason, rather than experience, in order to establish the basic "essence" of things. Such views were also later championed by other "rationalist" philosophers such as Leibniz (1646–1716), who claimed that a priori truth in fact amounted to objective knowledge (i.e., knowledge of the world as it *actually* is). However, during the eighteenth century, the rationalist perspective endured substantial challenge and critique from "empiricists" such as David Hume (1711–76).

It was the argument of the empiricists that the only thing we can truly know is what our senses tell us, and correspondingly that we can have objective truth of nothing and certainly no understanding beyond that of the individual. It was not until the arrival of Immanuel Kant more than a century after Spinoza's death that these opposing schools of thought were reconciled; and in successfully combining empiricist and rational positions, Kant served to usher in a new epoch in terms of how we might come to view rational and reasoned behavior. Specifically, Kant's work recentered notions of rationality by focusing on two key aspects: (1) how we might come to know the world and (2) how we should act in relation to it.

Kantian Epistemology and Ontology

Kant begins his reconciliation of Leibniz and Hume by restating their opposing rationalist and empiricist positions. The former, he argued, situates understanding as something that is dependent on the existence of innate principles that the self knows intuitively to be true and that do not depend on experience for any sort of verification. The rationalist position thus ultimately stems from the idea that reality "is accessible to reason alone since only reason can rise above the individual point of view" (Scruton 1982: 16).

Similarly, Kant sets out Hume's diametrically opposed position as one that denies the possibility of knowledge through reason. This is because reason must be situated within ideas and in themselves; ideas can only stem from sense data. Ultimately, however, sense data is only ever experienced at the level of the individual and so knowledge of the world can only be as each individual perceives it. As a result, empiricists argue that objective knowledge becomes a spurious concept and phenomenon that appears to operate independently of our perceptions (e.g., causal effects) and should be viewed as nothing more than sets of experiences that we come to regularly perceive in consistent ways.

Kant reconciles these two positions through his argument that neither experience nor reason alone is able to provide knowledge: no knowledge can exist without it being some combination—some synthesis—of reason and experience. The natural extension of Kant's analysis is that judgment results from the application of reasoning to data: experience provides concepts with meaning and in doing so provides the grounds for the application of a concept. That judgments might be *objective*—in other words, externally valid explanations rather than simply representing subjective interpretations of the world—can be derived from proving the existence of objects in time and space, a notion that had been thrown into doubt by the skeptical empiricism of Hume and by Leibniz's desire to explain the world as existing as a form of abstract reason.

In other words, by demonstrating that the world conformed to the laws laid down by Newtonian science for all perceivable things, the existence of objects in time and space were fixed. A key aspect of Kantian analysis thus involves his treatment of cause and effect: Kant posits that it is only by finding causal relationships that we can believe in the objectivity of the world. In turn causality is dependent on the endurance of things in time and space: their ability to exist even when we are not experiencing them, which in itself can be assessed by observing their altered state over time. Kant's work on epistemology and ontology, therefore, provides one of the first philosophical backings to scientific method as a means of investigating and making sense of the world.

A Universal Moral Code

But Kant's work also provided a universal moral underpinning for rationality: while Kant rejected the idea of pure reason as a means to understand the world as is, he did, however, believe that a form of pure "practical" reason (in the Aristotelian sense) could serve to guide people's actions within it. It was Kant's argument that people exist, not only as self-conscious centers of knowledge but also as agents (i.e., people possess agency) who can and do make choices. Kant held however that, despite this, objective practical reason could be established independent of agency, with it being possible to employ such reason that it might recommend both means and ends to choices while simultaneously justifying and motivating our actions.

Such motivation, Kant argued, materializes through the idea of the moral imperative: imperatives that tell you what to do uncategorically (typically signaled by the presence of an "ought") (Scruton 1982). A moral imperative is thus something that we are intuitively drawn toward, knowing that it is right—that we "ought" to do it. Since the autonomous being is both an agent (i.e., can act) and someone who possesses values, categorical imperatives as universal "law" must relate to both these attributes.

Kant therefore describes his notion of the overarching categorical imperative in the following way: that we must respect the existence and endeavors of rational beings. In other words, the constraint of our freedom is that we must respect the freedom of all. In this sense, Kant's universal code encapsulates concepts such as justice within an intuitive understanding of what is right. It is thus a compelling dictum, but one quite different from interest or desire—we know we should follow it, whether or not we actually do.

The End of Enlightenment?

Kant's work helped to usher in the enlightenment, a movement concerned with progress and the Baconian ideal that developing and organizing empirical knowledge could immeasurably improve mankind's lot in life: in other words, it promoted the banishing of traditional philosophy (broadly viewed as an amalgam of Christianity and Aristotelian philosophy), replacing it instead with scientific method.

Specifically, the types of epistemologies and ontology generally thought of as being realist/positivist in nature (i.e., those that view the world as knowable and prone to being accurately explained via the application of scientific method and the development of broad overarching theories that set out universal or macro-level notions of cause and effect). The privileging of the scientific and universal that followed Kant has not been without problem, however. And this has been noted elsewhere with regard to the needs of individual contexts and the costs of recontextualization (Brown 2019). I have also previously discussed in some detail the notion of social constructivism, and that while there may be social "facts," in relation to other social facets such as opinion and belief, there can be no all-encompassing understanding of the social world (Brown 2013).

As you might expect, given the aim of this book, extensive critique of this impact of the enlightenment is also provided by the critical theorists of the Frankfurt School: for example, that set out by Max Horkheimer and Theodor Adorno, who concern themselves with enlightenment's "self-destruction." In discussing the enlightenment, Horkheimer and Adorno suggest it has "always aimed at liberating men from fear and establishing their sovereignty .... The program of the enlightenment was the disenchantment of the world; the dissolution of myths and the substitution of knowledge for fancy" (1972: 4).

Somewhere on the "road to modern science," however, such ideals became lost: "Men renounce[d] any claim to meaning. They substitute[d] formula for concept, rule and probability for cause and motive" (1972: 5). In other words, Horkheimer and Adorno argue that, as the enlightenment became enveloped by empiricism, scientism, and ultimately positivism, that verification and falsification became the bywords and supposed features of good science and of good understanding generally. This, as a result, served to stifle new, original, and unproven or untested thought: the ability to critique and reason, engage in creative philosophical acts became lost.

So too, however, did values: "Substance and quality, activity and suffering, being and existence: to define these concepts in a way appropriate to the times was a concern of philosophy after Bacon—but science managed without such categories. They were abandoned as *idola theatri* of the old 'metaphysics'" (Horkheimer and Adorno 1972: 5). Rationality, they suggest, thus became a concept associated simply with attempts to understand and verify claims to the universal, test for cause and effect at a macro level, and develop ways of explaining the world that subsumed the complexities of the individual: essentially rationality came to represent a concern for "what is" not "what ought to be."

Simultaneously, the unexplicated or implicit concepts that underpinned these universal theories became elevated to the level of true social realism: the status quo became rigidly locked in place, but done so unassumingly and in a way disguised by the neutrality of scientific discourse. Falsification of such assumptions (e.g., in relation to the inferiority of those of specific class, gender, or race) subsequently took time, since this process both represented and required discursive challenge to the status quo: a revolution of ideas.

The analysis by Horkheimer and Adorno helps to illustrate how the notion of the scientific ideal, the universal explanation of phenomenon, came to prominence in terms of how it was expected social science should contribute to the production of solutions (e.g., in terms of policy and practice). More than this, however, Horkheimer and Adorno suggest that in privileging a scientific approach, the notion that social scientists might also contribute to society's conceptions of ethics and values (the things that are good or bad for society) has been diminished and undermined and that these things have become the domain of the politician. That the current situation facing social science might be considered problematic has been illustrated by Flyvbjerg, who argues that social science is not able to develop the types of theory considered "normal" (in a Kuhnian sense) in the natural sciences.[1] Conversely, that social science is better placed than the natural sciences at providing aspects of practical wisdom (i.e., the notions of ethics and values described by Horkheimer and Adorno).

As I will now explore, Kant's moral legacy—the notion of the imperative that might guide us all—appears in the modern world, specifically in relation to consumption, to be increasingly difficult both to enforce and adhere to. Social scientists would therefore seem to find themselves facing the irony that they are being asked to produce the types of scientific knowledge they are ill-placed to provide while being unable to contribute to wider value-laden notions regarding the roles of rationality and morality in a post-Kantian world.

The End of a Universal Moral Code?

I now assess the difficulties the moral code currently faces in more detail, beginning with the idea of enforcement, where I suggest that contemporary conceptions of power and its distribution serve to illustrate the difficulties in establishing any kind of mechanics that might police the moral code. This is perhaps best illustrated by juxtaposing the work of Jürgen Habermas and Michel Foucault: both of whom are political thinkers and who agree on the need for reason and the importance of Kant (Foucault 1984). Their analysis differs in their treatment of power and its effects on rationality: in other words, if and how a universal moral imperative can be upheld. I begin by examining the work of Jürgen Habermas that is principally concerned with how rational decision-making can be facilitated in modern democratic societies.

Habermas's thesis is dependent on his theory of "communicative action": action oriented toward reaching an agreement, which, Habermas contends, is *the* fundamental type of social action. In turn, communicative action depends on a further premise: the notion that discourse is used by people as an everyday process of making claims to validity.

These two premises enable Habermas to conceive of civic life as comprising networks of relationships that display two principal characteristics: firstly they are cooperative—this is because the success of any interaction depends upon the interdependent activity of both narrators and audiences (respectively as producers and receivers of the communicative act); secondly, that discourse must have a rational dimension: a narrator will seek to provide reasons for the validity of their communicative act, knowing that their counterpart (the audience) may either accept it or counter it with a better argument. Habermas's twin premises of mutual agreement and discursive validity also allow him to set out a vision that positions valid and rational arguments as the basis for all major decisions.

In other words, in a Habermasian society, public acts of praxis are ultimately determined by what Habermas describes as "the unforced force of the better argument" (2003: 37), which represents a "cooperative search for *truth*" (75, my emphasis). Habermas thus conceives of power as something that is constantly ameliorated by rationality: power is only afforded to individuals or institutions in instances where they can successfully argue their case. The notion of the better argument, meanwhile, is "policed" by rules established by Habermas to uphold the validity of arguments (Habermas's five "tenets" of discourse ethics) (as cited in Cooke 1999).

The Habermasian approach would appear to reflect much of the essence of Kantian moral imperative and, at the same time, the rhetoric of being "evidence-informed." For example, the consequence of Habermas's analysis emphasizes decision-making that is informed by widespread public participation, the extensive sharing of information that might inform decisions, consensus reached through public dialogue rather than the exercise of bureaucratic power, a reduction of the privilege afforded to policymakers based solely on their position, and the morphing of the role of policymaker from policy technician to that of the reflective practitioner (Argyris and Schön 1974).

As such, Habermas argues that the legitimacy of praxis should be viewed in terms of not only whether individuals (undertaking public roles) have acted *intra vires*, but also on the nature and the quality of the deliberation that preceded this action. Evidence therefore has a key role to play in shaping decisions via actions such as informing citizens with regard to issues, or providing decision-makers or social actors with a myriad of perspectives with which to inform their decisions/actions. Researchers in a Habermasian system are thus afforded pivotal positions as both gatekeepers to and the interpreters of knowledge while using this to uphold the freedoms of individuals.

Habermas's model for democracy can be critiqued, however, precisely because it represents an ideal (i.e., it represents a type of government that should be aspired to), and Habermas does little to address how power materializes in actuality (Flyvbjerg 2001). Instead, Habermas immerses himself within a perspective of structures: he principally concerns himself with establishing what might be required for rational argument to flourish, as well as with identifying procedures to establish democratic consensus based on the outcomes of argument. Habermas's solution is to resort to "the legal institutionalization of those forms of communication necessary for democratic will formation" (n.d.: 15). This focus on how democratic processes should work, rather than how they do currently, leads Flyvbjerg to contend that "the basic weakness of Habermas's project is its lack of agreement between idea and reality, between intentions and their implementation" (1998: 215).

But Habermas's work is also open to even more basic critique: while the Habermasian system is centered on consensus-building as *the* fundamental type of social action, many other social commentators and philosophers believe that the exact opposite is in fact true. English philosopher Thomas Hobbes

(1588–1679), for instance, painted a bleak picture of people as self-interested and prone to baser instincts; similarly, Niccolò Machiavelli suggests human beings are "ungrateful, fickle, liars and deceivers" (1984: 96).

If human beings truly behave in such a way, what incentives do decision-makers/social actors have to systematically consider evidence? Firstly, for instance, why should they trust the motivations of researchers to provide them with the most appropriate (as opposed to the most self-serving) evidence? Secondly, if individuals are self-interested, they are unlikely to be willing to cede power to a democratic system that might require them to bend their will to the force of a well-argued case, particularly if that case doesn't suit their needs.

Such critique implies that, instead, we should enquire as to how claims to validity are constructed, how institutions operate, and so what comprises the wider discursive milieu in which acts of praxis are formulated. To ask whether validity really is characterized by consensus-seeking and the amelioration of power, or whether it, and the process of communication that leads to it, is in itself part and parcel of the exercise of power (Flyvbjerg 1998).

Michel Foucault

A counter to Habermas's democratic utopia is found in Michel Foucault. Habermas's concept of power and its amelioration by legal and democratic frameworks juxtaposes that of Foucault. Instead, Foucault claims that his analysis is feasible only due to it having "abandon[ed] the juridical model [that] makes the law the basic manifestation of power" (2004: 265). Although Habermas calls for a system of universally accepted and applicable democratic principles (i.e., one that implies processes for establishing consent and a normative validity), Foucault contends that these principles are simply not achievable (268).

Instead, Foucault proposes that the worldviews of social groups are contextually grounded (and therefore truth is "perspectival and strategic"). This stance not only rejects Habermas's general principle of "the better argument"; given there is no neutral or a priori manner by which this is judged, it also rejects the likelihood that social groups or institutions can operate in ways that would be seen as "value-neutral" or in accordance with any universal *imperative*.

Consequently, rather than adopt the construction of mechanisms that provide a blueprint for how a utopian government might operate, Foucault frames his work as "genealogical." Foucault's genealogy describes the genesis of a situation in order to illustrate how it was arrived at. Foucault demonstrates that what is often given or presupposed has not always been the case. As such, alternatives are possible. Foucault specifically describes the task of laying open norms and the identification of alternatives as "criticiz[ing] the working of institutions which appear to be both neutral and independent; to criticize them in such a manner that the political violence which has always exercised itself obscurely through them will be unmasked, so that one can fight them" (Chomsky and Foucault 1974: 171).

A natural extension of this line of argument is that those in power are better placed to promote their perspectives as "normal." Foucault describes this notion as the "will to knowledge"—the desire by social groups to advance their version of events. Key to the successful operation of the "will to knowledge" is how knowledge might be disseminated: this affects how power is enforced or maintained and how it is undermined. Foucault suggests that this role is played by discourse.

For instance, in terms of maintaining power, Foucault (1980) argues that each society has a "regime of truth"—discursive realities that are not only accepted as true but which are also made to function as true (e.g., via affording status to those charged with pronouncing the truth). In such cases, the dissemination of discourse facilitates control over what those in power wish to promote as the truth: power is synonymous with the promotion of the "true" knowledge of the status quo, and the discourse that results is specifically designed to uphold the current, specific "regime of truth."

Foucault (1978: 100–101) also notes that "discourses are not once and for all subservient to power ... discourse can be both an instrument and an effect of power, but also a hindrance, a stumbling block, a point of resistance and a starting point for an opposing strategy." Discourses formed as part of the appropriation of knowledge can also be used, therefore, to seek to undermine existing power relations through the promotion of alternative "truth regimes." It is clear then that, for Foucault, power determines both rationality and truth, with the result that rationality and truth are contextual, not universal in nature. That is to say, these notions are subject to competing discourses that work to promote given ideologies while also serving to remove others from general circulation.

This leads Foucault to suggest that the Kantian notion of a universal moral imperative is no longer tenable: "Perhaps too, we should abandon a whole tradition that allows us to imagine that knowledge can exist only where power relations are suspended and that knowledge can develop only outside its injunctions, its demands and its interests" (1977: 27).

Code

There are other concepts that serve similar functions to the "regime of truth" since they suggest that rationality is contextualized by the milieu within which individuals operate. For example, Jean Baudrillard (1998) conceives of code in a similar way as Foucault positions discursive power: as something that serves to program reality (via the construction of simulacra that subsume the real) in ways desired and preferred by those in power. In other words, codes equal the subordination of existence within given forms of representation.

Baudrillard's notion of power differs from that of Foucault's in several ways, however. For example: (1) Baudrillard's conception of power as produced through signs allows for a wider conception of discursive control. In other words, it allows for the influence of brands, branding, and advertising; and (2) that "code" can construct both physical and social reality (e.g., the former would be achieved via the production of original DNA, the production and overlaying of virtual reality onto the social real, and so on; the latter via the production of signs). Within this analysis, I concentrate solely on power as it relates to the social,[2] and while Baudrillard presents a more extreme and unbending position, I prefer to engender people with a certain amount of agency and so regard the notion of the code as something that can be resisted (i.e., via the acts/actions described by Foucault as "ethics").

The Impossibility of Consuming in Line with the Moral Imperative

Remaining with the notion of (social) code for the moment, Baudrillard perhaps failed to anticipate the economic and social situation facing the West from the 2010s to now and that might accompany his notion of code: he does not posit, in the same way that Foucault does, that there might be several different codes struggling for hegemony, or at least requiring action. In a globalized and connected world, however, the multitude of perspectives that are transmitted via the hyperreality means that we are often faced with a myriad of conflicting messages.

Not only this, but in the West, our consumer society and the marketing machine that accompanies it also mean that we are also faced with a constant bombardment of a multiplicity of sign seeking to influence our thoughts and behaviors. In terms of consumption, which I suggest is how the use of research might best be conceived (Brown 2014), we are also faced with numerous choices (often provided by the same supplier) for every consumer object imaginable. But perhaps, more importantly, in a world of globalized mass consumption, there are "externalities"—our acts of consumption have implications for others (both in the future and geographically).

These implications might realize themselves in terms of our carbon footprint; the pollution more generally that accompanies production; the conditions of the labor force producing the work compared to more expensive Western labor; that diverting resources into one good will, at some point, mean that someone else cannot have it, and so on. In the modern world then, for the act of consumption, the notion of freedom and respecting the freedom or rights of others becomes almost impossible: almost all acts of consumption have a consequence that have implications for others.

As individuals, we are often left wondering which source of information (or signs) to believe and how to act since there is no perfect value-free information upon which we might make our choices: the moral imperative thus becomes an unattainable ideal and we are left instead with pragmatic compromise—trying to live life in the Kantian tradition as much as we are able.[3]

What Next for Rationality?

Through my analysis above, I have suggested that the two types of Kantian universals that have previously underpinned notions of rationality (the moral imperative and the "scientific" approach to theory) are now increasingly untenable as hallmarks of rational behavior: (1) the moral imperative is something that only exists in relation to local, not universal, discourse, and it is, in terms of consumption, impossible to act in ways fully congruent with it; in addition, (2) the social world is not fully amenable to the scientific method, and acting as though it is will negate or relegate the other roles social science can play in suggesting what is good or right for society.

Consequently, I suggest we need to revisit conceptions of rationality to ensure their relevance to contemporary society. We need first to remove the notion of the universal from the moral imperative and then consider that which works best to guide context-specific situations at a given point in time. Second, we need to remove the notion of the universal from the development of theory by acknowledging that cultures, subcultures, groups, or institutions are likely to work in a way that suits their setting best: thus, the more effective a theory will be to explain a given phenomenon, the more grounded it is within that phenomenon. This is not to say that more generalized theories cannot be produced, simply that their explanatory power will wane the more detached from the empirical they become.

Given this need to remove these two types of universality, a second ironic twist then is to argue that, for acts of consumption, the way forward for rationality is perhaps located in the past, specifically via a repositioning of Aristotelian ethics. This repositioning is not undertaken, however, with a view to emulate the past but to learn from it. In other words, I agree with Foucault when he suggests that "this idea that the Greek civilization is something like a model, which has been forgotten … doesn't make a lot of sense because history is history. There is no way, no hope, no positive meaning in turning back on something" (Maas and Brock 1983: 21).

Nonetheless, it is also Foucault's observation that in the ancient world we can find examples of ethics and values different than ours and not rooted in the same sociohistorical contexts (e.g., in terms of contemporary religion, civil law, or science) (Flyvbjerg 2001)—a civilization where values and the philosophy of ethics are strong. Foucault cautions, however, that our solutions must be very different from those proposed by the ancient Greeks (Maas and Brock 1983).

I argue then that what might best be learned from Aristotle is twofold: first, that reason may exercise both theoretically and practically (we intuitively know that we regularly fail to consume in ways we know are "best" for us, and I will illustrate this with concrete examples below); second is the lack of the universal in Aristotle's notions of theoretical and practical reasoning. With regard to the latter, Aristotle makes no attempt (as Kant did) to distill via reasoning a moral imperative designed never to be refuted; he simply refers to happiness, a concept that can always be achieved but is totally dependent on context.

A Departure from Aristotle

My repositioning also departs from key aspects of Aristotle's position in two key ways. First, I argue there will be a number of aspects of rationality, and I suggest we must broadly disaggregate these so that we might understand the full gamut of perspectives through which to view rational behavior. For example, rationality is likely to range, on the one hand, from universal rationality (which is concerned with behavior in relation to society as a whole) to individual rationality (how individuals might behave), and, on the other hand, from short-term behavior to that which concerns the long term. In each case, however, these are likely to be concerned with maximizing "well-being." By this, I do not mean the type of welfare maximization described by economists who equate it directly to economic action/activity; instead, my suggestion is that acts to enhance well-being represent actions that individuals "know" are "needed" at a given point in time.

These acts of *practical rationality* thus represent the actual courses we take in life and are as much driven by emotion, feeling, intuition, expertise (in a Flyvbjergian sense), and an unconscious desire or motive as any conscious decision we may think through in detail: it is how we behave on a minute-by-minute, hour-by-hour, and day-by-day basis no matter what our state of mind—we might be drunk, stoned, or sober, but attempting to meet our desires and maximize our welfare in these states will nonetheless represent rational behavior in the practical mode. In other words, unlike Aristotle, I treat emotion as a valid motivator of, not something that gets in the way of, rational behavior.

Second relates to the need to incorporate concepts designed to explain society's role in instilling values or norms into individuals, which act to influence or shape behaviors, such as Foucault's *regime of truth*, or Baudrillard's concept of *code*. These provide the theoretical yardstick of reason, which I will reterm *cultural rationality*,[4] or that which producers, society, subcultures within society, or perhaps even more localized cultures, such as schools or government departments, deem as vital to the wider well-being and seek to embed in practice and enforce via discourse or through signs. A fundamental difference between these two forms of rationality relates to the "aspects" of rationality they are concerned with and the forms of welfare they are aimed at increasing.

Broadly, although not exclusively, practical rationality tends to be concerned with the individual and the short term: often we act in ways that suit our own immediate needs for the here and now. Cultural rationality then relates to the wider group and/or the longer term: how do our actions affect the well-being of our coworkers, neighbors, friends, or family; and/or how will our behavior today affect our well-being tomorrow? In considering how the two modes of cultural and practical rationality interrelate or affect behavior, either one or both may operate at a given point in time. It is not unreasonable that we might seek to pursue an entirely practical path (which will likely amount to individuals focusing on the welfare of the short-term self), nor simultaneously that we might criticize individuals (from an external standpoint) for pursuing this type of action.

Indeed, it is in an individual's interest that everyone else in society sticks to behaving in ways entirely consistent with what its cultural reasoning suggests. An approach that is not only rational but also optimal from the standpoint of both the individual and the group (which ultimately will be the same) ensures that on aggregate there is balance or alignment between the two. This is because at a point of balance, when an individual or subgroup pursues their desires, they do so in ways congruent with approaches that also benefit either society or themselves in the long term.

Perhaps a better way to explain this contemporary interpretation of Aristotelian rationality is to relate it to real-life examples: thus, if we assume that being rational is to consume in a way that maximizes our well-being, then we equate it to improving the positive experiences we have. Personally I enjoy eating at more gourmet restaurants, or going to more gigs. I also like drinking *Corona* and eating *Ben & Jerry's*. While doing these things in the short term might be fun, I know that if done, say, daily, these actions will not be conducive to my long-term well-being (I might become obese, die younger from a heart attack than I ordinarily might do, get tired from too many long nights, and so on).

So, what is needed here is a balance between what I know will give me short-term well-being and what is probably best for my future well-being (my ability to consume longer term). At the same time, I may also do things that might not necessarily give me pleasure now, but act to benefit me in the long term (e.g., save money, or go to the gym four times a week). At the same time, while the well-being I maximize is personal, it is done within familial and cultural norms and the "structural" influences that exist at societal level: the maximization of my welfare is thus contextualized by both the signs (transmitted by the producers of consumer goods: brands, marketing activity, etc.) and the norms of the wider groups to which I belong (family, friends, work colleagues, bosses, stakeholders, customers, religious perspectives, etc.). I do not therefore act or consume in entirely selfish ways, or solely influenced by messaging: I understand the societal requirements related to my acts of consumption and bear them in mind as I act.

In other words, my understanding of the long-term negative consequences of beer and ice cream is part informed by the messages and signs promulgated by certain parts of society that have a vested interest in my staying sober and healthy (e.g., the National Health Service and the police who would otherwise have to spend money on remedial activity, such as heart bypass operations or prosecution). My wife too would probably prefer that I stay trim, lean, and coherent.

This notion of balance and optimality thus requires individuals or groups to act as often as possible in ways sympathetic with society's notion of reason, but simultaneously it requires society to provide an incentive to do so: for example, by setting in place disincentives to dissuade people from pursuing their whims too often (or to excessive levels) to the detriment of others, or by educating (e.g., with regard to health and fitness) so that individuals seek to balance themselves in their acts of consumption. At the same time, "abandoning" Kant in this way does not necessarily need to result in relativism or extremist dominance (as relates to cultural rationality), since it is clear that the universal itself can be bent to meet the needs of a particular will to knowledge: for example, Foucault has previously illustrated how the Kantian position itself was adopted by those sympathetic to Nazi Germany (in particular Foucault refers to Max Pohlenz) (Tully 1999). In other words, espousing a theory doesn't necessarily mean adhering to it.

Instead, cultural rationality must be continuously revisited and challenged in order to ensure that the dominant discourse or the prevailing code is not allowed to be unconsciously or unwillingly perverted so that it affects people's ability to maximize their well-being, or ensures that we act with the best available understanding of the implications of our actions. Perhaps the best way to envisage such a challenge is via the idea of a discursive feedback loop between practical and cultural rationalities: acts of practical rationality, directed as they are at maximizing the being of the individual, can—should they deviate significantly from current cultural rationalities—be positioned as instances of resistance. Where there are consistent commonalities and themes, this deviation might then be positioned as alternative regimes of truth and serves to challenge the discourses that form any given cultural rationality. The notion of promoting discursive challenge directly addresses both Horkheimer and Adorno's (1972) and Flyvbjerg's (2001) critique of the enlightenment and its effects on social science. What is now needed, however, is to take the analysis above and apply it to educational decision-making, specifically to consider what rational behavior "looks like" as it relates to employing improving educational decisions, and what the role of social science might be in promoting more specific versions of rational behavior.

Notes

1 This is because Flyvbjerg (2001) argues that scientific theory must be (1) explicit (clearly laid out and not dependent on interpretation), (2) universal (applies in all

places at all times), (3) abstract, (4) abstract (does not require reference to concrete examples), (5) systematic (it represents a whole in which elements are related by laws), (6) complete and predictive (precise predictions can be made).
2. While the physical is regarded as less relevant for this analysis, there is, however, one aspect where it may have salience: if copies of reality (simulacra) can one day be perfectly constructed, then might we not use these resultant virtual realities to test out the efficacy of and media/public reaction to government policy in situ – to examine how these play out in context and when combined with other initiatives and social phenomena? Similarly, we could do the same with classrooms and evidence-informed practice. Surely this would provide the ultimate in evidence-informed policy.
3. Quite possibly the difficulties I raise of consuming in adherence with the moral imperative existed before the modern consumerist age. Rousseau (writing during the time of the enlightenment) argued that the enlightenment served to usher in a moral decay: that Bacon's grand hope of creating abundance could be equated to luxury, which in itself is a breeder of corruption. For Rousseau then, only a simple (i.e., austere and frugal) life could also be virtuous; certainly such an approach means we are faced with less complex choices when it comes to understanding the implications of our actions.
4. I use the term rational rather than reasoned since an action, belief, or desire is rational if we *ought* to choose it. This then can be simply and easily applied to the notion of welfare maximization at the level of the individual. Reason, however, is more commonly associated with the power of the mind to think, understand, and form judgments by a process of logic—which is often difficult to prove and likely to depend on one's state of mind being unimpaired.

References

Argyris, C., and D. Schön (1974), *Theory in Practice: Increasing Professional Effectiveness*, San Francisco, CA: Jossey-Bass.

Baudrillard, J. (1998), *The Consumer Society: Myths & Structures*, London: Sage.

Bell, M., P. Cordingley, P. Crisp, and M. Hawkins (2012), *Understanding What Enables High Quality Professional Learning: A Report on the Research Evidence*, London: Pearson School Improvement. www.pearsonschoolmodel.co.uk/wp-content/uploads/2011/09/CUREE-Report.pdf.

Brown, C. (2013), *Making Evidence Matter: A New Perspective for Evidence-Informed Policy-Making in Education*, London: UCL IOE Press.

Brown, C. (2014), *Evidence Informed Policy and Practice: A Sociological Grounding*, London: Bloomsbury.

Brown, C. (2019), "Exploring the Current Context for Professional Learning Networks, the Conditions for Their Success, and Research Needs Moving Forwards," *Emerald Open Research* 1 (1): 1–20.

Cain, T., S. Brindley, C. Brown, G. Jones, and F. Riga (2019), "Bounded Decision-Making, Teachers' Reflection and Organisational Learning: How Research Can Inform Teachers and Teaching," *British Educational Research Journal* 45 (5): 1072–87.

Chomsky, N., and M. Foucault (1974), *The Chomsky-Foucault Debate: On Human Nature*, New York: New Press.

Coldwell, M., T. Greany, S. Higgins, C. Brown, B. Maxwell, B. Stiell, L. Stoll, B. Willis, and H. Burns (2017), *Evidence-Informed Teaching: An Evaluation of Progress in England. Research Report*, London: Department for Education.

Cooke, M. (1999), "A Space of One's Own: Autonomy, Privacy, Liberty," *Philosophy & Social Criticism* 25 (1): 23–53.

Cordingley, P. (2013), "The Contribution of Research to Teachers' Professional Learning and Development." www.bera.ac.uk/wp-content/uploads/2013/12/BERA-Paper-5Continuing-professional-development-and-learning.pdf.

Flyvbjerg, B. (1998), *Rationality and Power: Democracy in Practice*, trans. S. Sampson, Chicago, IL: University of Chicago Press.

Flyvbjerg, B. (2001), *Making Social Science Matter: Why Social Inquiry Fails and How It Can Succeed Again*, Cambridge: Cambridge University Press.

Foucault, M. (1977), *Discipline and Punish: The Birth of the Prison*, trans. A. Sheridan, New York: Random House.

Foucault, M. (1978), *History of Sexuality, Vol. 1: An Introduction*, trans. R. Hurley, New York: Random House.

Foucault, M. (1980), *Power/Knowledge: Selected Interviews and Other Writings 1972–1977*, trans. C. Gordon, L. Marshall, J. Mepham, and K. Soper, New York: Pantheon.

Foucault, M. (1984), "What Is Enlightenment?" in P. Rabinow (ed.), *The Foucault Reader*, 32–50, New York: Pantheon.

Foucault, M. (2004), *The Birth of Biopolitics: Lectures at the College de France, 1978–79*, New York: Pantheon.

Godfrey, D. (2014), "Creating a Research Culture: Lessons from Other Schools." www.sec-ed.co.uk/best-practice/creating-a-research-culture-lessons-from-other-schools.

Godfrey, D. (2016), "Leadership of Schools as Research-Led Organizations in the English Educational Environment: Cultivating a Research Engaged School Culture," *Educational Management Administration & Leadership* 44 (2): 301–21.

Gough, D., J. Tripney, C. Kenny, and E. Buk-Berge (2011), *Evidence Informed Policymaking in Education in Europe*, London: EIPPEE.

Greany, T. (2015), "How Can Evidence Inform Teaching and Decision Making across 21,000 Autonomous Schools? Learning from the Journey in England," in C. Brown (ed.), *Leading the Use of Research & Evidence in Schools*, 11–29, London: IOE Press.

Habermas, J. (2003), *Truth and Justification*, trans. B. Fultner, Boston, MA: Massachusetts Institute of Technology.

Hammersley, M. (2013), *The Myth of Research-Based Policy & Practice*, Los Angeles, CA: Sage Publications.

Handscomb, G., and J. MacBeath (2003), *The Research Engaged School*, Chelmsford: Essex County Council.

Horkheimer, M., and T. W. Adorno (1972), *Dialectic of Enlightenment*, trans. J. Cumming, New York: Herder.

Maas, P., and D. Brock (1983), "The Power and Politics of Michel Foucault," *Inside* 7: 21.

Machiavelli, N. (1984), *The Prince*, New York: Bantam.

Malin, J. R., C. Brown, G. Ion, I. van Ackeren, N. Bremm, R. Luzmore, J. Flood, and G. M. Rind (2020), "World-wide Barriers and Enablers to Achieving Evidence-Informed Practice in Education: What Can Be Learnt from Spain, England, the United States, and Germany?," *Humanities and Social Sciences Communications* 7 (1): 1–14.

Mincu, M. (2014), "Inquiry Paper 6: Teacher Quality and School Improvement: What Is the Role of Research?," in British Educational Research Association/The Royal Society for the encouragement of Arts, Manufactures and Commerce (eds.), *The Role of Research in Teacher Education: Reviewing the Evidence*, 1–15.

Oxman, A. D., J. N. Lavis, A. Fretheim, and S. Lewin (2009), "Support Tools for Evidence-Informed Health Policymaking (STP) 17: Dealing with Insufficient Research Evidence," *Health Research and Policy Systems* 7 (1): 1–7.

Scruton, R. (1982), *Kant*, Oxford: Oxford University Press.

Tully, J. (1999), "Deparochializing Political Theory and Beyond: A Dialogue Approach to Comparative Political Thought," *Journal of World Philosophies* 1 (5): 1–18.

Part 2

Critical Educational Leadership for Improving School and Society through the Pragmatic and Active Lenses

Charles L. Lowery with insights from contributors

Introduction

In the first chapter of this section, Taylor Hines points out for us that an enduring project of the Frankfurt School was to understand and define the contours of a new kind of capitalist subjectivity that was emerging under conditions of modernity. Grounding his discussion in Horkheimer and Adorno's notion of a "new anthropological type," Hines presents how this new type of subject has the tendency to uncritically accept rigid, predefined social categories. This new type also tends to adopt an instrumental, positive rationality over the pursuit of "sublimation" in creative expression, satisfied by the "repressive desublimation" offered by mass-distributed culture industry products. Hines builds on Adorno's *The Authoritarian Personality*, where the authors contend that this type of subject might be more willing to submit to authoritarian or totalitarian administration. The authors also note that authoritarian personality traits are to some degree characteristic of late capitalist subjects overall. Therefore, Hines argues, the new anthropological type is less a distinct personality type than a suite of adaptations to the totalization of monopoly capitalism. In response to decreased opportunities for independent entrepreneurs and increased affective demands on corporate or service workers, argues C. Wright Mills, a "competitive personality" is adopted to succeed in the "market of personality."

In doing so, the new anthropological type is better adapted than its predecessors to life in late capitalist society. To counter these trends, Hines offers the study of character formation and social adaptation as a particularly important aspect of K-12 education. The function of modern schooling is, at least in part, to reproduce, discipline, and cultivate future workers in response to the demands and dynamics of the labor market. Continuing the Frankfurt School's project to understand how capitalism registers at the level of thought, this chapter attempts to understand how public school educators and administrators might participate in—or resist—the increasingly rigidified administration of character. Adopting the analytical toolkit of *The Authoritarian Personality*, while maintaining that character traits are not the cause of totalizing social structures but are their precipitate, this chapter considers the way market demands are mediated by K-12 schools and internalized by students in turn. As school psychologist and critical theorist Jonathan Chabrier notes, today "students are 'classified' instead of diagnosed, without a clinical psychologist's input, yet able to receive medical services, accommodations, expensive placements, and collect social security." As Chabrier shows, increasingly positivistic and rigid administration on the part of educational institutions is internalized as increasingly competitive and rigid character on the part of students. In looking to understand how educators and school administrators mitigate alienating market demands on students, this chapter also keeps in mind Adorno's warning that "however necessary they may be, pedagogical reforms alone are not sufficient." This chapter argues that more effective therapeutic techniques are necessary, but insufficient without structural changes in the social and material circumstances of schoolchildren and their families. Without critically-oriented social reforms, attempts to repair the damage caused by alienating circumstances, and risks intensifying repression on the part of students rather than offering relief.

Gennaro and Kellner, drawing on the work of Herbert Marcuse, present a companion piece discussion to Hines's chapter. They offer a chapter intended to contemplate practice in education (in this case, critical media literacy) as a force for cultivating literate and informed individuals at all levels of schooling and leadership. Marcuse's notion of resistance provided a framework for transforming society within institutions (both primary/secondary schools and universities). Marcuse viewed the university as a utopia where students could organize and effect change. Although the organization can and in many ways must be the primary locus of change, the intimacy and primacy with which the apparatus of contemporary media and technology engages individuals, Marcuse's university-based utopia for social change is now being repositioned to primary and secondary (i.e., K-12) settings. The lack of critical consciousness underscores the growth of culture industries—or what can be thought of as the passive acceptance of entertainment and consumerism over a citizen's agency, advocacy, and activism. The anecdote to this mass deception is the development of critical media literacy. Therefore, the need to expand critical media literacy to the K-12 curriculum is pivotal.

Betty Alford et al. focus on Freire's work as a long-recognized influence for improving the practice of adult education. The preparation of school leaders is a concern for adult education. As such, they note that Freire drew implications from critical theory and made the ideas of critical theory accessible for the practice of adult education. Yet, Freire's theoretical ideas have not always received prominence in educational leadership preparation programs. According to Alford and her student collaborators, Freire's view of the adult educator's role is to "enter into reality so that knowing it better, he can transform it." As adult educators integrate this into the preparation of school leaders, they are, as Freire put it, "not afraid to confront, to listen, to see the world unveiled." Without a doubt, an essential role of the adult educator is to promote dialogue, trusting the wisdom that people hold as individuals and believing in their inherent worth. As Freire stated, "A real humanist can be identified more by his trust in the people in the struggle than by a thousand actions without trust." These ideas are implied in the development of educational leaders but are equally impactful for educational leaders as they work with teachers, parents, and the community to transform schools into equitable learning spaces for all students.

Rhonda Humphries, Bakari Lumumba, and Anthony Walker operationalize and analyze critical educational leadership theory by examining the systems that create and perpetuate racist practices and policies. Humphries notes that the research on Black leadership and its impact on building sustainable school cultures while raising student achievement is limited in scope. Accordingly, the interaction and socialization of Black men and women leaders into K-12 educational spaces require further investigation to unpack how societal prejudice and systemic racism are further projected onto these self-same leaders in the school buildings where they lead. The traditional path to leadership would lead school leaders to have once served inside the classroom as a teacher—sites that can be problematic in terms of power. Too often minorities, specifically Black women and men, are *absent* from classrooms as teachers. Humphries's research reveals that during the 2017–18 school year, nearly 80 percent of US teachers were white, while only 7 percent identified as Black. The implications for this underscore the importance of further investigating the relationship between

Black men and women in K-12 spaces, how these relationships are derived, the norms they exist around, and how schools influence their dysfunction. She sees critical theory as an approach educational leaders can take to confront social, historical, and ideological forces that replicate societal norms that dismantle marginalized communities.

No text concerning critical theory would be complete without a critique of critical theory. Lumumba takes on a critical analysis of the American education system as historically and contemporarily a site of anti-Black violence while taking the opinion that critical theory is not critical enough for a proper analysis of racial issues. Historically, the pervasive violence experienced by Black students in schools can be situated during the Holocaust of enslavement that deprived countless Africans of their freedom and fostered a legal system that ensured their descendants were barred from reading, forced to attend underfunded segregated schools, indoctrinated them with a Eurocentric curriculum, and promoted arbitrary white standards while suffering assaults from those who are supposed to protect them (school resource officers). This analysis brings to light how this system has remained oppressive for decades after emancipation and as a result has caused psychic, cultural, and physical harm in the aftermath of *Brown v. Board* (1954). Lumumba views these "disruptions" as contributing factors behind issues of school dropout, pushout, and underachievement for people who have historically viewed education in high regard. Critical educational leadership can leverage the means to counter and combat these issues. K-12 school leaders must disavow commonplace piecemeal, incremental remedies and commit to a more critically oriented curriculum and school culture where educators promote critical consciousness, individual agency, and self-authorship for African American youth in their schools. More recent critical theorists, such as Freire and John Taylor Gatto, offer leaders a way of understanding the links between class consciousness and Black Critical Theory (BlackCrit) to engage in an authentic education for liberation.

Walker explores the founding principles, values, and vision of critical theory that he views as still relevant to twenty-first-century education. This is a response to the perspective that instead of directly embracing the core principles of critical theory, much of today's education system continues to function in what Freire described as a banking model. Standardized curricula and high-stakes assessments driven by neoliberalism have become the key drivers in teaching and learning—systems that depend on knowledge being a commodity bestowed "by those who consider themselves knowledgeable upon those whom they consider to know nothing" (Freire 1970). As a result, education's curriculum and pedagogical designs systematically reinforce traditions and values of a normalized and unquestioned status quo. This neoliberal approach to education silences the voices of marginalized groups and dampers the potential of education as an equitizing and emancipatory possibility. Under these guises, creativity and inquiry are dulled. Critique and innovative thinking are squelched. Voices inspired by criticality, justice, and equity-mindedness are silenced. Educational leadership grounded in critical theory, drawing on values of Marxian critique and stressing the need to critique and analyze ideological foundations that frame definitions, practice, and politics of education, offers an alternative. For Walker, an educational leadership practice framed in a critical theory will seek to initiate transformational and revolutionary change by identifying, questioning, and contesting acts that allow and support systems of power and oppression. Walker employs a critical theory framework to examine questions about the purpose and potential of education that finds origins in the teachings of Habermas and proposes a connection to the culturally relevant pedagogy frameworks offered in Ladson-Billings. Specifically, he points his discussion toward Habermas's cultural debating and the public sphere with values of Ladson-Billings's culturally relevant practice to demonstrate the relevancy, value, and need for a critically oriented and culturally relevant leadership.

In conclusion, Charles L. Lowery explores Fromm's notion of productive love as a framework for a critical educational leadership. This chapter presents a discussion on the relationship of Fromm's "productive love," Nodding's ethics of care, and Dewey's democracy as an associated way of living. The intersection of these concepts is used to demonstrate the complexity of productive love as the work of critical educational leaders in primary and secondary schools. In *The Sane Society*, Fromm (1955) discusses brotherly love, or what he called productive love, as foundational to forming relationships of constant unity and equality. Productive love is the only kind of love that fulfills "the condition of allowing one to retain one's freedom and integrity while being, at the same time, united with one's fellow man." Fromm referred to this in terms of a syndrome of attitudes: care, responsibility, respect, and knowledge. As such, this chapter attempts to demonstrate how Fromm's ideals of "care, responsibility, respect and knowledge" are integral aspects of democratic education, as defined by John Dewey, and the ethic of care, as developed by Nel Nodding. The author proposes that these are inherent to the critical literacies necessary to being an educational leader in schools of today's societies. Current neoliberal metrics applied to contemporary education systems fail to prepare learners for life and citizenry in local or global communities (e.g., businesses, cities/towns, cultures, political arenas). It creates environments of learning that drive dedemocratization, political divisiveness, and loss of the ability to recognize commonalities through individualistic separation in our various social settings as human beings. Individualism, or what Fromm calls alienation or separateness, leads to aggression and destruction, be it symbolic or otherwise. This is an issue of integrity. Unless citizens are integral in a community there is no relatedness, no connectedness or completeness. Integrity implies soundness of moral principle and character, entire uprightness or fidelity, especially in regard to truth and fair dealing (etymology). Fundamentally, integrity then replies to wholeness. Therefore, my application extends this to include closeness—not only closeness in proximity such as a neighbor but closeness in the sense of affection or care for others. I also hold that this is why Fromm interchanges the terms "brotherly love" with "productive love." This aligns quite expressly to Dewey's concept of democracy and a democratic social efficiency grounded in community, common aims, and communication. In alignment with this, productive educational leaders who embrace a leadership grounded in care, respect, responsiveness, and knowing are positioned to generate and foster climates and cultures of productive love in their schools. As such, they then are positioned to model these values to their teachers, students, and partnering parents.

7

Competitive Character in Education and the Frankfurt School's Theory of a New Anthropological Type

Taylor Hines

The subjective impact of our relationship with technology can be felt acutely in our experience of the Covid pandemic, and especially the ways it has changed education. In particular, when educational institutions transitioned from in-person to distance learning, symptoms such as anxiety, depression, and social withdrawal have seen sharp increases among students. Yet, many studies of remote-learning technologies tend to focus on "efficiency" or "effectiveness" only by measuring traditional learning metrics. While these educational benchmarks are doubtlessly important, such a framework foregoes a critique of the rationality behind remote-learning technologies themselves. In this chapter, I argue that the symptoms often attributed to remote learning—isolation and the increased use of technology in the classroom—are not necessarily caused directly by the increased use of digital technology, but in fact represent intensifications of trends that have arisen for material reasons—in the case of education, from the requirement to produce and adapt a workforce to the demands of contemporary labor. Distance learning and remote educational platforms prefigure the world of work for many students, in which employment is increasingly isolated, automated, and lacks material protections for precarious workers. At-will service work, for example, lacks meaningful intersubjective connections but still demands a rigidly obsequious personal comportment, a contradiction that students must internalize as part of contemporary education. The psychological symptoms that have been reportedly increasing during lockdown should be understood in the context of the demands of these labor practices.

In this chapter, I reconsider the rise of technologically mediated educational practices from the perspective of the Frankfurt School's critique of advanced technological society, and attempt to map the way contemporary learning technologies require new modes of engaging with educational institutions on the part of both teachers and students. Applying Marcuse's critique of "technological rationality" to the world of education, I highlight how specific character structures are created and perpetuated in contemporary education and how educational institutions fulfill the task of adapting students to their future lives as producers of surplus value. More generally, I connect the understanding of remote-learning technologies to the Frankfurt School's study of authoritarian character and a "new anthropological type"—a character structure predisposed to uncritically accepting rigid categorical thinking. I argue that such a character is adapted to the contemporary world of work, and that educational institutions assist in developing these specific character structures.

Technological Rationality and Education

While acknowledging that isolation affects all aspects of student life, studies of remote teaching are often framed in terms of how well distance-learning technologies emulate the classroom experience, or how "effective" these platforms are in imparting information to students that was previously accomplished in the classroom. A 2022 UK study of remote learning in the context of the Covid lockdown has found that "certain participants considered that learning remotely online was beneficial for instant feedback, supported motivation and fostered communities of practice," while "negative perspectives related to feeling isolated, unmotivated and a preference towards face-to-face (F2F) delivery" (Baxter and Hainey 2022). A 2021 McKinsey study has found that "nearly 60 percent [of US teachers surveyed] rated the effectiveness of remote learning at between one and three out of ten. That barely beats skipping school altogether …. From missed assignments to falling test scores, teachers see the disengagement and learning loss, the effects of which could hurt the economic wellbeing of some students for life" (Chen et al. 2021). Indeed, what many studies of remote learning have in common is a measurement of traditional learning metrics, tacitly prioritizing the internalization of information instead of questioning the rationality behind educational practices themselves. Here I reconsider this framing and seek instead to understand what specific modes of learning are required in the remote-learning environment and what effects these modalities have on character development.

Remote learning, I argue, can be understood through Herbert Marcuse's critique of "technological rationality," first laid out in the essay "Some Social Implications of Modern Technology" and further developed in his book *One-Dimensional Man*. In his analysis of the way social relationships are mediated by technological processes, Marcuse argues that "under the impact of [the technological] apparatus, individualistic rationality has been transformed into technological rationality" (1982: 141). By this, Marcuse means that the machine process, as it becomes "the embodiment of rationality and expediency," transforms the nature of human rationality itself. When we use machines, we have no choice but to play by the machines' rules and adapt ourselves to their rhythms. In this way, Marcuse argues, it is the *machines* that use *us*, because they change the way we live and thus change the way we think. In the case of education, for instance, when student success is measured in terms of quiz scores, individual intelligence is equated with efficient performance on automated examinations, and conversely, these metrics confer validation on the individual. The more efficiently and effectively one can adapt themselves to the machine process, the better equipped they are to succeed in society.

More generally, as subjects of a technologically advanced society, our success is beholden to the prevailing metrics of achievement and efficiency. As these metrics are increasingly technologically mediated, it becomes the rational choice to adapt one's thinking to the technological process. As Marcuse describes, "Human behavior is outfitted with the rationality of the machine process, and this rationality has a definite social content. The machine process operates according to the laws of mass production. Expediency in terms of technological reason is, at the same time, expediency in terms of profitable efficiency, and rationalization is, at the same time, monopolistic standardization and concentration" (1982: 144). In this way, Marcuse observes, "technological rationality" becomes rationality *as such*. It is ultimately rational to adopt machine logic in a society wherein production is organized by the machine process.

In this framing, we can learn from the reportedly "beneficial" or "negative" outcomes of distance-learning technology what categories are considered to be beneficial or negative under the prevailing rationality of educational institutions. For example, a study of online university-level courses has found that "students who were given the opportunity to schedule their lecture watching in advance scored about a third of a standard deviation better on the first quiz than students who were not given that opportunity …. However, these effects diminish over time such that we see … no difference in overall course scores" (Baker et al. 2019). Overall, this study concluded that, while allowing for some added "flexibility" and "time management" opportunities, the benefits of the remote-learning medium are negligible at best.

We might reframe this conclusion as implying that remote-learning places additional burdens of course management onto students, without sufficient justification for whether this added burden improves the student's learning outcomes, and without questioning the subjective impact of this additional burden. In other words, a "beneficial" outcome would be a student learning to self-manage, without the "negative" side effects that arise when direct human guidance and supervision is replaced with technological surveillance and automated benchmarks of progress. Similarly, if "negative perspectives related to feeling isolated, unmotivated and a preference towards face-to-face (F2F) delivery," we can reinterpret this statement as arguing that technological mediation is only detrimental in the sense that technologically mediated criteria for success cannot seamlessly supplant human relationships. A student "succeeds" in this framework only to the degree that they can adapt themselves to the machine process with little to no human interaction.

The result of increasing technological mediation, in Marcuse's analysis, is what he terms a smooth, efficient, "authoritarian bureaucracy." Technological society is authoritarian, for Marcuse, in the sense that individuality is liquidated by the machine process. However, unlike the fascist authoritarianism of the interwar period, technological bureaucracy only unites subjects as individual economic agents, each scrambling for their own survival. Therefore, technological bureaucracy provides no sense of *community* in the traditional sense, and in fact represents its antithesis. In Marcuse's words, "True, the crowd 'unites,' but it unites the atomic subjects of self-preservation who are detached from everything that transcends their selfish interests and impulses. The crowd is thus the antithesis of the 'community,' and the perverted realization of individuality" (1982: 150).

Applying Marcuse's analysis to technologically mediated education when we read that remote learning "fostered communities of practice," we should question what kind of community is envisioned by this purported "benefit." Rather than a community of individuals, Marcuse might argue, what "communities of practice" actually reflect is a common compartmentalization into standardized categories, especially those that prefigure the world of work. Educational institutions in an advanced technological society aim not at fulfilling individual autonomy but at "fitting" the individual to a particular task. From this perspective, rather than remote-learning technologies failing to provide an adequate substitute for the classroom experience, they in some ways function *better* to adapt students to the demands of the modern workplace—and conversely, remote learning only fails insofar as it cannot properly incentivize students to conform to the rhythms of automated production.

Yet, concluding that technology is "bad" for education, or suggesting that the task for educators is to avoid its use, ignores the insight that technology rationality has "a definite social content." It makes sense that education *would* adopt the schemata that prevail in the era of mass production and mass surveillance, since educational institutions are tacitly tasked with preparing students to be members of society. Educational institutions are not immune to the demands of the labor market; it is not educators per se who enforce a particular criterion of success for students but the prevailing rationality that determines how success is understood. In Marcuse's words, "Individuals are stripped of their individuality, not by external compulsion, but by the very rationality under which they live" (1982: 145). As individuals, it is ultimately *rational* to adopt whatever set of dependable, mechanical behavior patterns is incentivized by technological society. The individual "can pursue their self-interest only by developing 'dependable reaction patterns' and by performing pre-arranged functions" (Marcuse 1982: 150–1), since these reaction patterns are expected and incentivized by educators, employers, and institutions of authority generally. Such patterns of behavior are ultimately determined by the social nature of production. The increasing use of lockdown browsers or antiplagiarism software, for example, betrays not simply a preoccupation with "cheating" but also the need to acclimate students to the era of workplace surveillance and efficiency-monitoring tools. In other words, educational technologies cannot escape the prevailing social rationality and are "effective" only to the degree that they communicate a specific rationality to students in a way that can be internalized. As Marcuse observes, the purpose of education and training is not simply the acquisition of knowledge; it is also the development of a specific personal comportment: "The abilities developed by [vocational] training make the 'personality' a means for attaining ends which perpetuate man's existence as an instrumentality, replaceable at short notice by other instrumentalities of the same brand" (Marcuse 1982: 151). Central to Marcuse's critique of technological rationality is the idea that technology extends into human interiority and redefines the nature of subjectivity. In the following sections, I seek to understand how remote-learning technologies develop in response to the *subjective* needs of production and the way they influence student character development as a result.

Authoritarian Bureaucracy and Competitive Character

In this section, I continue the critique of technological mediation by attempting to understand how technological rationality registers at the level of thought. Using the Frankfurt School's theorization of authoritarian character as a jumping-off point, I attempt to trace connections between technological rationality and the so-called authoritarian personality and show how these character traits are conditioned by contemporary working conditions. For this, I turn to mid-century sociologists like C Wright Mills and David Riesman, who theorize a shift in character development in response to the increasing concentration of capital in the era of monopolistic bureaucracy. Although not explicitly connected to education yet, I argue in future sections that these social forces are mediated by educational institutions and have a profound influence on students.

An enduring project of the Frankfurt School was to understand and define the contours of a new kind of capitalist subjectivity that was emerging under conditions of modernity—what Max Horkheimer and Theodor Adorno refer to as a "new anthropological type." This new type of subject, they argue, mirrors the technological rationality of an advanced industrial society. Specifically, the modern subject shows a tendency to uncritically accept rigid, predefined social categories; adopt an instrumental, positive rationality (goal-oriented, efficient, and unidirectional); and, rather than pursue "sublimation" of libidinal drives in creative expression, is satisfied by the "repressive desublimation" (in Marcuse's terms) offered by mass-distributed culture industry products. First published in 1950, *The Authoritarian Personality* is a sociological study of character that draws upon, and continues by empirical means, the Frankfurt School's study of late capitalist subjectivity. Perhaps most famously, the study develops what its authors call the "F-scale," a questionnaire that seeks to measure how amenable a respondent is to potentially fascist ideology. Containing questions such as "Any red-blooded American will fight to defend his property" (Adorno et al. 2019: 524) or "Obedience and respect for authority are the most important virtues children should learn" (525), the F-scale is designed to test how willingly a respondent submits to authority, how rigidly they make in-group vs. out-group distinctions, and a host of other psychological traits. This study provides important empirical justification for the Frankfurt School's sociological project, but it has often been misinterpreted as validating a kind of "personality quiz" that separates the high-scoring "fascists" from the low-scoring "liberals."

While *The Authoritarian Personality* contends that the "new anthropological type" that the Frankfurt School describes might be more willing to submit to authoritarianism or totalitarianism, Adorno also notes that authoritarian personality traits are to some degree characteristic of late capitalist subjects overall. It is not fascists who create authoritarianism, but it is authoritarianism that creates fascists. As Peter Gordon describes, Adorno was concerned that *The Authoritarian Personality* was misunderstood even in its own time, and that its contemporary interlocutors "had mistakenly reversed the directionality of causation in its theory of fascism." Rather than affirming the authoritarian personality as the actual *source* of its appeal, Adorno insisted that an authoritarian "character" be seen as the *introjection* of an irrational society (Gordon 2016). As Adorno himself explains, "Psychological dispositions do not actually cause fascism. Rather, fascism defines a psychological area which can be successfully exploited by the forces which promote it for entirely non-psychological reasons of self-interest" (Gordon 2016). The new anthropological type is not a distinct personality type but a suite of adaptations to the totalization of monopoly capitalism.

For Adorno, the hallmark of authoritarian culture is the internalization of rigid, stereotypical social categories, what he calls "ticket thinking," or *Vor-Sich-Hinleben* (living-straight-ahead) (as described by Fong 2016). Similar to the way Marcuse describes technological rationality as having a "definite social content," Adorno understands "the typification of men itself as a social function" (Adorno et al. 2019: 747). What bureaucratic society demands from its subjects is a dependable set of reaction patterns that "fit" the individual to his or her prescribed task. Subjects of a technological "authoritarian bureaucracy" must internalize the willingness to submit to injunctions whose rationale are not immediately obvious. As Adorno describes,

> [The individual] has entered a social constellation in which the reproduction of its life can no longer be carried out in the old sense by its "monadological" nature, that is to say its independent and antagonistic separation from its environment. The individual seems to be on the way to a situation in which it can only survive by relinquishing its individuality, blurring the boundary between itself and its surroundings, and sacrificing most of its independence and autonomy. (2009: 462)

Success in large bureaucratic institutions comes not through an intense struggle to master one's environment, but through the willingness to adapt oneself to serve the powers as efficiently and dependably as possible. Autonomy, we might bleakly conclude, is simply not achievable in such an environment. As Adorno writes, "Our [highly authoritarian] subjects do not seem to behave as autonomous units whose decisions are important for their own fate as well as that of society, but rather as submissive centers of reactions, looking for the conventional 'thing to do'" (Adorno et al. 2019: xlii).

In this sense, the authoritarian type defined by Adorno et al. is similar to that studied by mid-century sociologists like David Riesman and C. Wright Mills, who analyzed character development in the age of monopoly capitalism. In response to decreased opportunities for independent entrepreneurs and increased affective demands on corporate or service workers, argues C. Wright Mills, the personality itself becomes the terrain of competition. Workers are no longer expected to simply labor, but to adapt and cater to the perceived desires of others. Under these conditions, the worker must adopt a "competitive personality" to succeed in the "market of personality." Rather than skill and efficiency in immediate production, the service worker or office worker within a large corporation has much more nebulous criteria for success, which depends instead on the ability to appease and influence superiors and clients.

Mills compares the situation of white-collar workers with the traditional image of blue-collar factory workers: "If there are not too many plant psychologists or personnel experts around," Mills ([1946] 2018) writes, "the factory worker is free to frown as he works. But not so the white-collar employee. She must put her personality into it. She must smile when it is time to smile." Because success in corporate bureaucratic institutions depends on impressing one's colleagues and superiors, rather than concrete, objective criteria, there are intense demands on the contemporary workers' idea of self. "The competition in which [this] new entrepreneur engage[s] is not so much a competition for markets of commodities or services," Mills ([1946] 2018) continues, "it is a bright, anxious competition for the good will of the chieftain by means of personality …. She must make of her personality an alert, obsequious instrument whereby goods are distributed." By rigidly introjecting the properly "alert, obsequious" character traits and easily adopting a mask of polite personability, the new anthropological type is *better* adapted than its predecessors to life in late capitalist society.

Sociologist David Riesman, in a similar sociological analysis titled *The Lonely Crowd*, describes contemporary workers as developing a "radar"-like character structure in this environment. Unlike the early industrial bourgeoisie, which had a fixed moral "gyroscope" instilled by their parents and other authorities through intense oedipal struggle in childhood (what Riesman calls "inner-direction"), for the subjects of late capitalism, the most important directives of daily life come from without rather than within. Success for the modern worker in a professional or customer service role requires the ability to continually monitor subtle and ever-changing social signals to better adapt to the demands of a world dictated by the needs of concentrated capital. "What can be internalized," Riesman writes, "is not a code of behavior but the elaborate equipment needed to attend to [cultural] messages and occasionally to participate in their circulation. While guilt and shame, the primary controls of inner-directed society, never go away, a new psychological force—diffuse anxiety, comes to predominate" (Riesman et al. 1969: 15). In much of modern life, criteria for success are sustained interpersonally—benchmarks of achievement often don't exist concretely but rather *in the opinion of others*. The self becomes embodied not in the objective and material products of one's life but in the shifting perceptions of other people.

Competitive Character and Social Media

Under the conditions of the personality market, signal-monitoring tools like social media are perfectly suited to filtering and processing the cultural signals required for work and social life. Social media provides one's inner radar with the necessary data and enables constant broadcasting and monitoring of tastes and preferences necessary to function in the market of personality. Moreover, constant inputs from the social media enable one to check if their inner radar is working properly and provide the "inside dope" behind the polite veneer that often masks competitive workplace relationships. Under these conditions, social media specifically—and mass media more generally—performs a contradictory role. On the one hand, they help *construct* the self by enabling one to perform the basic functions of scanning and responding to interpersonal demands. But, on the other hand, they provide a means of *escape* from the pressures of having one's personality constantly attuned to the impositions of others. When, moreover, these contradictory tools become one's only medium of interaction with the outside world, one's self and one's reality start to blend together in a particularly disorienting way. During Covid, mediated forms of escape (television, social media, podcasts, etc.) become more readily accessible in isolation *and* more necessary in order to bear with the tedium and anxiety of lockdown. But because these same tools also mediate our interaction with the "real world," reality itself starts to seem more disorienting. And it is not only that reality, after Covid, takes on hallucinatory characteristics; reality itself, for many contemporary workers, was inherently hallucinatory before Covid began—being grounded in immaterial and ill-defined perceptions.

This perspective is only reinforced by the material and historical side to the story: the social landscape of the United States has been dramatically transformed since the 1970s. Membership organizations and labor unions have been hollowed out and replaced by "efficient" nonprofit organizations. As Wolfgang Streeck summarizes,

> In the absence of collective institutions, social structures must be devised individually bottom-up .... Social life consists of individuals building networks of private connections around themselves, as best they can with the means they happen to have in hand. Person-centred relation-making creates lateral social structures that are voluntary and contract-like, which makes them flexible but perishable, requiring continuous "networking" to keep them together and adjust them on a current basis to changing circumstances. An ideal tool for this are the "new social media" that produce social structures for individuals, substituting voluntary for obligatory forms of social relations, and networks of users for communities of citizens. (2017: 42)

This extreme marketization, fragmentation, and atomization of society has made technological society especially vulnerable to the perils of isolation and atomization. On the one hand, social media is more necessary to cope with the affective demands of the modern workplace, as well as the atomization and isolation of social life.

Yet, on the other hand, the increasing social-media-ification of work and social life only exacerbates the demands to rigidly internalize a particular set of affective demands. In other words, social media both accelerates and exacerbates social trends that have been developing for decades. As both a problem and a solution to the same problems it creates, social media exemplifies the contradictory nature of contemporary life.

Psychological Effects of Isolation

The understanding of social media and character development outlined in the previous section helps explain a common symptom that is often reported in studies of education under Covid lockdown and the increasing virtualization of life generally—withdrawal. Psychoanalyst Frantz Fanon writes that "in the hallucinatory process, we see the collapse of the world turn into a system of reference. Hallucinatory time and space bear no pretension to reality. As Sartre claims, hallucination coincides with a sudden annihilation of perceived reality. It is a perpetual flight; its spatio-temporal frame is unreal, fictitious" (Fanon and Asselah 2018). As Fanon argues, hallucination is intimately connected with isolation. "The rejection of the real world," he writes, "is only possible thanks to the emergence of a pseudo-world based on new relations and new significance. The denial of reality ... requires substantiation and nourishment .... From this perspective, isolation is the authorization of hallucination" (Fanon and Asselah 2018). Life in bureaucratic institutions is supported and made bearable by tools like social media and micro-doses of viral media—short, easily accessible reprieves that provide both "nourishing isolation" and schema for making sense of a confusing reality. But as social life becomes more isolating—due in part to increasing technological mediation—Fanon's framework suggests a wholesale condonement of hallucinatory escape.

This may in part explain the sudden increase in withdrawal symptoms reported following the transition to distance learning during Covid. In the isolation brought about by distance learning, for instance, interpersonal criteria for success grow increasingly more muddled and obscure, and in a sense, pieces of the self also start to dissolve. Of the metrics reported in a 2021 McKinsey study, "social withdrawal" made the largest leap in pre- to postpandemic comparisons (Dorn et al. 2021). According to the study, "Parents also report increases in clinical mental health conditions among their children, with a five-percentage-point increase in anxiety and a six-percentage-point increase in depression. They also report increases in behaviors such as social withdrawal, self-isolation, lethargy, and irrational fears" (Dorn et al. 2021). The same McKinsey study has found that "high schoolers have become more likely to drop out of school, and high school seniors, especially those from low-income families, are less likely to go on to postsecondary education" (Dorn et al. 2021). The pandemic and its fallout is a perfect storm for overanxious and understimulated students: an enforced isolation, saturated with social media and culture industry modes of escape, could not have been better designed to distract from the problems of life in capitalist society while nevertheless contributing to the propagation and intensification of those very problems. Under these circumstances, it makes sense why someone would stop attending school in the same way they might turn off a television program. Sharing the same screen and performing the same subjective function, neither bears much pretension to reality.

Competitive Character, Isolation, and Education

Primary school is often a child's first contact with administrative institutions, and increasingly competitive and rigid administration on the part of educational institutions is internalized as competitive and rigid character on the part of students. Adopting the perspective that character traits are not the *cause* of totalizing social structures but are their *precipitate*, we seek to understand how a "radar"-like or competitive character is internalized by students. Like all agents on the personality market, students are not immune from the pressure to monitor and conform to the ever-changing cultural landscape. Success in school—no less than in the modern workplace—requires careful monitoring and response to the prevailing taste consensus. Study after study has linked social media use with increased anxiety, but we can understand the immense pressure social media puts on students not as a problem of social media per se but as mediated by the demands of the labor market. Social media, which presents students with direct metrics of popularity, can be seen as prefiguring the world of work, where those same markers of popularity might one day determine success or failure.

The material dimension of technology in the classroom also mirrors the material dimension of atomized and isolated social life. Technology is presented as a silver bullet to underfunded and understaffed public schools, which are given electronic devices to create "hybrid learning" environments instead of the funds necessary to hire sufficient teachers and staff. When these stopgaps fail, online and remote-learning schools step in to provide "alternative options" and further justify withholding public funds. Social media is promoted as a method for engaging students with learning material, yet the same vicious cycle that exists more generally is apparent in schools: technology is both more necessary to cope with the failures of isolating and hollowed-out administrative institutions, yet also exacerbates the very problems it purports to solve.

School psychologist Jonathan Chabrier is particularly incisive in his description of these dynamics, and his experience working in Brooklyn public schools provides an insightful case study of student character generally. As he notes, contemporary education has always been a way to discipline and subjectify future laborers, and thus necessarily mediates the demands of the labor market. As Mills and Riesman argue, the demands of monopoly capital for "global competition, service economy social skills, and digital fluency are all impressed onto students through increasingly market-mediated competitive anxieties, cognitive-behavioral discipline and, for the growing relative surplus-population, expressed enigmatically by unconvinced teachers" (Dorn et al. 2021). The effects of these social forces on students, Chabrier (2018) argues, has been catastrophic. He goes further:

> No Child Left Behind (NCLB) reduced teacher interactions and increased "data-driven" encounters within a scripted curriculum, [and] the national Common Core Learning Standards forced teachers to push children to and beyond the developmental limits of their age. Since their inception, critics of these currents across the political spectrum recognized the cultivation of a barren and anxious competitive spirit that is educationally counterproductive, if not disastrous. Yet the intensification of globalized value production during a period spanning two major capitalist crises has animated the drive to have children "maintain America's competitive edge," as they were now posed to compete with students "from all across the globe for the jobs of tomorrow."

Educational institutions, in Chabrier's analysis, do little to ameliorate the demands of the personality market placed directly onto students. Students are exposed to social forces over which they have little understanding and even less control, and the hallucinatory worlds of technology are offered as an easy escape. Although educational institutions offer some assistance in the form of counseling, accommodations, or individualized education programs, these tools are designed to preserve students as efficient workers rather than helping them develop autonomy. Ultimately, in Chabrier's critique, schools fall victim to the same vicious cycles that plague late capitalist society as a whole.

Where We Go from Here

In this chapter, I have attempted to outline the ways educational institutions mediate the demands of the market and adopt the prevailing rationality of production. Beginning with Marcuse's critique of technological rationality, I argue that distance-learning technologies tacitly assume that the task of education is to fit individuals to specific tasks. Next, I considered the affective dimension of technological rationality and how the demands of the "personality market" shape character development in contemporary society. Social media plays an important role in character development, I argued, since it distracts one from the contradictions of contemporary life while nevertheless contributing to the propagation and intensification of those very problems. Finally, I argued that educational institutions can adopt and mediate these social forces with students and play an important role in imparting the demands for competitive character onto students.

We might question what a proper response should be to the social forces that cause the anxiety and withdrawal so often reported in studies of remote education. Here I am not easily convinced by calls for better therapeutic remedies. In my opinion, school psychologist Sal Henderson (2018) says it best:

> All bureaucratic institutions that care about the well-being of their members (students, workers, soldiers, slaves), insofar as that well-being is seen as a precondition of efficient system functioning, run up against an elemental problem: *the introduction of a therapeutic element in the absence of any explicit acknowledgment of the social and material context in which tensions arise intensifies repression rather than relieves it.* [emphasis in original] Disarming a generation well-trained in emotional intelligence, one that is not at all ready to register emotional, interpersonal, and physical needs, requires pointing to an *outside* that is in error.

Our task as educators and critical theorists should be to understand and critique the social forces that damage subjectivity. Absent this, no matter how well-intentioned we may be, any solutions we may propose can only reinforce the status quo.

References

Adorno, T. (2009), "The Problem of a New Type of Human Being," in *Current of Music: Elements of a Radio Theory*, Cambridge, MA: Polity.

Adorno, T., E. Frenkel-Brunswik, D. J. Levinson, and R. Nevitt Sanford, with B. Aron, M. H. Levinson, and W. Morrow (2019), *The Authoritarian Personality*, London: Verso.

Baker, R., B. Evans, Q. Li, and B. Cung (2019), "Does Inducing Students to Schedule Lecture Watching in Online Classes Improve Their Academic Performance? An Experimental Analysis of a Time Management Intervention," *Research in Higher Education* 60: 521–52. https://doi.org/10.1007/s11162-018-9521-3.

Baxter, G., and T. Hainey (2022), "Remote Learning in the Context of Covid-19: Reviewing the Effectiveness of Synchronous Online Delivery," *Journal of Research in Innovative Teaching & Learning.* https://doi.org/10.1108/JRIT-12-2021-0086.

Chabrier, J. (2018), "A New Type of Educational Illness in Brooklyn Public Schools," *Damage*, November 26. https://damagemag.com/2018/11/26/a-new-type-of-educational-illness-in-brooklyn-public-schools.

Chen, L.-K., E. Dorn, J. Sarakatsannis, and A. Wiesinger (2021), "Teacher Survey: Learning Loss Is Global—And Significant," *McKinsey*, 1 March, www.mckinsey.com/industries/education/our-insights/teacher-survey-learning-loss-is-global-and-significant.

Dorn, E., B. Hancock, J. Sarakatsannis, and E. Viruleg (2021), "Covid-19 and Education: The Lingering Effects of Unfinished Learning," *McKinsey*, July 27, www.mckinsey.com/industries/education/our-insights/covid-19-and-education-the-lingering-effects-of-unfinished-learning.

Fanon, F., and S. Asselah (2018), "The Phenomenon of Agitation in the Psychiatric Milieu," *Damage*, July 9, https://damagemag.com/2018/07/09/the-phenomenon-of-agitation-in-the-psychiatric-milieu.

Fong, B. Y. (2016), "The Psyche in Late Capitalism I: Theodor Adorno, Max Horkheimer, and the Crisis of Internalization," in *Death and Mastery: Psychoanalytic Drive Theory and the Subject of Late Capitalism*, New York: Columbia University Press.

Gordon, P. E. (2016), "The Authoritarian Personality Revisited: Reading Adorno in the Age of Trump," *b2o*. www.boundary2.org/2016/06/peter-gordon-the-authoritarian-personality-revisited-reading-adorno-in-the-age-of-trump.

Henderson, S. (2018), "The Psychoeducational Middle School," *Damage*, November 19. https://damagemag.com/2018/11/19/the-psychoeducational-middle-school.

Marcuse, H. (1982), "Some Social Implications of Modern Technology," in Andrew Arato and Eike Gebhardt (eds), *The Essential Frankfurt School Reader*, 138–62, London: Continuum.

Riesman, D., N. Glazer, and R. Denney (1969), *The Lonely Crowd: A Study of the Changing American Character*, London: Yale University Press.

Streeck, W. (2017), *How Will Capitalism End? Essays on a Failing System*, London: Verso.

Wright Mills, C. ([1946] 2018), "The Competitive Personality," *Damage*, November 5. https://damagemag.com/2018/11/05/the-competitive-personality.

Marcuse's Critical Theory for the Educational Practice of Critical Media Literacy

Steve Gennaro and Douglas Kellner

Why Critical Media Literacy?

Critical media literacy is "a pedagogical approach that promotes the use of diverse types of media and information communication technology (from crayons to webcams) to question the roles of media in society and the multiple meanings of the form and content of all types of messages" (Share 2007: 127). Media literacy skills prepare students to communicate and succeed as twenty-first-century learners in a digital economy. Elsewhere, we have defined media literacy as requiring not just an engagement with media but also a critical engagement to properly make visible all the contradictions between the modern individual and the embedded ideologies of heteronormativity, misogyny, white supremacy, and classism through which the culture industries mitigate the modern self's capitalist existence.

> Critical media literacy seeks to explore power and justice through understanding media and how new technologies create media that produce texts, stories, and images, often without adequately explaining them to the user. Therefore, the user requires some basic understanding of how those texts are created, for whom they are created, and how the texts themselves get taken up by audiences and influence society, often reproducing hegemonic ideologies. Critical media literacy involves active engagement with a text that employs a user's power to construct meaning that is not wholly reliant upon the intended or surface message. When activated, critical media literacy pushes individuals to think beyond themselves to ask questions about how systems of power and ideologies actively participate in our perception of the galaxy we live in. User involvement in producing meaning also helps individuals fulfill their civic duty as members of participatory democracy. (Gennaro and Miller 2020: 9)

Critical media literacy skills challenge students to activism and agency through a rights-based and social justice approach to understanding democracy. In response to changing social and political environments, the promotion of critical media literacy skills across all disciplines needs to be the primary task of educators, activists, and theorists.

The Frankfurt School and Critical Theory

The term Frankfurt School refers to the work of members of the *Institut für Sozialforschung* (Institute for Social Research), established in Frankfurt, Germany, in 1923 as the first Marxist-oriented research center affiliated with a major German university. However, in most cases, Frankfurt School refers to the work at the institute after 1930 when Max Horkheimer became its director. Under Horkheimer, the institute sought to develop an interdisciplinary social theory that could serve as an instrument of social transformation. For example, in the 1937 essay "Traditional and Critical Theory" (see Horkheimer 1972), Horkheimer argued that the *traditional theory* of philosophy and modern science tended to be overly abstract, objectivistic, and cut off from social practice. In contrast, *critical theory* was grounded in social theory and Marxian political economy. It carried out a systematic critique of existing society and allied itself with efforts to produce alternatives to capitalism and bourgeois society.

Under Horkheimer, the institute referred to its work as the *critical theory of society*. For many years, *critical theory* stood as a code for the institute's Marxism and was distinguished by its attempt to enact a radical interdisciplinary social theory rooted in Hegelian–Marxian dialectics, historical materialism, and the critique of the theory of revolution. Members argued that Marx's concepts of commodity, money, value, exchange, and fetishism characterized the capitalist economy and social relations under capitalism, where commodity and exchange relations and values governed all forms of life.

Critical theory produced a theoretical analysis of the transformation of competitive capitalism into monopoly capitalism and fascism and hoped to be part of a historical process through which socialism could replace capitalism. Horkheimer (1972) claimed:

> The categories which have arisen under its influence criticize the present. The Marxist categories of class, exploitation, surplus value, profit, impoverishment, and collapse are moments of a conceptual whole whose meaning is to be sought,

not in the reproduction of the present society, but in its transformation to a correct society. (218)

The term critical theory would become synonymous with the term Frankfurt School and this era, as a synthesis of philosophy and social theory that combed sociology, psychology, cultural studies, and political economy.

As predominantly Jewish intellectuals, members of the institute fled Germany with Hitler's ascendency to power. The majority emigrated to the United States, where the institute reemerged and became affiliated with Columbia University in 1931. After the Second World War, Adorno, Horkheimer, and Pollock returned to Frankfurt and reestablished the institute in Germany, while Lowenthal, Marcuse, and others remained in the United States. It would be incorrect to consider the postwar writing as belonging to one Frankfurt School. Whereas there was a shared sense of purpose and collective work on interdisciplinary social theory from 1930 to the early 1940s, theorists frequently diverged after that. During the 1950s and 1960s, the term Frankfurt School best described the work produced at the institute in Frankfurt by Adorno, Horkheimer, and others rather than the work of Fromm, Lowenthal, Marcuse, and those who did not return to Germany. While this chapter discusses contributions of the Frankfurt School, using the ideas of Marcuse that are clearly part of this postwar schism and not part of the Frankfurt School by this definition, it does so by engaging with ideas that emerged from within the institute during the 1930s and 1940s that Marcuse built upon in his later works.

For example, in 1937 Horkheimer wrote how the role of critical theory is to alter the core concepts that dominate our understandings of our social relations and the paradox, which underpin these relations.

> [The role of critical theory] consists of changing the concepts that thoroughly dominate the economy into their opposites: fair exchange into a deepening of social injustice; a free economy into monopolistic domination; productive labour into the strengthening of relations which inhibit production; the maintenance of society's life into the impoverishment of the people's. The goal of critical theory is to transform these social conditions and provide a theory of "the historical movement of the period which is now approaching its end."

Herbert Marcuse begins *One-Dimensional Man* in 1964, similarly arguing that

> this society is irrational as a whole. Its productivity is destructive of the free development of human needs and faculties, its peace maintained by the constant

threat of war, its growth dependent on the repression of the real possibilities for pacifying the struggle for existence—individual, national, and international.

As Horkheimer notes, motivated by an interest in emancipation, critical theory is a philosophy of social practice engaged in "the struggle for the future" and "a future society as the community of free human beings, in so far as such a society is possible, given the present technical means" (1972: 230). Likewise, Marcuse concurs, "to investigate the roots of these developments and examine their historical alternatives is part of the aim of a critical theory of contemporary society, a theory which analyzes society in the light of its used and unused or abused capabilities for improving the human condition" (1964: xl).

The Frankfurt School coined the term *culture industry* in the 1930s to signify the process of the industrialization of mass-produced culture and the commercial imperatives that constructed it. Like other areas of mass industrial production at the time, the culture industries mass-produced commodified and standardized objects for consumption. However, the commodified mass production of cultural artifacts also worked as essential agents of socialization and mediators of political reality. Again, returning to the opening pages of *One-Dimensional Man*, Marcuse notes:

> But here, advanced industrial society confronts the critique with a situation which seems to deprive it of its very basis. Technical progress, extended to a whole system of domination and coordination, creates forms of life (and of power) which appear to reconcile the forces opposing the system and to defeat or refute all protest in the name of the historical prospects of freedom from toil and domination. Contemporary society seems to be capable of containing social change—qualitative change which would establish essentially different institutions, a new direction of the productive process, new modes of human existence. This containment of social change is perhaps the most singular achievement of advanced industrial society. (1964: xlii)

Examining the cultural industries through a political lens, Frankfurt School theorists were among the first to examine the effects of mass culture and the rise of the consumer society on the working classes that were to be the instrument of revolution in the classical Marxian scenario.

Frankfurt School theorists analyzed how the culture industries' use of cultural artifact consumption integrated the working class into capitalist societies and stabilized contemporary capitalism. Marcuse promoted classical philosophers such as Plato, Rousseau, Kant, Hegel, Marx, Nietzsche, Heidegger, and Freud while presenting a critical theory of contemporary societies and projecting emancipatory alternatives to what he saw as a repressive contemporary civilization. In his 1967 public talk at the University of Notre Dame titled "The Obsolescence of Marxism," which garnered national coverage, Marcuse explained, "The title of my paper is not supposed to suggest that Marx's analysis of the capitalist system is outdated; on the contrary I think that the most fundamental notions of this analysis have been validated." Similarly, Horkheimer and Adorno (2002), in their collective book *Dialectic of Enlightenment* (originally published 1947), sketched out a vision of history from the Greeks to the present that discussed how reason and enlightenment became their opposite, transforming what promised to be instruments of truth and liberation into tools of domination. They argued that the system of cultural production dominated by film, radio broadcasting, newspapers, and magazines was controlled by advertising and commercial imperatives and served to create subservience to the system of consumer capitalism. Therefore, the culture industries should be seen as major institutions of contemporary societies with various economic, political, cultural, and social effects.

Adorno returns to this notion in his 1967 "Culture Industry Reconsidered," noting: "Although the culture industry undeniably speculates on the conscious and unconscious state of the millions towards which it is directed, the masses are not primary, but secondary, they are an object of calculation, an appendage of the machinery. The customer is not king, as the culture industry would like to have us believe, not its subject but its object" (12). While later critics pronounced Horkheimer and Adorno's approach as too manipulative, reductive, and elitist, it provides an important corrective to more populist approaches to media culture that downplay the way the media industries exert power over audiences and help produce thought and behavior that conforms to the existing society (see the discussions in Kellner 1989, 1995).

The Frankfurt School eventually became best known for their theories of the *totally administered society*, which analyzed the increasing power of capitalism over all aspects of social life and the development of new forms of social control. In their essay "The Culture Industry: Enlightenment as Mass Deception," Horkheimer and Adorno (2002) state: "There is nothing left for the consumer to classify. Producers have done it for him. Art for the masses has destroyed the dream but still conforms to the tenets of that dreaming idealism which critical idealism baulked at" (98). Mass culture and communications now stood at the center of leisure activity, and the culture industries provided ideological legitimation of existing capitalist societies, integrating individuals into a way of life. Marcuse argued this totally administered society was a *one-dimensional society*, whereby "it shapes the entire universe of discourse and action, intellectual and material culture. In the medium of technology, culture, politics, and the economy merge into an omnipresent system which swallows up or repulses all alternatives. The productivity and growth potential of this system stabilize the society and contain technical progress within the framework of domination" (1964: xlvii).

In the next two sections, we will argue, first, that Herbert Marcuse provides useful perspectives on educational leadership that we should embrace to respond to the ever-proliferating forms of media culture and recent technologies that are shaping youth today and that produce new challenges for education to provide critical media and digital literacies that will empower youth and enable them to better participate in and produce a democratic future. Educators today, like the Frankfurt School theorists, can use critical media literacy as a teaching philosophy across public education in K-12, exactly as the institute used critical theory, seeking new political change strategies, agencies of political transformation, and models for political emancipation that could serve as norms of social critique and goals for political struggle. In this spirit, we argue that Marcuse's critical perspectives on education and the Frankfurt School's critiques of technology and media culture provide the philosophical foundation for a transformation of education responding to the challenges of recent technologies with critical media literacies.

Marcuse and Education

In the 1960s, Herbert Marcuse emerged as one of the most important intellectuals in the United States. His works and influence cannot be overstated. Herbert Marcuse was a self-proclaimed Marxist radical, a father figure to New Left and countercultural activists, an influential author, public speaker, and teacher. Yet, his ideas on education remain removed from the ongoing development and redevelopment of curriculum and public education in the United States and elsewhere around the world. His most prominent books all remain as key pieces of the introduction of social and political theory to English-speaking American audiences. For example, *Reason and Revolution* (1941) introduced the ideas of Hegel and Marx; *Eros and Civilization* (1955) provided a synthesis of Marx and Freud; *One-Dimensional Man* (1964) radicalized earlier critiques of "advanced industrial society" from the Frankfurt School, each providing powerful critical perspectives on contemporary US society.

Although Marcuse suggested "the long walk through the institutions" as a strategy of social change that included education as a transformative force, he spoke largely to the university as a utopia to teach, cultivate, and organize students to make them capable of being subjects of individual thought and action and democratic citizens who are able to transform society. Marcuse was right that the locus of change must be the institutions themselves. Yet, given the intimacy, primacy, and expediency with which today's media culture, digital technologies, and administrative-technological apparatus engage with individuals, the utopia for social change that Marcuse once believed to be the university now requires a reclaiming of K-12 learning spaces, whereby K-12 leadership and teachers in cooperation with students reclaim these spaces for transformative radical education and democracy.

In the 1967 essay, "The Obsolescence of Marxism," Marcuse (2014) argues that the focus of education must be to promote truth in a society where information is deliberately suppressed, and facts are the casualty of media propaganda.

> And as repression is flattened out and extended to the entire underlying population, the intellectual task, the task of education and discussion, the task of tearing, not only the technological veil but also the other veils behind which domination and repression operate—all these "ideological" factors become very material factors of radical transformation. (Kellner et al. 2009: 417)

In an era of neo-conservative hegemony, Marcuse's critical perspectives are more needed than ever and provide moments of critique and alternative vision needed to keep hope alive and envisage a different and better future.

Ironically, there has been more engagement from neo-conservative critiques of Marcuse's impact on contemporary education rather than from those seeking to harness Marcuse's work as an energy for emancipatory alternatives. For example, one of the earliest works to engage Marcuse's implications for education, by Joseph DeVitis (1974), claimed Marcuse's educational ideas to be "repressive" at the same time as reducing the rich complexity of Marcuse's positions to pan-rationalism and Platonism. It is true that a tension exists in Marcuse's theory between Hegelian–Marxian critical theory and an aesthetic ontology grounded in Schiller, Freud, and a subjectivist aestheticism. However, this complexity is what makes Marcuse's work as important today as it was when he preached it more than half a century ago. His combination of critical philosophy, social theory, aesthetics, and radical politics mediates aesthetic education, the humanities, and the sciences with a critical theory of the contemporary era and radical politics aiming at emancipation and a nonrepressive society.

Similarly, right-wing critiques of Marcuse by Allan Bloom in *The Closing of the American Mind* (1987) and by Kors and Silvergate in *The Shadow University* (1998) gained popularity by labeling Marcuse's influence on education as antithetical to democracy in the same vein that the FBI once labeled Marcuse a threat to national security.

> To effectively construct Marcuse, then a 70-year-old Professor as a clear and present danger to American society, the Bureau worked to paint him as an individual who stood at odds with the core values of U.S. democracy, and this battle was waged through the emphasis on representing Marcuse as the "other," that is, as "a self-proclaimed Marxist," a Jewish-German intellectual and immigrant, as an anarchist, and as a revolutionary ... highlighting the differences in Marcuse's life with the social construction of what it meant to be an American. (Gennaro and Kellner 2009: 291)

Bloom claimed that Marcuse's significant influence on the 1960s counterculture was part of the spread of a corrosive nihilism that seduced the youth with theories that led to "the betrayal of liberty on America's campuses" (1987: 152). Revealing his inability to grasp the philosophical dimension and challenges of Marcuse's thought and the contradictions at play in combining Marxist and Freudian analysis, Bloom writes of Marcuse: "He ended up here writing trashy culture criticism with a heavy sex interest" (1987: 226), a simply ludicrous claim.

Kors and Silvergate (1998) argued that Marcuse was responsible for speech codes in the university, whereby a newly imposed "political correctness" promoted intolerance toward conservatives by promoting critical race theory, gay and lesbian studies, and militant feminism. Attributing the totality of struggle to one individual is an attempt to discredit the fight of many scholars and activists and negate the power they democratically reclaimed. This divisive discourse toward socially marginalized groups is consistent with an era of neoliberal hegemony and right-wing attacks on education.

> The totalitarian tendencies of the one-dimensional society render the traditional ways and means of protest ineffective—perhaps even dangerous because they preserve the illusion of popular sovereignty. This illusion contains some truth: "the people," previously the ferment of social change, have "moved up" to become the ferment of social cohesion. Here rather than in the redistribution of wealth and equalization of classes is the new stratification characteristic of advanced industrial society. (Marcuse 1964)

Marcuse actively opposed racism, sexism, homophobia, and imperialism while promoting the rights of oppressed groups and multicultural education. However, to credit Marcuse with establishing academic programs in Critical Race Theory, Women's Studies, or Chicano Studies, among others—as Kors and Silvergate propose—is an attempt to depoliticize the protest critical theory as pedagogy presents to neo-conservatism.

It is only in recent years that Marcuse's critical perspectives have been engaged and discussed in educational circles. For example, a wealth of his thought was probed in a series of presentations at a panel on "Marcuse and Education" at the 2005 AERA organized by UCLA graduate students. This of course is directly in line with Marcuse's ideas on the connections between education and social change; as he continually noted, the nexus of radical social change must come from student-organized protests, even calling youth "the intelligentsia of the new left." The presentations from the panel were published in a coedited collection, *Marcuse's Challenge to Education* (2009). Some of the papers collected focused on critique, others on alternative educational praxis and pedagogy, with many combining these poles and, in some cases, proposing a reconstruction of Marcuse's thought. This follows the two poles of the Marcusian dialectic between domination and emancipation. Together, they show how the work of Herbert Marcuse continues to challenge the institutions and practices of the contemporary education establishment while providing emancipatory alternatives.

Bildung and the Transformation of Education

Marcuse's critics do not engage his ideas or his ability to present both systematic critique and positive alternatives for education. Instead, critiques of Marcuse's potential contribution to education are simply replications of a neoliberal education system, which holds a reputation steeped longer in disenfranchisement than citizenship training. This is why returning to the ideas of Marcuse today, as educators and critical theorists seeking solutions to emerging global problems in a technologically mediated twenty-first century, connects us to the importance of a critical media literacy grounded in theory. As argued by Marcuse, "Today's capitalist society is increasingly shaping thoughts, behavior, needs, and aspirations and that liberation requires new needs and consciousness" (Gennaro and Kellner 2009: 305). Hence, for a radical social change, there "must be new social institutions and a new way of life" (305).

For Herbert Marcuse, education was a force for cultivating individuals—that is, *Bildung*—and he argued that education was required to produce the ideas, skills, and critical consciousness for active citizens in a participatory democracy. Originating in the German *bild* and *bilden*—the first a neutrum (like an English noun) that translates to "image" and the second a verb that refers to the process of building or formation—*Bildung* connects human learning to meaning of human life. As Jennifer A. Herdt notes in *Forming Humanity: Redeeming the German Bildung Tradition*, humans are "oriented toward a telos conceived as the harmonious development of all their various capacities … into a balanced, unified whole" (2019: 82).

In the present moment, the concept of *Bildung* has reemerged as an approach to education, socialization, and citizenship to combat the changing technologies, literacies, and digital competencies required to navigate The Googleburg Galaxy. In his 2017 TEDx talk, describing the establishment of the *Bildung* academy in Amsterdam in 2015, Koen Wessels describes *Bildung* as the idea that education is not only about knowledge and skills, but it concerns the development of the whole human being, promoting an integral understanding of what education is for. Recently, a report by Erasmus+—the European Union's program to support education, training, youth, and sport in Europe—defined it like this:

> Bildung is the combination of the education and knowledge necessary to thrive in your society, and the moral and emotional maturity to both be a team player and have personal autonomy. Bildung is also knowing your roots and being able to imagine the future.

With a budget of over 26 billion Euros, Erasmus+ has established its priorities for 2021–7 on social inclusion, the environment, digital literacy, and promoting young people's participation in democratic life. In explaining the role of *Bildung* in this expansive program, Erasmus+ points out four key areas where education and educational leadership can play a pivotal role: transferable knowledge, nontransferable knowledge, a sense of responsibility, and civic empowerment.

Similarly, we argue that critical media literacy as a pedagogical process is harmonious to the Marcusian definition of *Bildung*. As a response to globalization and technological revolution, transformations in pedagogy must be as radical as the technological transformations that are taking place. Education should be reconstructed to consider the importance of citizenship and participation, thus linking education and democracy. Education occupies three essential roles in the lives of young people: *social*, *vocational*, and *civic*. Critical media literacy has an opportunity to bring together all three roles of education: the socialization component of establishing or destabilizing social norms, the vocational component of mastering the science and technology of the future workforce, and the civic component of active citizenship. Even if educational institutions cannot develop curricula at a pace equivalent to the rate of technological change, a pedagogy that explores these media relationships through a critical lens is required.

Firstly, education occupies *a socializing role*. Young people must occupy a physical space in society, and the curriculum provides a template for cultural norms and social expectations on how to occupy such spaces. Childhood or youth itself is a binary and oppositional term to adulthood. Therefore, the lives of young people, the representations of these lives, and the inherent power imbalance that structures their lives necessitate a recognition of youth culture as subcultural a priori. Subcultures exist primarily as a response to unequal power relations and as an organic feedback channel to ideology. The most apparent problem for an education designed by adults is that outsiders craft such a system with little understanding of contemporary children's culture. As a result, the system more clearly represents the hopes, fears, needs, desires, and expectations of adults at a particular social moment, instead of representing the crisis of the social moment to which young people must engage, ask critical questions about, and respond to with a pedagogy of hope.

One component of critical media literacy that addresses the socializing aspect of education sees literacy as a tool for receiving or decoding the media messages we interact with daily. Here students can participate in expanding a critical awareness of the power of the culture industries in their lives. Students can engage with activity-based learning to question their current relationships with media and technology using cultural studies, political economy, critical theory, and intersectionality inside the classroom. Examples include students unpacking their daily social media existence critically. Educators can challenge students to see the world they live in—and their existing relationships with technology, media, and capitalism—through a different lens and provide students with social justice narratives to what previously may have been ordinary life experiences. At the same time, including young people in the discussion of how to implement critical media literacy into the curriculum ensures that schools in the future will include space for social justice narratives and not just those stories that perpetuate the dominant norms of capitalism: patriarchy, white supremacy, and heteronormativity.

Schools must also provide *vocational* training for the workplace. To address current workplace needs and the future of work in the twenty-first century, this component of critical media literacy recognizes literacy as a tool for producing or encoding messages. In *Pedagogy of the Oppressed*, Paulo Freire (1970) notes that liberation can only come from having the power to participate as active agents in naming the world around us. The grading components of courses need to be built into practical projects, which ensure students learn media literacy skills for encoding. Examples include designing a webpage, starting a blog, writing a copy for magazines or newspapers, podcasting, and creating a YouTube channel. More recently, students can now participate in an *hour of code* project, learning the basics of coding from playing *Minecraft* or similar games. In 2021, UNICEF (2022) identified coding as an area of primary importance for increasing gender and racial equity in STEM (science, technology, engineering, and mathematics) education around the globe, highlighted in UN Sustainable Development Goal 4 (Quality Education), Goal 5 (Gender Equality), and Goal 10 (Reduced Inequality). Providing all young people with access to a digital means of production can empower actions toward social change. When young people can produce their own media, they also produce their own realities. A transformative education, which sees the world as a problem to be solved, uses education as a space to ask questions, and challenges knowledge dissemination that reinforces cultural indoctrination.

Citizenship training is perhaps the most crucial function of a public education system in a democratic society. However, this is complicated by a structure that allocates an age of majority for civic participation that is not in alignment with the ages of public schooling in modern democratic societies. The twentieth century witnessed enormous changes in the right to vote in Canada, for example, which saw the legal voting age lowered from twenty-one to eighteen. In the spring of 2020, Bill C-10 was introduced in Canada—a private members bill to lower the voting age in federal elections from eighteen to sixteen. Arguments against extending the vote to young people suggest that children are not smart enough to vote appropriately, or engaged enough to vote correctly. Other scientific arguments suggest that since children's brains are not fully developed, they cannot understand the magnitude of their decisions or are more prone to being manipulated. The arguments used to deny youth the right to vote are the same arguments voiced to deny political rights to women, minorities, and Indigenous peoples since the establishment of democracy. These are also precisely the areas where training in critical media literacy could help fulfill the civic duty of the education system.

Citizenship training needs to place our young people directly in the middle of the political arena. This is the opposite of the neoliberal education system across the last half century, which has attempted to legislate and mandate the removal of transformative action from our pedagogy. Yet, this is exactly what an education grounded in critical media literacy must do to encourage students to see how power is always bound up in the most mundane and the most extreme aspects of human activity and why this requires people of action—fully present in the current moment and committed to meeting the challenges of tomorrow. Marcuse rightly points out in *One-Dimensional Man*:

> Today, in the prosperous warfare and welfare state, the human qualities of a pacified existence seem asocial and unpatriotic—qualities such as the refusal of all toughness, togetherness, and brutality; disobedience to the tyranny of the majority; profession of fear and weakness (the most rational reaction to this society!); a sensitive intelligence sickened by that which is being perpetrated; the commitment to the feeble and ridiculed actions of protest and refusal. These expressions of humanity, too, will be marred by necessary compromise—by the need to cover oneself, to be capable of cheating the cheaters, and to live and think in spite of them. In the totalitarian society, the human attitudes tend to become escapist attitudes, to follow Samuel Beckett's advice: "Don't wait to be hunted to hide." (1964: 247)

The year 2022 has continued to bring with it a series of unfortunate global events and uncertainty. The pandemic of Covid-19 remains widespread, and more recently, the actions of Russia in Ukraine pose a significant danger to human life, and to global security. Yet, the media spectacle of these events continues to depoliticize global citizens from concrete action. News continues to polarize opinions, fragmenting publics and placing them in direct opposition to each other at the same time as obfuscating the drastic gap in global wealth that continues to make the world's top 3 percent of wealthier richer than the combined 97 percent of the global population. Therefore, critical media literacy and a political economy of information are essential building blocks for reclaiming our democracy. As Marcuse (2014) noted:

> What we see is the rapid transformation of our own society into an unfree society which already shows the tendencies which we so valiantly deplore in other countries … the restriction of the freedom of the press, a self-imposed censorship, a moratorium on criticism, a misinformation of the public, and [the emergence of the importance and value invested in] the cult of personality. (155)

Our interactions with the media and technology present reflections of the limiting aspects of education, when it is used as a tool for indoctrination, and the revolutionary potential for democracy at large, when education is informed by critical media literacy. As explained in a recent news article "Media Literacy Is Desperately Needed in Classrooms around the Country, Advocates Say" on TheHill.com (the largest independent political news site in the United States), there is an increase in the amount of time young people spend online and the uses of online spaces as gathering points for information or knowledge. However, there is a deficit in the amount of time spent in schools teaching young people how to "apply critical thinking skills to the onslaught of content available on a slew of different devices." Precisely because "children aged 8 to 18 spend an average of 7 hours and 38 minutes per day with media outside of school." Education must act as a space for training for critical media literacy. Critical media literacy gives us a framework to challenge dominant norms and work together to improve the lives of young people locally and globally. A commitment to social justice pedagogy provides students with spaces to be seen and heard and ensures that regardless of background or circumstance every student is equipped with the knowledge, transferable skills, and values to navigate the challenges of tomorrow with a compassionate approach.

Our task as educators is akin to the shaking of a snow globe. A snow globe can easily be found in most souvenir shops across the United States, where a popular Canadian image sits inside of a glass sphere. When a person picks up the snow globe and shakes it, the picture becomes blurred by what appears to be a large amount of snow-like confetti rolling around throughout the globe. And yet, when the shaking of the globe stops, only moments later the snow settles and the image UNMOVED and UNAFFECTED remains! However, the individuals' perspectives of the globe and all its contents have forever been changed. In our work as educators, students come to our classrooms with their own experiences, contexts, ideologies, and understandings of the world they live in; this is their snow globe. Challenging students to see the world they live in and their existing relationships with technology, media, and consumption through a different lens provides an opportunity to engage young people with social justice narratives than what previously may have been their ordinary life experiences. Education can play a primary role in the civic training of young people and can provide additional tools to help activate agency. Students can engage in a critical pedagogy that unpacks social media platforms, the stories that get told on social media platforms, and the resulting social relations. A public education informed by critical media literacy can provide improved opportunities for young people to participate in decision-making, especially when those decisions directly impact their lives.

References

Adorno, T. W. (1967), "Culture Industry Reconsidered," in T. W. Adorno (ed.), *Ohne Leitbild*, 12–19, Frankfurt: Frankfurt am Main.

Bloom, A. (1987), *The Closing of the American Mind*, New York: Simon & Schuster.
De Vitis, J. L. (1974), "Marcuse on Education: Social Critique and Social Control," *Educational Theory* 24 (3): 259–68.
Freire, P. (1970), *Pedagogy of the Oppressed*, trans. Myra Bergman Ramos, New York: Seabury Press.
Gennaro, S., and D. Kellner (2009), "Under Surveillance: Herbert Marcuse and the FBI," *Nature, Knowledge and Negation* 26: 283–313.
Genarro, S., and B. Miller (2020), "Critical Media Literacy in the Googleburg Galaxy," *Media Literacy and Academic Research* 3 (2): 6–22.
Herdt, J. A. (2019), *Forming Humanity: Redeeming the German Bildung Tradition*, Chicago, IL: University of Chicago Press.
Horkheimer, M. (1972), *Critical Theory: Selected Essays*, trans. M. J. O'Connell, New York: Continuum.
Horkheimer, M., and T. W. Adorno (2002), *Dialectic of Enlightenment: Philosophical Fragments*, Stanford, CA: Stanford University Press.
Kellner, D. (1989), *Critical Theory, Marxism, and Modernity*, Baltimore, MD: Johns Hopkins University Press.
Kellner, D. (1995), *Media Culture. Cultural Studies, Identity, and Politics between the Modern and the Postmodern*, London: Routledge.
Kellner, D., T. Lewis, C. Pierce, and K. D. Cho (2009), *Marcuse's Challenge to Education*, Lanham, MD: Rowman & Littlefield.
Kellner, D., and J. Share (2019), *The Critical Media Literacy Guide: Engaging Media and Transforming Education*, Leiden: Brill.
Kors, A. C., and H. A. Silvergate (1998), *The Shadow University*, New York: Free Press.
Marcuse, H. (1964), *One-Dimensional Man*, London: Routledge & Kegan Paul.
Marcuse, H. (2014), *Marxism, Revolution and Utopia: Collected Papers of Herbert Marcuse*, vol. 6, London: Routledge.
Share, J. (2007), "Young Children and Critical Media Literacy," in R. Hammer and D. Kellner (eds.), *Media/Cultural Studies: Critical Approaches*, 126–51, New York: Peter Lang.
UNICEF (2022), *Using Data to Achieve the Sustainable Development Goals (SDGs) for Children*, New York: United Nations International Children's Emergency Fund.

9

Perspectives of the Relationship as an Enduring Message of Hope through Dialogue, Reflection, and Action in Freire's *Pedagogy of the Oppressed*

Betty J. Alford, Rene Levario, Sergio Chavez, and Alberto Medina

In adult education and ethnic studies, Freire's work has long been recognized as influential to the improvement of practice (Brookfield 1986; Cranton 1994; Merriam and Caffarella 1991; Merriam and Cunningham 1989). Merriam and Cunnningham (1989) pointed out that Freire's work was influential to "adult education, working for social change" (89). Freire drew implications from critical theory and "popularized these ideas for the practice of adult education for empowerment" (Merriam and Cunningham 1989: 156). However, although Freire's books were translated into multiple languages and were powerful in furthering adult learning through dialogue, Freire's works have not always received prominence in educational leadership preparation programs (Starratt 2014).

As described in *Pedagogy of the Oppressed*, Freire's view of the adult educator's role is to "enter into reality so that knowing it better, he can transform it. Not afraid to confront, to listen, to see the world unveiled. Not afraid to meet people and enter into dialogue with them" (1972: 24). Indeed, one of the primary roles of the adult educator is to promote dialogue, believing in the wisdom that people hold and of their inherent worth. Freire (1972) stated, "A real humanist can be identified more by his trust in the people in the struggle than by a thousand actions without trust" (47). These ideas are impactful for educational leaders as they work with teachers, parents, and the community to transform schools into equitable learning spaces for all students.

Educational leaders are called to be transformative leaders who, with the community and all stakeholders, will work to achieve equity and excellence for student success (Shields 2014). As we emerge from the two pandemics of Covid-19 and growing recognition of racial injustice (Ladson-Billings 2021), working with all stakeholders as equal partners, not as oppressors, the educational leader is called to engage in dialogue through ongoing praxis (reflection and action) toward meeting identified student needs. Drawing on the experiences of learners, Freire (1972) stated that "reflection is essential to action" (38). He reinforced that all individuals are persons of worth with valuable experiences that should not be discounted but further built upon in learning, and emphasized that we are all in the process of becoming or growing. He further expressed a belief in the ability of individuals to transform and have a role in the transformation of the world. Through problem-posing education, individuals "develop their power to perceive critically the way they exist in the world, and they come to see the world as a reality in process, in transformation" (Freire 1972).

This chapter will provide an overview of Freire's professional experiences. Then, a discussion of tenets of Freire's philosophy as expressed in *Pedagogy of the Oppressed* will be provided in relation to teaching and educational leadership. Then, through the perspectives of two educational leaders and a university professor, the relevance of Freire's perspectives to the roles of educational leaders today will be shared. Each of these individuals will share reflections of their first encounter in reading Freire's *Pedagogy of the Oppressed* and describe what was influential in the process of reflecting on Freire's perspectives and what has been influential in their work as educational leaders. The chapter will conclude with a discussion of implications to the preparation of educational leaders.

Overview of Freire's Professional Experiences

Freire's chief ideas, arguments, and recommendations for adult learning remain relevant in the twenty-first century and provide a conceptual foundation that remains relevant for the field of educational leadership. Over fifty years ago, Freire first published *Pedagogy of the Oppressed*. In this book, Freire provided a definition of praxis that includes action and reflection as equally important in transformative leadership. He argued that the teacher should not be a dispenser of knowledge and should recognize that the teacher is also a student just as the student is also a teacher. Freire (1972) illustrated this belief through sharing a story of a worker's interaction with him in which the worker said, "Excuse us, we ought to keep quiet and let you talk. You are the one who knows; we don't know anything" (50). Freire rejected this viewpoint of the teacher as the authority and instead supports the educator's role as one of promoting dialogue, believing in the wisdom that people hold and of their inherent worth. The learner has significant life experiences that the teacher should build upon as they engage in dialogue to "enter into reality so that knowing it better, he can transform it. Not afraid to confront, to listen, to see the world unveiled. Not afraid to meet people and enter into dialogue with them" (24).

Over time, Freire held to the belief that dialogue was needed for self-understanding (Merriam and Cunningham 1989). Merriam and Cunningham stated that the range of his ideas grew, but there were not shifts in the basic tenets of his beliefs. Freire was with the World Council of Churches in the middle to late 1970s where his ideas of dialogue and praxis "challenged many literacy and adult basic education practitioners in both Canada and the United States" (Merriam and Cunningham 1989: 74). His ideas were also shared through the work of World Education.

In 1985, Freire published *The Politics of Education: Culture, Power, and Liberation*. He drew implications from critical theory and "popularized these ideas for the practice of adult education for empowerment" (156). Shor and Freire wrote *A Pedagogy for Liberation* in 1987. In this book, they presented a role of a facilitator of learning as to be "engaged in presenting alternative scrutiny of previously unchallenged and uncritically accepted assumptions … and help learners locate their personal troubles within the context of wider social forces and structures" (Merriam and Cunningham 1989: 202). Another point that received clarity in Freire's later works was that the facilitator should "avoid crucifying themselves on the cross of perfection" (207). Facilitators should employ parallel pedagogies. This means that the facilitator varies their methods, has a range of materials (visual and written), and makes efforts to individualize the curriculum (207). Freire's work speaks directly to social and political change, which was an enduring focus throughout his writings.

Freire's Educational Background

Freire's initial education was in philosophy and law, but while he worked as a labor union lawyer in Brazil, he became very interested in teaching workers to read. What he had observed was a very authoritarian approach that was ineffective in teaching them. At the same time, he had been involved in discussion groups in democratic reform with the workers and had used pictures to promote discussion. He used a modified version of this method as a way of teaching reading within forty-five days to the workers using 16–18 words that had the following characteristics: personal meaning to the workers, three syllables, and representative of phonetic sounds of the language. He used an interdisciplinary team of a sociologist and a psychologist to engage in initial dialogue with the workers to generate themes of importance and the resulting words that would be used in teaching reading. Then, pictures were made to capture the meaning of the words to be used as an instructional tool. This method is similar to an approach Sylvia Ashton Warner used with children, termed the language experience approach; however, Freire's approach strongly included words of liberation and freedom. Due to the success of the program, he had planned in 1964 to establish 20,000 discussion groups; however, Freire was accused of using the literacy method to spread revolution, and in April 1964, Freire was jailed. After seventy days in jail, Freire and his family sought exile in Chile before then coming to the United States as a visiting professor for the Harvard Center for Studies in Education. From 1971 until his death, Freire made his home in Geneva where he served as special education consultant to the World Council of Churches.

In his early works, Freire was strongly influenced by "Christian personalism, that emphasized the place of the individual in the face of a growing technological and scientific culture" (147). Merriam (1980) stated that *Pedagogy of the Oppressed* was a "turning point in his writing, more analytical and dialectic and moving from citing advantages of social democracy to a plea for Marxist thought with a radical Christian theology" (147). Throughout his life, Freire saw "domination as a fundamental theme and liberation as a goal" (Langenbach 1988: 98). Griffith and McClusky (1981) noted that Freire placed an emphasis throughout his career that "education leads to social and political actions" (25). Freire continued to view "adult learning as a process of becoming aware of one's assumptions, beliefs, and values and then transforming these into a new perspective or level of consciousness" (Merriam and Caffarella 1991: 15). Freire emphasized "critical thinking and the liberation of learners" throughout life (Hammond and Collins 1991: 15) with "problem-posing and equality of the teacher and learner as themes" (Candy 1991: 55). Boyd and Apps (1980) maintained that Freire's stance toward life was one of "hope for the future, the importance of faith in oneself, and the importance of the courage and willingness to risk failure" (162).

Tenets of Freire's Beliefs as Provided in *Pedagogy of the Oppressed*

Inherent in Freire's beliefs as expressed in *Pedagogy of the Oppressed*, first published in 1970, was that the teacher should not approach other learners from a position of power. Both the teacher and the student should grow and benefit from the discussions in a reciprocal process of learning. Both dialogue and critical analysis serve as ways that students can grow in recognition that there are possibilities beyond their present level of existence and dependency. Freire (1972) advocated for committed involvement, "not pseudo-participation" (56) and advocated that the adult educator should engage students in critical thinking instead of depositing learning into each student as an empty vessel. In doing so, the teacher should demonstrate a "profound trust in men and their creative power" (62) instead of providing a "ready to wear approach" (63) through a scripted, structured lecture. He argued that learning should be an active process of dialogue and reflection, not a passive process of listening to a lecture. He further argued that problem-posing education is needed where "men develop their power to perceive critically the way they exist in the world, and they come to see the world as a reality in process, in transformation" (71). In this way, students can gain consciousness that they have a role in the transformation of the world.

Freire also advocated in *Pedagogy of the Oppressed* that education should be a liberating or freeing process including the freedom to make choices, think critically, and reflect. He further stressed, "Hope does not consist of crossing one's arms and waiting," but leads instead to the "incessant pursuit of the humanity denied by injustice" (80). The value that Freire advocated is a critical perception of the world, a process of gaining "real consciousness" (108) of individuals who open their eyes to domination, injustice, and lack of hope. He advocated that the teacher's role is to listen to students but also challenge them, "posing as problems both the codified existential situation and their own answers" (140). In critical reflection, it is key not to impose the teacher's view of the world encouraging "men to become masters of their thinking" (18) in an *I–Thou* relationship not *I–It*, as Martin Buber the German theologian pointed out. Freire argued that educators should have consistency between words and actions with "boldness, radicalization, courage to love, and faith in people" (177). This viewpoint remains relevant to educational leaders today who strive to foster authentic relationships with students, faculty, parents, and the community and engage in problem-posing and resolution through collaborative planning and implementation of needed changes to promote educational equity and excellence.

Beliefs about Learning

In *Pedagogy of the Oppressed*, Freire expressed a belief in the ability of individuals to grow and transform, stressing that we are all in the process of becoming or growing. Believing in the worth and value of the individual, Freire (1972) referred to them as "those who are marginalized are now transformed" (ix). The learner, a seeker, one who is struggling to gain a "fuller ideal, is a searcher after the good life and wants to count for something" (14). Freire stressed that individuals are the masters of their own destiny. There is pain evident in Freire's words, a pathos of caring and concern for the oppressed who must yet gain consciousness that they are in control of their fates.

For Freire, the role of the teacher is that of a colearner. The teacher is viewed as no more important than the student, and the roles will naturally shift at times during a discussion or dialogue. Freire (1972) posed a statement of action when he said, "To affirm that men are persons and as persons should be free, and yet to do nothing tangible to make this affirmation real, is a farce" (34). The teacher's role is that of an activist working side by side with the oppressed to bring change. For educational leaders, this tenet of Freire's philosophy provides a challenge to engage in this way with all stakeholders not as an authority but as a colearner.

Illumination can be a result of learning. Freire (1972) used the metaphor of light in saying, "We were blind; now our eyes are open" (xii). He further stated that "conversation to the people requires a profound rebirth. Those who undergo it take a new form of existence and are no longer as they were" (47). Freire referred to this process as transformation. He stated that "the complete situation must be transformed" (35). Consciousness-raising leads to a fuller humanity according to Freire, the ability to live life with meaning.

In the opening of *Pedagogy of the Oppressed*, Freire (1972) expressed a viewpoint based on the concept of hope as he stressed that "from these pages the following will endure: my trust in the people, my faith in men, and in the creation of a world in which it will be easier to love" (24). He did not view life pessimistically. Freire expressed a belief that circumstances can change. The oppressed do not need to stay in this state. Change can occur. Freire (1972) referred to freedom as "an indispensable condition for the quest of human completion" (31). He further stated, "When they discover within themselves the yearning to be free, they perceive the yearning can be transformed into reality only when the same yearning is aroused in their comrade" (32). He continued, "An action is oppressive when it prevents man from being fully human" (42). In other words, freedom is something all should attain. Freire did not place limits on capacity; instead, he stressed more fully the role of fellow learners in actions to bring forth freedom with freedom as a goal.

Freire (1972) expressed that power comes in realizing the "reality of the oppressed not as a closed world from which there is no exit, but as a limiting situation they can transform" (34). The power he would desire individuals to seek is the recognition that they have power over their lives. While Freire (1972) defined pedagogy of the oppressed as the "pedagogy of men engaged in the fight for their own liberation" (39), this must be "forged with the oppressed in the struggle to regain their humanity" (33). It is also a quest toward a fuller humanity. Freire sought transformation through adult learning. He suggested that raising consciousness is part of adult learning leading to a fuller humanity and that "reflection is essential to action" (38). Freire advocated that the purpose or goal of education was to help the oppressed "become fully human" (42). He expressed a belief that educators must work side by side with the oppressed to help alleviate the oppression. The role of the educator was described as one who builds on the experiences of the students through the method of dialogue.

Relevance of Concepts Presented in *Pedagogy of the Oppressed* to Educational Leadership

In considering the relevance of Freire's ideas for the current practice of educational leadership, his tenets in *Pedagogy of the Oppressed* remain pivotal. Learning should lead to consciousness and a fuller humanity. Man's search for meaning is ongoing, and it is this theme that influences Freire to be referred to as an "emancipatory theorist" (Cranton 1994: 16).

The emphasis on real experiences seems to be an idea that is also enduring. Freire advocated that we open our eyes through discussion or dialogue, recognizing the power of rebirth, of transformation, of change. While specific methods have been added for stimulating dialogue in the past fifty years through technological advances, educators may use virtual reality to evoke dialogue or a discussion rather than a dramatization or a chapter from a book, as Freire recommended, to emphasize the importance of listening, caring, and sharing. Even if all outside oppression or inequalities ceased, the need to fight against the barriers from within would endure. The need to learn what it is to be more fully human is an ongoing quest. In these ways, Freire's illumination of concepts that can foster growth remains as relevant to educational leaders in the twenty-first century as when they were expressed in *Pedagogy of the Oppressed* over fifty years ago.

Four Reflections

Through discussion and dialogue, the process of enlightenment and transformation can begin. The next section of this chapter will provide ways that current educators describe the influence of Freire's writing on their praxis as educational leaders who are committed to educational equity and quality learning experiences for all learners.

Reflection of the Impact of Freire's Concepts to Educational Leadership

Rene Levario, EdD

Love. The first time I heard the name Paulo Freire was from Dr. Sergio C. Chavez, a student and future mentor of mine, as we started the doctoral program at Cal Poly Pomona. It was about a month into our program, and we were sharing our own educational journeys as students and educators within the education system. I expressed that some of the ideas that I was thinking and feeling didn't quite mesh with the paradigm of education that exists in our lives today. In that moment, as Dr. Chavez was listening to me and questioning me, he asked if I had ever read *Pedagogy of the Oppressed* by Paulo Freire and encouraged me to consider it. The following class, Dr. Chavez came with a copy of the book and gave it to me. I have never let it go since. At that moment, I had never experienced an exchange where someone listened to my innermost thoughts, questions, and feelings about the conditions of our education system and knew where I was coming from. Thus began not only my journey as a doctoral student at Cal Poly Pomona but also my education with Dr. Chavez.

I vividly remember the first time I read the book and then having to reread passages. I remember reading a sentence and then having to reread four to five sentences before the one I was reading. I had to read recursively in a sense to better understand the idea and connections that Freire was describing. The reason that this style was so influential for me was that Freire has a way of connecting his ideas, and it is through connecting those main ideas that he was able to establish his own personal reflection. And as you read his own personal reflection, it is almost as if you are reading your own reflection or, at least, a model of how you can reflect on your own.

Another part that is also influential is the language Freire gives us to describe and use in our work as educators, especially in terms of praxis as action and reflection, our pedagogical framework and the banking concept, and the impetus to hold sacred the values of generosity and trust. In a way, this language gives us a way to breathe life into and from our reflections as educators in this historical moment.

Listen. What is important for an educational leader is to think, act, and reflect on not only the visible structures and processes of the education system but also the hidden structures and processes (Yosso 2002) that lie in plain invisibility within the traditional education system. When you learn to understand that structure and process, then as an evolving transformational educational leader, you can begin to formulate ways on how to transform this system in a way that serves the community where your school is located. More specifically, what I mean by transformation is not looking for the cracks or breaks in the system that allow for small incremental victories, which for some cases might be appropriate, but rather looking for ways to truly change and transform the schooling experience with the children, families, community, and educators who are immersed in it. For me, there is no better place for praxis than the classroom.

Lead. What has been most influential to me—as an educator who has recently returned to the classroom by my choice after serving as an assistant principal and having been assigned to a new school—has been to embrace the utmost urgency to center praxis as action and reflection. I have spent the past few weeks listening to how students, educators, and families describe our school. In these dialogical moments, I listen for the language that Freire gave us in terms of generosity, trust, and the banking concept. As I listen and learn from these moments, I reflect on two important items for praxis that Duncan-Andrade (2017) posed to leaders who are seeking to transform their schools: (1) in order to understand the community your school sits in, you must be an ethnographer of the community, and (2) how proximate are you willing to get to the pain, suffering, and joy experienced by the people in the community of your school? These two items are critical because Freire (1972) points out "conversion to the people requires a profound rebirth" (61). Learning and reflecting on these dialogical moments gives me a better sense of my own transformational process within this system. Just as Freire (1972) asks us to transform ourselves, it is the same with this system. Because humans created this education system, it is humans who can transform it in a way that struggles for humanization, generosity, trust, love, and liberation (Freire 1970).

Reflection of the Impact of Freire's Concepts to Educational Leadership

Sergio Chavez, EdD, School Superintendent

The book *Pedagogy of the Oppressed* was referred to me by a friend in the late 1980s. I started reading it, and I couldn't put it down. It was a very difficult one to read, so I had to read the book with a dictionary. I think I would have read *Pedagogy of the Oppressed* six or seven times since then. When I began teaching, the book totally changed my perspective on education from switching from the traditional banking method of instruction to a much more liberating perspective. Reading the book was very timely for me because Freire was teaching adults, and at that time I was teaching English as a second language classes to adults in the evening while an undergraduate student even before I became a teacher in the K-12 system. I started applying a lot of things from the book in teaching the class and worked to create that dialectic. I've been using this method since that time. The book is profound and timely. Even though it was written over fifty years ago, it is still timely today.

The literature in and of itself is very polished and intriguing. The book is one that every time I go back to reference it, I end up reading the entire book again. Part of why I do this is to reignite and because I want to make sure I get it right. Each time I return to the book, it is to try to polish my thinking, and each time, I learn something new.

One of the main things Freire talks about is the rehumanizing of education when education is done right. One of the things that historically has happened with marginalized populations—in particular the Latino population, the Mexican American population, the African American population, and the Native population—is this whole sense of invisibility. Historically, they have not been seen. Decisions have been made on behalf of the group instead of with the group. Decision-making in this manner does not truly humanize the people we are working with and thus prevents us from addressing the issues that speak to the true concerns of the community. Conversation needs to be conducted in a very respectful manner with the understanding that the oppressed hold the secret to overcoming the oppression.

I think a prerequisite to reading the book is to ask the question, "Is the educational leader willing to become an agent of change?" I think that is a prerequisite because I can see how some people might be turned off not only by the style of writing but by perhaps even the content if they do not have empathy with the people who are most marginalized. Like most literature, the concepts in the book are open for interpretation. The book validates those individuals who are committed to social justice. It ignites, energizes, and gives a sense of hope to people to try to commit to concepts that were proposed. It is easy to become burned out when going up against an entire mindset, an entire institution, that was never designed for difference.

I would encourage a new leader to first engage in self-reflection and ask themselves, without judgment, the true reason they want to seek a leadership role, and if the answer has anything to do with creating change, then, I encourage them to read this book. If the individual's goals do not include creating change, certainly they are still encouraged to read this book, but they may misunderstand the book or get lost in its style of writing.

Freire's message of hope is extremely powerful, with education being a tool for creating educational and economic justice. Subsequent authors like Jeffrey Duncan-Andrade have taken this message of hope and further clarified that we're not just talking about regular hope, but instead *audacious hope*. The difference between audacious hope and regular hope is that you maintain hope alive even if the oppressors have already walked away from it. That requires a lot of inner strength, and you need that sense of clarity even in the complexity. Freire makes the concept of hope very clear. Instead he motivates us to be liberators of hope who demonstrate a love that reframes the oppressed as individuals in the process of becoming.

I think a key concept presented in the book is rehumanization. It is important to have faith in humanity, as Freire advocates. It is so easy to get discouraged in the age of industrialization and in social media that is more centrally controlled and much more Orwellian. In this context, sometimes things seem insurmountable, but Freire shared his belief, over fifty years ago, that this humanization would eventually be realized. The solution is of no material cost although there can be a cost of consequences if the system serves as the oppressor. In some countries, several people had lost their lives when seeking to confront injustice. For example, throughout Latin America, people have paid with their life. All are lucky if they live in a country that values freedom. As educational leaders, we can seize this opportunity to enact needed changes, working in collaboration with our community. Freire's *Pedagogy of the Oppressed* encourages our journey in doing so.

Reflection of the Impact of Freire's Concepts to Educational Leadership

Alberto Medina, Educator, Doctoral Student

"Alberto, may the wisdom of Freire help guide you on your journey, your compañero, Gilbert R. Cadena." Just before handing me his personal copy of *Pedagogy of the Oppressed*, Dr. Cadena inscribed the aforementioned statement on the 15th of March, twenty-one years ago. I remember well meeting Professor Cadena for office hours at that time. Having experienced social inequality, Dr. Cadena was keenly aware that if there exists a pedagogy of and for the oppressed, logically there is an oppressed class and a need for leadership to engage in the praxis to work to overcome injustices. Being introduced to Freire validated my struggle to attain access to a college degree.

At that time, I was completing my second year in the classroom, and I was working for a charter school that operated in the greater Los Angeles County. The charter school's mission was mainly to provide support to students who were identified as "at-risk." For the most part, students were on expulsion or on probation and lived in local detention facilities for delinquent and rehabilitation programs. My goal was to complete my undergraduate degree and then enter a credential program to become a teacher. Reflecting on that day and that conversation with my professor influenced my educational journey. At that time in accessing higher learning, I was determined to attain my undergraduate degree, having the resilience through struggle as I was at the end of my late twenties when typically an undergraduate degree should have been well behind me. Nonetheless, I made the transition from community college to a four-year institution, and I enrolled in a newly established Gender, Ethnicity, and Multicultural Studies (GEMS). Although I did not have any concept of Freire's philosophy in critical pedagogy when I first enrolled at the university, I was well on the path to Freire's *conscientização*, my consciousness-raising. As a novice educator beginning my professional career, I recognized the need to build relationships with students and create a classroom climate of openness and respect.

Freire states that critical pedagogy—pedagogy of the oppressed—is an endeavor to be enacted by radicals. So then, who is better suited than those who have been oppressed to know what it means to counter oppression and not conform? Who is better equipped to resist the subordination of their traditional education—an education that relegates them to the margins? Who better to push back against the status quo, and embrace newly constructed roles outside of the social and cultural norms that will almost guarantee them a better quality of life? To empower others and give a voice to the struggle as posited by Freire, the "culture of silence," education can hinder growth when outdated, outmoded teaching practices (e.g., banking system) are used, as these practices are ineffective and disengaging and serve to ensure what statistics have for years demonstrated that many minority youth, second-language acquisitioning youth, and other youth who have been identified as requiring special education support attain poor educational experiences, limiting or reducing a better quality of life.

Pedagogy of the Oppressed teaches us that in praxis one must commit to the transformation of oppression as the first stage of liberation through pedagogy. Unfortunately, for many minoritized youth in the K-12 public education system and at a higher institution of learning, a love of learning advocated by Freire has not been fostered. The experience for many minorities in the United States, instead, has been deficit-based where many did not reach their true potential to exercise self-determination that promotes a better quality of life in a free, democratic society. Dialogue is needed to empower students by supporting them through a pedagogy that empowers them.

In my own personal journey, having overcome unhealthy and risky adolescent practices while recognizing that my life could have easily gone down a grim and darker path, as an adult, I was able to not only leave behind a reckless and unhealthy lifestyle but also have the opportunity to meet a professor who nurtured my *consienctizacão* and who validated my struggles to overcome adversity. I was leaving behind my life as an object, and becoming the subject of my own reality.

Reflection of the Impact of Freire's Concepts to Educational Leadership by a University Professor

Betty Alford, PhD

One of my first thoughts in reading *Pedagogy the Oppressed* was to reflect on the timelessness of the message. When reading this book, Freire's deep commitment and his vision of the importance of the quest for meaning in life was clear. His writing provides a glimpse of ways life can be lived more abundantly by recognizing the barriers that we ourselves erect. If there is a physical oppressor, we should fight the injustice side by side with the oppressed; but we also should become aware and overcome the oppressors within, which are the barriers we ourselves create. Our goal should be to move to a fuller humanity.

As Dr. Levario shared, the power of the book may not be recognized in a quick reading of it. Freire's writing promotes reflections and action, praxis, and serves as hope in the possibilities of a deeper, richer life as well as an educational future where all students, faculty, and administrators continue to grow and learn without barriers that oppress or hinder them.

I remember the first time I read this book. I was completing my doctoral studies in educational administration at the University of Texas at Austin and taking a class on adult education. I read the book on a Saturday while sitting in my car under the shade of a lovely tree as I waited for my son to complete his scuba diving certification, a day-long process. I needed to remain at the site but had no responsibility for supervision of my son. As the day passed, I enjoyed reading the book slowly and reflecting on the message. This provided a wonderful afternoon that I still recall. I often have the thought, as we required this book for reading in doctoral courses, that this book should be read in a space without interruption, a place of quietness, and a place that encourages reflection.

Moving forward through the years, as a faculty member in an educational leadership doctoral program for over ten years that required this book as assigned reading for all students, I remember a student, a director of curriculum and instruction, walking into class the day of our discussion of the book and saying, "I just don't get it." She had used the technique of quick-scan reading and had lost the essence of the book. From the dialogue in class that day and hearing the importance of certain passages from other students, she returned to the book. After a two-week break between Saturday classes, as she entered the classroom, her first words were, "I get it." With animation, she shared what she recognized as the importance of the concepts of criticality, reflection, and hope that emerged for her when she entered a dialogic reflective space with the reading and slow rereading of some sections that other students had shared that had special meaning for them. This reflection always reminds me of the power of dialogue in adult learning, of providing spaces for reflection and honest sharing, of fostering criticality, of fostering introspection but also influencing positive actions to work with others toward the elimination of inequities.

As I write this reflection, it is early morning. The birds are chirping, and otherwise, it is very quiet. Early-morning sunlight is streaming across my face much as the sun had done years ago when I first read the book. As an educational leadership professor, I am reminded again of the central importance of our classes in providing readings that encourage reflection as well as positive actions so that we as educators truly make a difference through and with others in our work, through the authentic dialogue with others, and through providing spaces of equality and mutual respect evidenced by words and actions.

I am reminded again that we all do not come to new learnings at the same pace. Through our dialogue with others, we can grow and learn. We have different backgrounds, experiences, and cultural understandings that open us to immediately connect with the topic of oppression, while others may not have the experience firsthand, and the concepts that Freire shared do not immediately prompt a connection for them. Through dialogue, as learners, we seek to understand, and in doing so, our commitment to the principles of social justice can grow and strengthen.

Implications for the Preparation of Educational Leaders

Pedagogy of the Oppressed offers many implications for the preparation of educational leaders. It is important to note that educational leaders are not only the principals or superintendents but also classroom teachers. It is important to consider what goals or purposes each has that could also align with the goals and dreams of the community. As the often-repeated phrase, "It takes a village to raise a child," we must move beyond archaic frameworks and structures built for thinking other than for equity and excellence and ask, "Where do you find the cracks in the system? How do you imagine something different within an educator's role?" Freire refers to true generosity as an act of liberation, not just to be a teacher in the class or a principal at the school but to connect with the community. An individual who walks in true generosity—not false generosity to move up in a professional position or to achieve a school district's goal—is brave and courageous and willing to challenge those paradigms of justice. This person can be an example of an effective leader.

The implications of Freire's work are not just on liberating the oppressed; it is also liberating the oppressor to be more empathetic, less bound by tradition or the "way things have always been," but serving as an advocate for change considering, for example, "How do we move beyond just a concern for academics to the social-emotional well-being of students, their consciousness?"

Education provides a better quality of life in economic means, but in true education, the learner is part of the process. There are also opportunities for teachers and educational administrators to transform the system in a way that brings in the community. For example, a principal created a room designated for parents of students. He allowed the women in the community to redesign and renovate the room to be a place where they could share skills such as baking and sewing. This was an intentional project intended to bring the community to the school. Then, he reached out to the same community in attempts to raise parent consciousness by offering adult learning classes for parents. Through his efforts, he modeled true generosity as he offered health classes with Zumba, citizenship classes, and other conscious-raising classes for the community.

Many times, teaching frameworks or strategies are missing the critical element of criticality and respect for the community. Leadership involves problem-posing and asking questions such as "Why am I focusing on this concept? What am I not seeing? What do I need to do? Am I building trust? Am I listening?" In asking myself these questions, I start to form different answers. I ask, "Am I in an oppressor role or a liberator role? How do I get this across to students? Am I really listening to them or telling them? Am I trustworthy? Am I trusting the individuals I work with?"

Conclusion

Freire's *Pedagogy of the Oppressed* is a book one can return to for reflection concerning our progress in meeting each student's needs. Dr. Levario suggested, "I go to the first chapter and reread it. Then, I skip around to the parts that resonate with me. It may be in section 2 of the third chapter or in another part. The key is to use the concepts of critical theory to ground an individual's reflections."

Our current time of emerging from a worldwide pandemic requires rethinking schooling, including the consideration of changes in instructional modes. Engaging with the students, faculty, and the community remains a priority during the pandemic and is in some ways intensified during this time as educators seek new ways of providing spaces for students' voices against racial injustices they were seeing or experiencing, spaces for encouraging healing, and spaces for understanding and joy. As educational leaders, our roles continue to expand to focus even more fully on the whole child, the whole community, and the entire school's practices, policies, and processes to alleviate inequities, rather than simply focusing primarily on academic success.

Our engagement with our community as colearners on the journey of seeking to remove barriers we created within ourselves, as well as barriers imparted by our education system in need of revision, is ongoing. *Pedagogy of the Oppressed* continues to serve as a source for reflection, action, and hope in the possibilities that will positively impact our lives and the lives of others as we engage in continued learning and school improvement processes. Therein lies the promise and the power.

References

Boyd, R. D., and J. W. Apps (1980), *Redefining the Discipline of Adult Education*, San Francisco, CA: Jossey-Bass

Brookfield, S. D. (1986), *Understanding and Facilitating Adult Learning: A Comprehensive Analysis of Principles and Effective Practices*, Buckingham: Open University Press.

Candy, P. C. (1991), *Self-Direction for Lifelong Learning: A Comprehensive Guide to Theory and Practice*, San Francisco, CA: Jossey-Bass.

Cranton, P. (1994), *Understanding and Promoting Transformative Learning: A Guide for Educators of Adults*, San Francisco, CA: Jossey-Bass.

Duncan-Andrade, J. (2017), "Equality or Equity?" www.youtube.com/watch?v=okBjLsFd58M&ab_channel=TalksatGoogl.

Elias, J. L., and S. B. Merriam (1980), *Philosophical Foundations of Adult Education*, New York: Robert E. Krieger.

Freire, P. ([1970] 1972), *Pedagogy of the Oppressed*, New York: Herder and Herder.

Griffith, W. S., and H. Y. McClusky (eds.) (1981), *Handbook of Adult Education*, San Francisco, CA: Jossey-Bass.

Hammond, M., and R. Collins (1991), *Self-Directed Learning: Critical Practice*, New York: Nichols.

Ladson-Billings, G. (2021), "I'm Here for the Hard Re-set: Post Pandemic Pedagogy to Preserve Our Culture," *Equity & Excellence in Education* 54 (1): 68–78.

Langenbach, M. (1998), *Curriculum Models in Adult Education*, Malabar, FL: Krieger.

Merriam, E. (1980), *Philosophical Foundations of Adult Education*, New York: Robert E. Krieger.

Merriam, S. B., and L. M. Baumgartner (1991), *Learning in Adulthood: A Comprehensive Guide*, San Francisco, CA: Jossey-Bass.

Merriam, S. B., and P. M. Cunningham (1989), *Handbook of Adult and Continuing Education*, San Francisco, CA: Jossey-Bass.

Starratt, R. J. (2014), "The Purpose of Education," in C. M. Branson and S. J. Gross (eds.), *Handbook of Ethical Educational Leadership*, 43–61, Oxfordshire: Routledge.
Yosso, T. J. (2002), "Toward a Critical Race Curriculum," *Equity & Excellence in Education* 35 (2): 93–107.

10

Unpacking the Intersections of Habermas's Critical Theory and Ladson-Billings's Culturally Relevant Practice

Anthony Walker

Introduction

Culture matters. The culture of an organization is the conduit of connection—it gives meaning to life and experience (Bates 1984). Fraise and Brooks (2015) described culture as the core beliefs, norms, practices, and traditions that span across an organization to create meaning for and of people. Education systems, like other organizations and systems, have a culture. For Carlson (2008), cultures in education are often reflections of economic and political interests of those with access to power and influence. Such a perspective counters the traditional discourse of education being objective and injects the presence and inputs of culture on education. Such a perspective highlights education systems as working entities that are microcosms of the cutler constructed by people leading and controlling narratives (Larson and Murtadha 2003).

A shift in viewing education from being a fact-based, objective entity to a critically subjective one influenced by socialization and people creates opportunities to think differently and ask different questions. One question then becomes: whose interests are being met and served through education? (Carlson 2008). A central tenet of education is its intimate connection and purpose-driven responsibility of preparing students for democracy and engagement that supports progress and advancement (Wolstein 2016). Spring (2008) argued that education systems are not designed to educate to empower the general populace. Rather, the primary function of education is to organize society in two ways. First, education teaches individuals and communities where their "correct" place is in society. Second, it assures that people learn and support those roles and expectations.

When considering education systems, factors such as leadership, curricula, pedagogies, assessment, and more play a role to teach and maintain hegemony and structure, what Young (2009) described as narrowly constructed frameworks of knowledge, values, and tenets that have guided, are guiding, and will hereafter guide if permitted to continue without being questioned or challenged.

For too long the structural roots of education in the United States have operated relatively free from critique or challenge that questions their dominant, mainstream influence on critical issues. Criticality has wavered in inspiring educators and students with the power to spark significant change in the modus operandi of the system (i.e., "the status quo"). Although critical examinations coupled with calls for change are not new, they have often been led by individuals, and communities that established structures of power have been able to discredit, distract, and silence. Such dynamics are not unique to the United States. Rather, marginalization and thriving are found within the systems and structures of education throughout the world where capitalism is the economic and cultural driver. Such systems serve a dual function of relegating some to the margins and creating platforms for others to thrive.

An imperative for today's education system is to reframe leadership and practice to include a mindfulness of how to expand platforms where more students thrive. More specifically, systems need to be designed to educate with equity and use praxis that is relevant to students from cultural identities that are often overlooked to minimize margins (Brown-Jeffy and Cooper 2011). When considering how to advance equity and relevancy, leaders can learn a great amount from those whose voices and experiences have been systematically and systemically suppressed. The focus of this chapter is to make a rational case for why change is needed and how Critical Theory offers a framework and justification for Culturally Relevant Practice being a pedagogical framework to operationalize Critical Theory and foster a more equitable education system.

Johnston (2012) asserted, "Change very often demands a strong argument in favor of exception to the rule" (118). Having and being able to articulate a vision of why change is needed and how change can occur is critical. As Kotter (2012) noted, a vision that connects people with goals and outcomes can galvanize people to think differently and expect different outcomes—to imagine possibilities. For leaders and practitioners who agree with Harsh and Merrow's (2006) belief that education is the backbone of a democracy, Critical Theory offers a framework to imagine such possibilities—and to imagine an education system invested in justice and equity (Shields 2004), democracy and freedom (Spring 2008), and criticality (Lowery et al. 2015).

Education is a space and place where curricula are used to teach, and values, ideals, and a sense of self are learned (Aronson and Laughter 2016). Leaders have the ability and position to define the culture of learning—the rituals, knowledge, language, and beliefs that are used to guide teaching and learning (Bates 1984). The question is what and whose values are presented and learned through leadership and practice? How are values of democracy, freedom, and identity modeled and taught? And by whom, for whom, and why? These questions are important to be mindful of because language becomes a tool for naming and giving meaning to the "world, thinking, and framing interpretations of experience" (Spring 2008: 59), and when it is relevant, education connects language with learning about personal cultures and the cultures of others (Aronson and Laughter 2016). However, if allowed to function without critique, education systems operate to manufacture that status quo (Bates 1984). And, as education systems often lack an authentic set of checks and balances to link learning and equity with outcomes, a systematic takeover of curricula that values principles of the dominant culture (Young 2009), and the devaluing, silencing, and sometimes removing of any narrative that may counter the status quo of power and privilege (Spring 2008), becomes both the norm and the narrative.

Critical Theory

Although systems of education are designed to reciprocate cultural values that further the entrenchment of power, privilege, and difference (Johnson 2005), frameworks built to dismantle systems of hegemony do exist. Critical Theory, focused on equity and change, is one of those frameworks. Hodges (2014) described Critical Theory as a "family of approaches" connected by a common set of goals. Those goals being to increase the knowledge of systems of power to challenge and disrupt the status quo (1043). Overall, the core tenets of Critical Theory are simple and straightforward. For example, as Johnson (2005) pointed out, Critical Theory is about engagement and change. For Habermas, this includes discourse and an acknowledgment that the culture and difference are real and impact a person's view and actions related to rights and democracy (Baumeister 2003). In his framework of Critical Theory as a tool for action, Habermas noted the importance of the roles the personal, cultural, and societal norms have on pedagogical frameworks of leadership and communication (Miedema 1994). The core tenets of Critical Theory, including equity, citizenship, and individual's rights, help maintain and sustain social and cultural engagement and rights

(Habermas 1998). While the values of teaching offer a framework to guide research, philosophy, and teaching, the true potential of Critical Theory is in how the tenets are translated into practice. It is where self-critique and reflexivity (Bohman 2005) intersect with a lens of empowerment and awareness of power dynamics (Kompridis 2014) that leaders can translate the potential of Critical Theory into practice that could result in a more just and equitable education system.

Critics argue that Critical Theory no longer offers a framework adept to meeting the challenges of contemporary social norms and behaviors (Freundlieb 2000). However, given that Critical Theory is about engagement, self-critique, and being reflexive (Bohman 2005), and fundamentally a theory simply offers *a framework* for understanding and explaining issues (Johnson 2005), the question might be less about the relevance of Critical Theory and more about how leaders use such a framework. Critical Theory offers a language to identify, explain, and examine power dynamics (Wolstein 2016). Do leaders of today have the courage to translate the principles of social justice, empowerment, and equity into action? As Hodges (2014) noted, leaders who practice the teachings of Critical Theory are committed to change, not the status quo. And, when awareness unmasks inequities and systems of oppression, those invested in the principles of Critical Theory will hear a call to action.

Culturally Relevant Practice as Critical Theory

How a leader leads reflects who they are—their values, principles, and beliefs. Individuals who lead through a lens of Culturally Relevant Practice demonstrate an investment in the potential and promise of education (Gay 2013). Gloria Ladson-Billings, considered the architect and leading scholar of Culturally Relevant Practice (Milner 2011), described culture- and identity-affirming teaching and leading as that which empowers learners to think critically, develop a critical consciousness, and become an advocate for equity (Ladson-Billings 1995a). Gay (2010) added that a lens of cultural relevancy utilizes lived experiences as a point of reference to connect curriculum, learning, and growth. Culturally Relevant Practice is critical to today's education system as it emphasizes both connections between pedagogy, student success, and practitioner responsibility (Hyland 2009) and the need to foster spaces and places where empowerment, equity, and engagement intersect and interface.

Leaders and practitioners who integrate Culturally Relevant Practice into their work agree with Bates's (1984) view that culture matters and shapes the operations and identity of an organization. As Morrison et al. (2008) noted, practice established through a lens of cultural relevance offers a framework where the "hegemonic epistemological assumptions about knowledge, teaching, and learning" (444) are questioned and critiqued. It is, as Habermas (1984) noted, about connecting dots between cultural norms with personal and societal aspects of lived experiences while recognizing that a person's lifeworld is simultaneously unique and linked to group and community lifeworlds. When core tenets of Culturally Relevant Practice are translated into practice, the result is a model of practice that empowers individuals to become aware and critical of "domination, discrimination, subjugation, and dehumanization of individuals and groups" (Bassey 2016: 5). School leaders who are critically conscious and culturally aware are needed to cultivate systems of education that teach for equity and empower learners to challenge unjust policy and practices. They design structures and examine issues through frameworks that dismantle systems of oppression that marginalize and minoritize those whose culture(s) run counter to privileged and socially privileged norms of being and doing.

A framework for practice that emphasizes cultural relevance has three key elements. First, practice results in individuals learning and achieving success. Second, individuals become aware, develop, and maintain cultural competency. And third, individuals learn to be critically conscious consumers of knowledge (Ladson-Billings 1995b). As leaders increase their awareness and knowledge of their sense of self, how the world around them operates, and how and where they fit into the world (Milner 2011), they become better equipped to challenge traditional norms and advocate for education systems that address inequities and enhance learning for all (Irvine 2010). The emphasis on empowering and enhancing learning for all is critical to the story, tenets, and goals of Culturally Relevant Practice. For example, translating Kendi's (2019) perspective on being not racist versus antiracist in an educational context, practice is either producing or disrupting the status quo; neutrality is not an option.

Culturally Relevant Practice is, for some, a reimagining of what educational leadership and practice look like and what this practice results in. A culturally relevant leadership practice imagines and sets goals for education systems and practices that are *student-ready* (McNair et al. 2016) rather than students being ready for education. A simple shift in phrasing and language can transform values, approaches, and expectations of leadership and practice. For example, many traditional pedagogical approaches that place the onus of responsibility on students reinforce a deficit-thinking mindset that separates lived experiences, culture, and identity from learning (Schmeichel 2012). However, a Culturally Relevant Practice approach embraces a cultural wealth framework (Yosso 2005) and leverages personal narratives and experiences to connect dots between the learner and their learning (Esposito and Swain 2009; Ladson-Billings 1995a). When governing from a traditional paradigm of thought—if lacking a focus or a charge to dismantle systems or to advance systems—the leader will reinforce a framework of education that is not designed to produce equity in outcomes and learning (Irvine 2010).

Practicing Culturally Relevant Practice as Critical Theory

To move forward, it is important to establish a baseline of assumption, perspectives, and purpose. By establishing parameters on the front end of a discussion, the audience is more informed and thus a space for productive communication is set. Therefore, before transitioning into how Culturally Relevant Practice and the central tenets of Critical Theory are not only relevant but also needed in contemporary education, it is warranted to restate a platform of assumptions and values that guide my research, practice, and leadership. Examples of such values include the following:

- Education is a key component of democracy and a well-informed, engaged society (Hersh and Merrow 2006).
- Education reflects culture, values, and norms and is both subjective and objective (Bassey 2016).
- Education teaches learners what and who is important as well as what and who is not valued (Ladson-Billings 1995a).
- Curriculum and pedagogy that is culturally relevant empowers individuals, affirms identities, emphasizes equity, and increases personal consciousness (Quezada 2008).
- The core tenets of education systems in the United States and other capitalist societies such as the UK are invested in maintaining a status quo of power and privilege, rather than equity and empowerment (Spring 2008).

With the aforementioned principles acknowledged, the next part of this chapter will address the brilliant and often neglected questions that connect the what and the why together. For example, why do conversations about cultural relevance, education, and systems matter? One critically important reason is because "language and culture are constitutive for the lifeworld itself" (Habermas 1987: xxv). Additionally, practice designed within the principles of cultural relevance uses a critical lens to bring focus to human suffering being an optional component of society, and inequities being a product of constructed suffering and social norms, both of which can be eliminated (Kincheloe 2008); the root causes of many inequities in education come from how we think and view experiences that do not reinforce the dominant culture (Ladson-Billings 2014); and practice that is culturally relevant embraces a holistic approach to teaching, leading, and learning that affirms and integrates individual and group cultures into learning (Quezada 2008). These, along with the core tenets of Culturally Relevant Practice, including academic success, sociopolitical awareness, and cultural competence (Ladson-Billings 1995b), as well as the belief that education should advance the public good (Kezar 2005) and values of democracy (Carlson 2008), highlight the need for cultural relevance in today's schools.

Culturally Relevant Practice as Critical Theory offers a framework to question, practice, and assess the impact and outcomes of education. As Durden and Truscott (2013) noted, when a critical lens is used, educational practices become a constant state of questioning if and how students' voices and experiences are not only a part of the learning experience but also affirmed. When structures that combine attributes of culture, society, and personal identities with norms and socialization are disrupted or not congruent with the principles of justice, equity in teaching and learning is lost. And thus, memories are lost, foundations are shaken, and confusion about identity and ethics occurs (Habermas 1984). And, as Ladson-Billings (2006) discussed, when a Culturally Relevant Critical Theory is a driver of practice, a mindfulness of how teachers view their students becomes a marker of teaching and learning. Further, practitioners who employ cultural and critical relevancy demonstrate a critical consciousness (Gay and Kirkland 2003) through their asset-based approach and reject deficit frameworks that cause harm to students whose identities don't align with status quo ideologies and norms (Howard 2021).

Instead, teachers who embrace the principles of cultural relevance operate from a place of "recognizing student strengths and seeks to build on them" (2). Such practice is not easy, and good intentions should not overshadow outcomes and impact. As Fraise and Brooks (2015) articulated, a practitioner who fuses the principles of cultural relevance into teaching and leadership is more than employing an approach or lens to practice, and integrating an authentic framework of cultural relevance into teaching and leading is a "paradigm of practice" (9). A lens of cultural relevance is critical for the purpose of advancing the ideals of democracy, equity, and success through education. In order to actively engage in a critical-oriented practice that is culturally relevant, a practitioner needs to blend moral courage and bravery, self-confidence and assurance, as well as competence so as to engage, empower, and challenge people, policies, and practice to produce equity in outcomes (Bassey 2016).

To be a leader embodying critical and culturally relevant leadership, one has to focus their efforts on identify, unpacking, and challenging the dynamics of power, privilege, and difference (Gay and Kirkland 2003). Much of the work to be a competent and effective leader who is prepared to foster equity-minded learning environments starts with personal work. As Howard (2003) pointed out, to become a culturally relevant and responsive practitioner, an individual must use an authentic and critical lens to reflect on how socialization and positionality influence their practice as well as how students think, learn, and understand the world they live in. Part of utilizing Culturally Relevant Practice to lead educational frameworks is to invoke a critical consciousness to evaluate if and how identities, values, and experiences are included in curriculum and assessment, particularly those that have been victimized or overlooked by the dominant culture. That is what it means to be a practitioner who embraces Culturally Relevant Practice as Critical Theory—to evolve and grow with a mindfulness that the cultures and experiences that students bring with them offer pathways for more effective teaching, learning, and leading (Ladson-Billings 2006).

It also means having an awareness that critically oriented self-reflection leads to a deeper awareness of how culture and identity evolve and shape a person's view of the world, their students, and their practice (Howard 2003). By combining these two modes of thinking and practice, practitioners will be better positioned to lead a twenty-first-century education system in need of learning environments that are culturally relevant, critically oriented, and student-ready.

Conclusion

The education of today and the future is vastly different from its origins. As society continues to become more diverse (Parrado 2011), decisions will need to be made to ensure practitioners are prepared to lead education systems that meet the demands and needs of a more diverse society and student body (Howard 2003). For example, will those having the power and ability to influence how systems of education function hold on to an outdated model that fails to adhere to the potential and purpose of education? Or, will they seek out opportunities to transform education into what it can and should be—spaces built on tenets of cultural relevance, equity-mindedness, and justice. For those who choose the latter, Culturally Relevant Practice and Critical Theory offer a viable pathway to translate potential into impact and outcomes. As Morrison et al. (2008) noted, Culturally Relevant Practice is necessary if leaders and practitioners truly believe that quality education engages all students well. Howard (2021) articulated what Ladson-Billings (1995b) described as simply "good teaching" into a tangible practice, stating that Culturally Relevant Pedagogy embodies a professional, political, cultural, ethical, and ideological disposition that supersedes mundane teaching acts. Nonetheless, it is centered in core fundamental beliefs about teaching, learning, students and their families, communities, and an unyielding commitment to see student success become less rhetoric and more reality. It also operates from a standpoint that teachers must have a firm and authentic belief in a student's ability to succeed.

Such work is not easy. Rather than allowing the status quo to continue and countless students to be harmed by the very institution that espouses itself to be a space and place of opportunity where all are welcome, leaders and practitioners who aspire for equity are taking the road less traveled. As Gay (2013) noted, to accept the responsibility of challenging the system of education is to accept the necessity of struggle that comes with disrupting the power dynamics to reimagine and redistribute knowledge. And, as Lowery (2016) discussed, this requires practitioners to engage in critical and reflexive reflections of the self. Self-work focused on critical reflections, equity-mindedness, and cultural relevance is an impetus for fostering education systems where inclusive excellence is the norm and learning is viewed as being a holistic experience, meaning practitioners embed formal and informal, in-school and out-of-school experiences into curricula, pedagogies, and assessment (Fraise and Brooks 2015). For practitioners, having an awareness of how their life worlds work to either maintain or challenge systems that result in harm to students and society is critical. Leading with an awareness of the importance of culture in mind means utilizing practice that views experience as an asset. It creates a space for intersubjectivity, critical thinking, and perspective building (Habermas 1987). A failure to not embrace the charge to disrupt current models of practice and integrate Critical Theory and Culturally Relevant Practice as pillars of democratic leadership and education will mean a continued eroding of education systems and a growing number of undereducated citizens. And that, as Ladson-Billings (2014) highlighted, an undereducated citizenry is not good for democracy.

References

Aronson, B., and J. Laughter (2016), "The Theory and Practice of Culturally Relevant Education: A Synthesis of Research across Content Areas," *Review of Educational Research* 86 (1): 163–206.

Bassey, M. O. (2016), "Culturally Responsive Teaching: Implications for Educational Justice," *Education Sciences* 6 (35): 1–6.

Bates, R. J. (1984), "Toward a Critical Practice of Educational Administration," in T. J. Sergiovanni and J. E. Corbally (eds.), *Leadership and Organizational Culture: New Perspectives on Administrative Theory and Practice*, 260–74, Chicago: University of Illinois Press.

Baumeister, A. T. (2003), "Habermas: Discourse and Cultural Diversity," *Political Studies* 53: 740–58.

Bohman, J. (2005), "We, Heirs of Enlightenment: Critical Theory, Democracy and Social Science," *International Journal of Philosophical Studies* 13 (3): 353–77.

Brown-Jeffy, S., and J. E. Cooper (2011), "Toward a Conceptual Framework of Culturally Relevant Pedagogy: An Overview of the Conceptual and Theoretical Literature," *Teacher Education Quarterly* 38 (1): 65–84.

Carlson, D. (2008), "Are We Making Progress? The Discursive Construction of Progress in the Age of 'No Child Left Behind,'" in D. Carlson and C. P. Gause (eds.), *Keeping the Promise: Essays on Leadership, Democracy, and Education*, 3–26, New York: Peter Lang.

Durden, T. R., and D. M. Truscott (2013), "Critical Reflectivity and the Development of Culturally Relevant Teachers," *Multicultural Perspectives* 15 (2): 73–80.

Esposito, J., and A. N. Swain (2009), "Pathways to Social Justice: Urban Teachers' Uses of Culturally Relevant Pedagogy as a Conduit for Teaching for Social Justice," *Perspective on Urban Education* 6 (1): 38–48.

Fraise, N. J., and J. S. Brooks (2015), "Toward a Theory of Culturally Relevant Leadership for School-Community Culture," *International Journal of Multicultural Education* 17 (1): 6–21.

Freundlieb, D. (2000), "Rethinking Critical Theory: Weaknesses and New Directions," *Constellations* 7 (1): 80–99.

Gay, G. (2010), *Culturally Responsive Teaching: Theory, Research, and Practice*, 2nd ed., New York: Teachers College Press.

Gay, G. (2013), "Teaching to and through Cultural Diversity," *Curriculum Inquiry* 43 (1): 48–70.

Gay, G., and K. Kirkland (2003), "Developing Cultural Critical Consciousness and Self-Reflection in Preservice Teacher Education," *Theory into Practice* 42 (3): 181–7.

Gur-Ze'ev, H. (ed.) (2005), *Critical Theory and Critical Pedagogy Today: Toward a New Critical Language in Education*, Haifa: University of Haifa.

Habermas, J. (1984), *The Theory of Communicative Action, Vol 1: Reason and the Rationalization of Society*, trans. T. McCarthy, Boston, MA: Beacon.

Habermas, J. (1987), *The Theory of Communicative Action, Vol 2: Lifeworld and System—A Critique of Functionalist Reason*, trans. T. McCarthy, Boston, MA: Beacon.

Habermas, J. (1998), "The European Nation State: On the Past and Future of Sovereignty and Citizenship," *Public Culture* 10 (2): 397–416.

Hersh, M., and J. Merrow (2006), *Declining by Degrees: Higher Education at Risk*, New York: Palgrave Macmillan.

Hodges, R. D. (2014), "When I Say ... Critical Theory," *Medical Education* 48: 1043–4.

Howard, T. C. (2003), "Culturally Relevant Pedagogy: Ingredients for Critical Teacher Reflection," *Theory into Practice* 42 (3): 195–202.

Howard, T. C. (2021), "Culturally Responsive Pedagogy," in J. A. Banks (ed.), *Transforming Multicultural Education Policy & Practice*, 137–63, New York: Teachers College Press.

Hyland, N. E. (2009), "One White Teacher's Struggle for Culturally Relevant Pedagogy: The Problem of the Community," *New Educator* 5: 95–112.

Irvine, J. J. (2010), "Culturally Relevant Pedagogy," *Education Digest* 75 (8): 57–61.

Johnson, R. (2005), "Habermas: A Reasonable Utopia," *Critical Horizons* 6 (1): 101–18.

Johnston, J. S. (2012), "Schools as Ethical or Schools as Political? Habermas between Dewey and Rawls," *Studies of Philosophy and Education* 31: 109–22.

Kendi, I. X. (2019), *How to Be an Anti-racist*, New York: One World.

Kezar, A. J. (2005), "Challenges for Higher Education in Serving the Public Good," in A. J. Kezar, T. C. Chambers, and J. C. Burkhardt (eds), *Higher Education for the Public Good: Emerging Voices from a National Movement*, 23–42, San Francisco, CA: Jossey-Bass.

Kincheloe, J. L. (2008), "The Vicissitudes of Twenty-First Century Critical Pedagogy," *Studies of Philosophy and Education* 27: 399–404.

Kompridis, N. (2014), "Re-envisioning Critical Theory: Amy Allen's *The Politics of Our Selves*," *Critical Horizons* 15 (1): 1–13.

Kotter, J. P. (2012), *Leading Change*, Boston, MA: Harvard Business Review Press.

Ladson-Billings, G. (1995a), "Toward a Theory of Culturally Relevant Pedagogy," *American Educational Research Journal* 32 (3): 465–91.

Ladson-Billings, G. (1995b), "But That's Just Good Teaching: The Case for Culturally Relevant Pedagogy," *Theory into Practice* 34 (3): 159–65.

Ladson-Billings, G. (2006), "Yes, But How Do We Do It: Practicing Culturally Relevant Pedagogy," in J. G. Landsman and C. W. Lewis (eds.), *White Teachers/Diverse Classrooms: Creating Inclusive Schools, Building on Student's Diversity, and Providing True Educational Equity*, 33–46, Sterling, VA: Stylus.

Ladson-Billings, G. (2014), "Culturally Relevant Pedagogy 2.0: a.k.a. The Remix," *Harvard Educational Review* 84 (1): 74–84.

Larson, C., and K. Murtadha (2003), "Leadership for Social Justice," in J. Murphy (ed.), *The Educational Leadership Challenge: Redefining Leadership for the 21st Century*, 134–61, Chicago: University of Chicago Press.

Lowery, C. L. (2016), "The Scholar-Practitioner Ideal: Toward a Socially Just Educational Administration for the 21st Century," *Journal of School Leadership* 26 (1): 34–60.

Lowery, C. L., C. Gautam, A. Walker, and C. D. Mays (2015), "The Scholar-Practitioner and Democratic Professional Practice in Education (DPPE): An Ethic of Care, Collaboration, Criticality, and Commitment," in P. Tenuto (ed.), *Renewed Accountability for Access and Excellence: Applying a Model for Democratic Professional Practice in Education*, 261–78, Lanham, MD: Lexington Press.

McNair, T. B., S. Albertine, M. A. Cooper, N. McDonald, and T. Major (2016), *Becoming a Student-Ready College: A New Culture of Leadership for Student Success*, San Francisco, CA: Jossey-Bass.

Miedema, S. (1994), "The Relevance for Pedagogy of Habermas' 'Theory of Communicative Action,'" *Interchange* 25 (2): 195–206.

Milner IV, H. R. (2011), "Culturally Relevant Pedagogy in a Diverse Urban Classroom," *Urban Review* 43 (1): 66–89.

Morrison, K. A., H. H. Robbins, and D. G. Rose (2008), "Operationalizing Culturally Relevant Pedagogy: A Synthesis of Classroom-Based Research," *Equity & Excellence in Education* 41 (4): 433–52.

Parrado, E. A. (2011), "How High Is Hispanic/Mexican Fertility in the United States? Immigration and Tempo Considerations," *Demography* 48 (3): 1059–80.

Quezada, S. (2008), "Critical Pedagogy: Dynamic Thinking and Teaching within the Confines of No Child Left Behind," *Radical History Review* 102: 35–8.

Schmeichel, M. (2012), "Good Teaching: An Examination of Culturally Relevant Pedagogy as an Equity Practice," *Journal of Curriculum Studies* 44 (2): 211–31.

Shields, C. M. (2004), "Dialogic Leadership for Social Justice: Overcoming Pathologies of Silence," *Educational Administration Quarterly* 40 (1): 109–32.

Spring, J. (2008), *Wheels in the Head: Educational Philosophies of Authority, Freedom, and Culture from Confucianism to Human rights*, 3rd ed., New York: Taylor & Francis.

Wolstein, A. (2016), "Critical Theory: A Language for Questioning the World and the Status Quo," *Literacy Today*, November: 28–9.

Yosso, T. J. (2005), "Whose Culture Has Capital? A Critical Race Theory Discussion of Community Cultural Wealth," *Race, Ethnicity, and Education* 8 (1): 69–91.

Young, A. V. (2009), "Honorary Whiteness," *Asian Ethnicity* 10 (2): 177–85.

11

A New Critical Theory and the Black Divide

Rhonda T. Humphries

A New Critical Theory

According to Eltis (2007), "The human misery quotient generated by the forced movement of millions of people in slave ships cannot have been matched by any other human activity" (1). The transatlantic slave trade set into motion a series of phenomena that continue to plague American democratic values—equity, access, and inclusion. The subsequent events that would follow paint a harsh reality of a colonial chattel culture that paralleled the nation's quest for independence and self-governance as an autonomous entity. The ripened relationships sewn on board the slave ships that departed the coast of Western African to the Americas created the precursor for the treatment and socialization of the African—later African American—within colonized America. That being their treatment and socialization that occurred between intercommunal and owner to the enslaved. The cartilage of the atrocities onboard and across the Middle Passage and early colonial life within America (Eltis 2007), coupled with present-day calls for reform, access to quality education, and diverse bureaucrats at the local school and district level, has forced us as a nation to consider how the socialization of Black women and men in K-12 spaces perpetuates remnants of plantation/colonial life under the lens of a New Critical Theory (Wilkerson and Paris 2001).

New Critical Theory implores us to consider the immediate and long-term implications for professional development in a critically conscious, active approach to ensuring that as a nation we are also, directly and indirectly, passing messages to our youth who are charged with leading our country in the future. This chapter will review the historical and sociological factors that have contributed to the hairline fractured relationships that may be common in

K-12 spaces. As well, I aim to also examine how to unweave stitches instead of layering the quilt with more patches.

Theoretical Framework

Aspects of New Critical Theory, as described by Wilkerson and Paris (2001), are "linked to a second level self-appropriation of the cognitive and existential self-knowledge and self-choice of the subject as experiencing, understanding, judging, and choosing in relation to being … (and) put the ethical humpty-dumpty back together by linking 'is' to 'ought,' right and good, duty and happiness, formal and material, and universal and particular" (56). The New Critical Theory consists of a set of norms:

1. respecting everyone's security and subsisted rights;
2. a maximum system of equal fundamental liberties;
3. a right to an equal opportunity to attain social positions and offices, an equal right to participate in all decision-making processes in institutions of which *you are* a part, and an equal opportunity for meaningful work; and
4. that social and economic inequalities are justified only insofar as they benefit the least advantaged, are inconsistent with the just savings principle, and do not exceed levels that will undermine the equal worth of liberty and the good of respect.

Chattel slavery, the fight for emancipation, equal and equitable representation, and legislative maneuvering to push the finish line back have undeniably impacted the socialization of the Black community (Thomas Jefferson Monticello n.d.). The 1965 Moynihan Report described slavery as having an indelible impact on the socialization of neighborhoods and homes preoccupied with Black Americans. The report asked, "Why was American slavery the most awful the world has ever known?" While no clear answer was provided to the question, Moynihan (1965) did conclude that when measuring the brutality and viciousness of American slavery, "the only thing that can be said with certainty is that this is true: it was."

A comparison of American slavery to slavery in other parts of the Americas—Brazil—was that the humanity of the enslaved was not stripped of their person. Rights were afforded to the Brazilian enslaved that were systematically denied to Black women and men, that is, marriage; baptism into the Catholic Church; familial security, for example, family members could not be sold or broken upland; the Brazilian enslaved could work without censor to purchase their freedom. The enslaved Brazilian man knew of his manhood, whereas the enslaved American was property and taught manhood from imitation. The enslaved Americans had no forms of protection, were removed from all forms of organized society, and could not meet among one another without the presence of someone White except for religious gatherings authorized by the enslaver. A striking comparison made in the report was the treatment of Jews in the Nazi internment camps during the Second World War. Forced isolation and a single "omnipresent authority" created a child–parental dependency of Jews imitating or regressing childlike behaviors and attaching themselves to SS guards as father figures. Obedience was the reward that depressed the need for achievement among all people.

Presently within our school structures, Black women and men are underrepresented in leadership roles in many states across the United States. The removal and movement, involuntarily or not, has led this researcher to begin unpacking our structural systems from the perspective of Blackness, centered on the relationships that were developed and socialized through trauma and fear on the plantation and after and its present-day impact on K-12 development.

Plantation Life: A Brief Synopsis

While economic profit was the central apparatus of plantation life, creating a civilized society was a distinct and crucial aspect of colonial life. The legitimacy of slavery against attacks rested on a binary of savage and civilized. Whiteness became the marker for social hierarchy in colonial life as debate about slavery in a democratic society was "just" or not echoed throughout the colonies. Conditions for enslaved men and women vary in description from deplorable to consummate. Accounts from colonial life on the plantation describe Black women and men beaten or "broken" into submission. Black women and men were sexually assaulted, ripped apart from their families, and bred to produce children only to see them sold to other plantation owners, breaking familial connections and leaving both sexes in a continuous state of traumatic fear. Accounts of early colonial life on the plantation also led to alcoholism and the debauchery of imitating aspects of a free life in private spaces.

Few descriptions and narratives about day-to-day life exist about plantation life from the perspective of the enslaved. Plantations replicated feudal manors, absent life-long captives based on race, and were considered complex machines producing mass crops for export. A formerly enslaved laborer in South Carolina, Henry James, described the living conditions of slave houses in an interview:

> The slave houses looked like a small town and there was grist mills for corn, cotton gin, shoe shops, tanning yards, and lots of looms for weaving cloth. Most of the slaves cooked at their own houses that they called shacks …. There was a jail on the place for to put slaves in. (Vlatch 1993: 185)

Plantations resembled small towns, with the main house belonging to the plantation owner and their wives, known as the headmistress (Vlatch 1993). Slave houses were tiny and in withered conditions that could often house up to three or more enslaved laborers. Captives from the continent of Africa were auctioned and purchased by colonists to work the fields and central parts of the house as servants. Black women and men were forced to engage in sexual acts with one another to produce "chattel" that would eventually lead to the breeding of future enslaved laborers in the Americas. While accounts about sexual assault are scarce for men, it was common knowledge (although unspoken) that enslavers would rape their female captives and, if they became pregnant, would either sell them off or enslave their children.

Enslavers enslaving their biological children with female captives was a well-known occurrence and practice of the framers of the US Constitution, including Thomas Jefferson (Ferris State University n.d.). Black males were often sent to other plantations to breed with other female captives. However, with exception only in particular circumstances, the relationships between parent and child were unable to remain a steady fixture in the home or on the plantation. This practice was in part to ensure that the children and the women were unable to build a relationship with the enslaved father/mate due to the threat of the Black household becoming strong. This also prevented the enslaved male from becoming a head of the family, which would have provided him the potential of becoming stronger than their owner. In some circumstances, plantation owners allowed enslaved laborers to live together or for the male enslaved to purchase his freedom or that of his family; however, due to instability across the familial structures of enslaved, many families were forged based on kinship and adapting or attaching to another family who lived in the slave houses as a form of survival.

Reconstruction and Early Schooling

In 1619, the first Africans arrived in Jamestown, Virginia, and were considered indentured servants (National Center for Education Statistics n.d.). Indentured servitude, unlike chattel slavery, was contingent on a contract, an exchange of goods and services for transportation to the colonies, clothing, and shelter. In

July of 1640, three indentured servants attempted to escape; however, they were captured and convicted by the General Court of Colonial Virginia. All three were convicted; however, the only African among the group was sentenced to a lifetime of servitude, where he became the first to be enslaved for life. The other two codefendants were white and received a sentence of additional years of captivity, but not a lifetime.

In 1705, the Virginia Slave Codes were passed, which limited the freedoms of enslaved people and increased the protections for enslavers to usurp consequences if accused of committing acts of violence against those they kidnapped and enslaved. Before the Emancipation Proclamation, many states had enacted slave codes that forbade enslaved laborers from learning to read or write. Punishment, if found to be aiding and abetting the education of enslaved laborers, included fines, whippings, and possible death. In 1863, when Abraham Lincoln declared that slavery had been abolished in the United States, the claim of freedom was a dream that remained as such for much of the South until 1865, the end of the Civil War. However, before the end of the Civil War, the US Senate passed the Thirteenth Amendment on April 8, 1864. As a result, US legislators declared involuntary servitude (slavery) illegal as a national policy but with no active enforcement at the state/local level.

Before the passage of the Thirteenth Amendment, enslaved laborers, although forbidden to do so, gathered in secrecy to educate one another. After the Civil War ended, the Freedmen's Bureau was established by the US Congress in 1865 to oversaw aspects of universal education in the South. Clandestine schools in Georgia, for example, began to open their doors to the public without fear of retribution from former Confederates. As schools began to sprout in the South, Northern missionaries and literate Black men and women began traveling to the South to support (financially) and have a proactive representative (active and passive) role in the education of freed laborers. As a result, Universal Education in American history saw an explosion of rural and southern children enrolling across the nation. As schools began to expand, schooling and operations did too, and so did the resentment of former enslaved laborers who felt that educating formerly enslaved people threatened the social hierarchy of white supremacy. W. E. B. DuBois noted during the Black Reconstruction that "public education for all at public expense was, in the South, a Negro idea." Fueled by the disruption of the status quo and intervention of the federal government, the South grew bitter, and restrictions on daily life and mobility were put in place to regulate the bodies and minds of African American women and men.

Black codes were laws designed to maintain the social status quo and whiteness across the South. Before the Black codes were passed in 1865 and 1866, slave codes existed under the premise of chattel slavery. In 1788, Congress codified the three-fifths rule by ratifying Article 1, section 2 of the US Constitution. Enslaved laborers were considered chattel property and not whole people. At the turn of the twentieth century, freed laborers began advocating and protesting for suffrage. As federal intervention and presence became prominent in the South, Blacks began to organize bureaucratically and thrive as newly freed people in the United States. During the era of Radical Reconstruction (1865–77), two subsequent amendments to the Constitution furthered the rights of African Americans—the Fourteenth and Fifteenth Amendments (National Center for Education Statistics n.d.). The Fourteenth Amendment guaranteed every American citizen equal protection under the law, and the Fifteenth Amendment guaranteed African American men their right to vote.

Later in 1921, after nationwide suffrage demonstrations, the Nineteenth Amendment would become ratified, and African American women were granted their right to vote—nearly fifty years later. Post-Reconstruction also saw a boom in African American representation at the local, state, and federal levels. Although whites contested many elections, African American males ran and won seats as legislators in previous slave-holding states due to their inclusion in the Union. While the ideals of emancipation were romantic, the harsh realities were that African American women and men were still being brutalized in their day-to-day lives, even with the protections of the Constitution in place. Thomas Nast's depiction of "Emancipation" demonstrates the contrasting realities ahead for enslaved laborers and the nation's (Northern) vision of freedom for Blacks by whites: freedom without mobility and freedom connected to whiteness.

As depicted in the picture by Nast, a white man, African American life portrays a white fantasy about Black women and men living in freedom. In the image, Abraham Lincoln is pictured below an African American family in a home, distinguished and gazing afar. To the left and right of the picture are two contrasting realities: freedom and the institution of slavery. Above the image of the African American family gathered in their homes is the word "EMANCIPATION," with several pictures of angels, military, and white settlers in the sky looking upward. While the imagery behind the political cartoon is subjective, the placement of Lincoln, the contrasting relationship between freedom and slavery, and the direct (or indirect) association to godliness as whiteness portray a life where Blacks were expected to adapt and assimilate into American "white" life.

In the "1619 Project," Nikole Hannah-Jones (2021) references how Lincoln had been the first sitting president to invite members of the Black "elite" to the White House to discuss the future of freed Negroes. Among the elite was Frederick Douglass, an abolitionist and formerly enslaved person who learned to read and write while in bondage, challenging Maryland slave codes at the time of his entrapment. Historian Bronner, as referenced in the 1619 project, states that Abraham Lincoln's ideals for African Americans' full inclusion into the Union were limited. While not an advocate of equality, the rapid changes made a short time before Lincoln's assassination also led to questions that continue to plague American society: What to do about the Negro problem? Bronner states:

> The last speech calling for partial inclusion of Black Americans, that's an evolution, and among the many tragedies of Lincoln's death is that he did change so much in such a short period …. Still, the final stages of Lincoln is a person who only believes in partial Black inclusion and is only advocating for the inclusion of certain black people on certain terms. (Hannah-Jones et al. 2021: 109)

Remnants of these changes and unanswered questions have lingered for over a century and have trickled into multi-agencies and bureaucratic structures, both public and private. Among these sectors are public schools across the country that promote democratic values, and assimilation into a system that harms the relationship structures between Black women and men, mimicking forms of plantation life and chattel slavery.

Historians, anthropologists, and sociologists all contend that the eras of Reconstruction and post-Reconstruction sought to keep the Black male in his place by limiting social mobility, access, and the perpetuation of fear and shame as the Black female was rarely perceived as a threat. The systematic denial or attempts to abridge the full inclusion of the Black man, and consequently the Black woman, into the Union are also evident today in school districts' calls for a diverse workforce and the provisions of alternative paths for school leadership, which still do not retain larger populations of Black male educators and cannot prevent the extinction of Black female teachers from the classroom in the name of performance evaluations, student achievement, and so on.

Leadership and Schooling

The machinery of schools changed drastically when the role of a principal/headmaster was introduced at the turn of the century. Schools no longer operated under the authority of a headteacher or master teacher, but were operationalized to incorporate a supervisory role over the work and production of multiple teachers' and students' success. Early descriptions of the principal's office that lacked role clarity created conflict, along with high standards of accountability from school operating agencies (e.g., school board, state, and federal government). With minimal authority but high accountability standards, schools began to systematize its day-to-day operations.

Leadership is broadly conceptualized in the United States as an idealist trait known as the Great Man Theory. Innate characteristics were first associated with the administration of schools that excluded nonwhites from participation and inclusion in academic settings that were not entirely minority-populated. While the creation of the principal's office revolutionized the internal organization of schools, it also anchored and solidified the specialization of schooling and the leadership role. Early accounts of minority-led schools (educators and leaders) often described tension among Blacks and whites due to access and quality. The role of the principal and the making of the principal's office also coincide with antigay campaigns in schools and campaigns against the feminization of the nation.

While there is information about the role, schooling, and impact of Black leaders, it is scarce and depicts impoverished conditions. Black leaders were viewed as cultural symbols within their communities and acted as liaisons between Black and white societal and, sometimes, political conflicts.

As schools began to evolve in the twentieth century and the US military began engaging in conflicts under the guise of democracy, schools, access, and equity were denied to Black women and men at home. Post–Second World War ushered in a period of significant crises within American schools. According to Mehta (2015), three external crises threatened American schooling during the twentieth century: the crisis of *standards* (1950), the crisis of *equity* (the 1960s), and the crisis of *efficiency* (1970s). Second, the role and concept of leadership continued to evolve and began to broaden its scope of inclusion to racial components and gender in schools. Third, the heterosexual, athletic male stereotype influenced perceptions about the role of the principal and the principal's office. As Rousmaniere (2007) claims, this also moved women out of leadership, and males into the principal's seat.

As veterans began returning home from the Second World War, incentives were provided via the Servicemen's Readjustment Act 1944. Returning soldiers and veterans were compensated for their service and provided funds for housing, insurance, and schooling. As more and more veterans returned home, schools and the path to school leadership benefited men primarily. Women were pushed back into classrooms, while men assumed leadership roles with higher pay, autonomy, and supervisory authority over predominantly female staff. The nuances of schooling and leadership, in conjunction with the continuous questioning of "what to do?" was again tempered by federal intervention but would soon explode.

Present-day leadership is overwhelmingly white, with white women outpacing their counterparts. According to the National Teacher and Principal Survey (NTPS) released by the US Department of Education in 2019, 78 percent of school-based leaders and principals are white; yet minority students compose more than 50 percent of the student population (National Center for Education Statistics n.d.). Similarly, we find women, regardless of race, outpacing males in the classroom by double-digit percentages. For example, Black males across the United States comprised 2 percent of teachers and 7.8 percent of school leaders in 2015–16 compared to their white male/female or Black female counterparts. According to the National Center for Education Statistics, Black females comprised approximately 5 percent of teaching positions. In 2016–17, 12.1 percent of school leaders across the United States were Black women. These statistics demonstrate the fragility of survival for Black males and, consequently, females in our current public school educational space, as well as the diminishing role and influence their active presence can have on the socialization process of Black and Brown youth in our schools.

Brown v. Board of Education

Shock waves were sent across the nation when the Supreme Court ruled that "separate but equal was inherently unequal" and desegregated public spaces, including schools across the South in the United States. The upheaval of social order in the South was again disrupted by federal intervention and met with the same/similar opposition as universal education during the Reconstruction era. Black principals were less visible in educational literature during this time; however, as described by Anderson, African American communities valued education and continued to promote ideals that favored full inclusion into the Union. As the 1954 decision of *Brown v. Board of Education* sent shock waves, a response by Southern states was to begin closing schools to subvert the federal government's authority. The forced closure of schoolhouses left thousands of

Blacks and low-income whites across the South without any public schooling options as tuition/private schools were made available to the privileged (Karpinski 2006; Rousmaniere 2007).

The Supreme Court's landmark decision also increased Black principal and teacher turnover within the South. The number of Black principals in Alabama decreased from 134 to 14; in Virginia, from 107 to 16; in Texas and North Carolina, 600 Black principals lost their jobs in less than a decade since the ruling of *Brown*. Smith and Lemasters (2010) estimated that 90 percent of Black principals were eliminated in the South due to desegregation. While Black principals and teachers faced extinction, white principal populations grew. For example, in the state of Maryland, white principals increased by 167 percent, while Black principalship decreased by 27 percent.

While the decision and intent behind *Brown v. Board of Education* were made to protect the welfare and maintain the democratic values of inclusion, Black women and men were forced out of their roles, schools, and sometimes their communities as they were left without a job for long periods. Again, another indirect impact of *Brown v. Board of Education* was the upheaval of Black women and men in predominantly Black schools. Southern disobedience led to another local, state, and national struggle within communities and among the nation.

Later, an effort by Lyndon B. Johnson post–Second World War was to reform education. Considered a critical component of the Great Society's plan, Johnson's administration created Head Start and passed the Elementary and Secondary Education Act of 1965. These initiatives sought to abolish inequality and improve the economic conditions of low-income students and families. As a result, schools began shifting their focus from measuring inputs such as reasonable classroom sizes and suitable classroom environments to outputs— metrics that justified decision-making in K-12 schools. According to Mehta, this increased accountability, evaluations, and test scores. The crisis of 1960 and 1970 led to scientific and systematic thinking on managerial logic, efficiency, and equity. A systemic view of present-day remnants of post-Second World War standardization continues to pit efficiency and equity against one another. This systemic efficiency model bleeds into schools.

The upheaval of *Brown v. Board of Education* left a Black workforce devastated as their roles and positions were swept from underneath them due to school closures and the replacement of Black staff (Karpinski 2006; Rousmaniere 2007; Smith and Lemasters 2010). Schools became more segregated than ever. With the forced and inevitable movement of Black leaders and teachers, communities began to lose their cultural symbols of success. In later decades, as school enrollments began to increase, *A Nation at Risk* and several federal initiatives designed to combat poverty and promote the general welfare of our schools also presented mindsets that severed the lifeline of Black women and men to schools, and put in place systems and policies that hindered these individuals from becoming leaders or autonomous and authoritative voices in education.

Implications for Schooling and Practice

We opened the chapter with the norms of a New Critical Theory. Since writing this chapter, a world pandemic has come to an end. As we've explored in several sections, the security of Black women and men within K-12 spaces has been deeply impacted by the socialization in colonial/plantation life. Insecurity in stable home structures alongside physical captivity, rape, and chattel slavery has plagued the mental health and psyche of Black women and men present day. Within a New Critical Theory, the first norm for every member of a representative Union is the security of everyone; however, since Blackness' pathology has not included aspects of humanity, the survival for Black women and men has been threatened at every level. Currently, Black women and men are nearing extinction within US schools without adequate representation at district school offices. This has ripple effects on the hiring, retention, and advancement of Black leaders across K-12 schools. To support K-12 schools, current and potential future leaders must also begin to delve into mental health and professional well-being development spaces that are able to identify the root causes of systemic problems, become exemplars of antiracism and abolitionism, and prioritize the intentional economic investment in creating pathways and pipelines for school leaders of color.

References

Borowski, J., and M. Will (2021), "What Black Men Need from Schools to Stay in the Teaching Profession," *Education Week*. www.edweek.org/leadership/what-black-men-need-from-schools-to-stay-in-the-teaching-profession/2021/05.

Eltis, D. (2007), "A Brief Overview of the Trans-Atlantic Slave Trade," Slave Voyages. www.slavevoyages.org/.

Eyewitness to History (2005), "Life on a Southern Plantation, 1854." www.eyewitnesstohistory.com/plantation.htm.

Ferris State University (n.d.), "Slavery in America," www.ferris.edu/HTMLS/news/jimcrow/timeline/slavery.htm

Hannah-Jones, N., C. Roper, I. Silverman, and J. Silverstein (eds.) (2021), *The 1619 Project: A New Origin Story*, New York: New York Times.

Karpinski, C. F. (2006), "Bearing the Burden of Desegregation: Black Principals and Brown," *Urban Education* 41 (3): 237–76.

Mehta, J. (2015), *The Allure of Order: High Hopes, Dashed Expectations, and the Troubled Quest to Remake American Schooling*, Oxford: Oxford University Press.

Moynihan, D. P. (1965), *The Moynihan Report*. www.blackpast.org/african-american-history/moynihan-report-1965.

National Center for Education Statistics (n.d.), "Characteristics of Public and Private Elementary and Secondary School Principals in the United States: Results from the 2017–18 National Teacher and Principal Survey." https://nces.ed.gov/surveys/ntps/summary/2019141.asp.

Rousmaniere, K. (2007), "Presidential Address: Go to the Principal's Office. Toward a Social History of the School Principal in North America," *History of Education Quarterly* 47 (1): 1–22.

Slavery and the Making of America (2004), "The Slave Experience: Legal Rights & Government." www.thirteen.org/wnet/slavery/experience/legal/history.html.

Smith, M., and L. Lemasters (2010), "What Happened to All the Black Principals after Brown?," *International Journal of Educational Leadership Preparation* 5 (4): 1–20.

Thomas Jefferson Monticello (n.d.), "Thomas Jefferson and Sally Hemings: A Brief Account." www.monticello.org/thomas-jefferson/jefferson-slavery/thomas-jefferson-and-sally-hemings-a-brief-account.

Vlatch, J. M. (1993), *Back of the Big House: The Architecture of Plantation Slavery*, Chapel Hill, NC: The University of North Carolina Press.

Wilkerson, W. S., and J. Paris (2001), *New Critical Theory: Essays on Liberation*, Lanham, MD: Rowman & Littlefield.

12

African American Education for Liberation in Twenty-First-Century America: From Critical Theory to Black Power

Bakari K. Lumumba

In his work *Awakening the Natural Genius of Black Children*, Dr. Amos N. Wilson stated, "I think it is vital that we understand that the major function of education is to secure the survival of a people" (1). The American education system is a site of historical and contemporary anti-Black violence (Pearman 2020). This pervasive violence began during the Holocaust of Enslavement, in which enslaved Africans and their descendants were legally barred from reading (Perry et al. 2003) or forced to attend underfunded segregated schools in dilapidated buildings after emancipation (Anderson 1988) and indoctrinated with a Eurocentric curriculum and arbitrary White standards (Woodson 1933) while suffering assaults from those who are supposed to protect them (i.e., school resource officers) (Ellis 2022), causing psychic, cultural, and physical harm in the aftermath of *Brown v. Board* (1954), and concomitantly enduring and combating the school-to-prison pipeline that seeks to usher Black[1] youth into a carceral state that ruthlessly exploits them for their cheap labor. These disruptions, as well as structural and institutional barriers in the education of African American youth, have contributed to contemporary issues of school dropout, pushout, and underachievement for a populace that has historically viewed education in high regard (Glover 2021).

These issues have exacerbated a historically vexed populace with a distinct historical legacy and identity, as African Americans are the only American racial/ethnic group that involuntarily migrated to America (Althouse and Brooks 2013). This peculiar fact serves as the aegis of a litany of institutions of social control (chattel enslavement, sharecropping, Black codes, Jim Crowism, the New Jim Crowism) that not only sought to deny African Americans their human and constitutional rights but also affixed them to a permanent racial caste system in which Black progress is not only inconceivable but also virtually impossible (Alexander 2010).

Central to this racialized caste system of social control was, and continues to be, the denial of a "quality" education. This chapter opines that to efficaciously combat anti-Blackness in American secondary education, K-12 school leaders and administrators must disavow the piecemeal, incremental remedies of yesteryear and embrace a curriculum and school culture that promotes culturally specific programming, critical consciousness, Afrocentric racial identity development, and Black Power for Black students. To do so, they should adopt a nexus of scholarship rooted in the work of turn-of-the-twentieth-century Black scholars (W. E. B. Du Bois, Dr. Carter G. Woodson, and Dr. Anna Julia Cooper). Their research sought to uplift the Black subaltern from the doldrums of anti-Black oppression by centering their lives and experiences through cogent scholarship and a focus on subverting anti-Black racism while fusing an African-centered ethos rooted in the philosophy of Black Nationalism.

Social-Political Context of Black Education

Black education developed in the crucible of anti-Black oppression (political disenfranchisement, social degradation, economic exploitation) rooted in the othering of African Americans as a subhuman species lacking the human qualities necessary for education and fundamental human rights (Zinn 1980). These vehemently deleterious anti-Black mandates formed the basis of a bilateral American system of schooling, rooted in schooling for democratic citizenship and schooling for second-class citizenship (Anderson 1988). This educational model stems from what Mills (1997) calls the Racial Contract (1997). This contract, according to Mills, "is a set of formal and informal agreements among whites to privilege themselves as a group through domination and exploitation of nonwhites as a group" (11). Thus, the contract provides the aegis of a "society that is not made up of free and equal individuals, as intimated in the US Constitution, Declaration of Independence, and other foundational American preambles, but rather a partitioned social ontology ... divided between persons and racial sub-persons" (16).

The Black educational experience in America is a casualty of the racial contract. Despite numerous protestations by the Black community, structural and institutional barriers remain due to anti-Black racism's pliable approach to

Black oppression. This approach is representative of the adaptability of the racial contract in which the rules and reasons employed evolve as they are challenged. This dynamic is what legal scholar Reva Siegel (1997) calls "preservation through transformation ... the process through which the racial contract is maintained through the rules and rhetoric of change."

History of Black Education

The Black past teaches us that periods of Black progress in America, whether real or imagined, are followed by periods of racial retrenchment. For example, the Reconstruction era (1865–77) resulted in the first nadir, one of the worst periods of racism in the nation's history (Logan 1965). The Civil Rights Movement (1954–68) was followed by the Nixon administration's emphasis on law and order and the momentous and historic election of Barack Obama as the nation's first Black president, which culminated in a resurgence of White Nationalist Hate Groups (WNHG), a surge in white vigilantism, and extrajudicial killings of African Americans at a rate that rivaled the first nadir (Lumumba 2020).

Black educational progress has also unfortunately bequeathed periods of racial retrenchment. For instance, the audacious quest for knowledge, literacy, education, and full citizenship that began during the antebellum era resulted in a cavalcade of setbacks, disruptions, and threats to Black peoples' physical well-being. For example, during the antebellum era, slave narratives recounted the intensity with which enslaved people's and ex-slaves' desire for education collided with the threat of beating, amputation, or death (Cornelius 1991: 66). Moreover, in *Young, Gifted, and Black: Promoting High Achievement among African American Students*, Perry et al. (2003) share:

> Enslaved people were hanged when they were discovered reading, and patrollers who went around breaking up Sunday meetings where enslaved people were being taught to read, beating all the adults who were present. Enslaved people cajoled white children into teaching them by trading marbles and candy for reading lessons. They paid large sums of money to poor white people for reading lessons and were always on the lookout for time with the blue-black speller (a school dictionary) or for an occasion to learn from their masters and mistress without their knowing. (13)

Additionally, in 1863, enslaved African Americans were "emancipated" to enjoy a brief reprieve from the horrors of the racial caste system known as chattel enslavement. Nevertheless, their campaign for first-class citizenship was "undermined by federal and state governments and extralegal organizations and tactics" (Anderson 1988: 2).

This led to a period known as the "nadir of race relations," in which Black civil and political subordination fastened them in a position to receive an educational curriculum rooted in second-class citizenship and miseducation (Anderson 1988; Logan 1965; Woodson 1933). Nevertheless, Blacks persisted in the fight for education and full humanhood via the largesse of Black and white churches, the Black elite and the Freedmen's Bureau, and, ultimately, *Brown v. Board of Education, 1954* (Painter 2007).

However, despite these advances in Black education, retrenchment was on the horizon, as numerous whitelash initiatives were implemented to halt Black educational progress. These initiatives include the educational misdiagnosis of Black boys, inequitable disciplinary standards, white flight, race riots, segregation academies, the school-to-prison pipeline, and school pushout (Ellis 2022; Glover 2021). These initiatives coalesced to create a volatile cocktail of anti-Black educational violence, rooted in destroying Black children's intellectual capability during the infancy of its development. To combat the onslaught of retrenchment initiatives, nontraditional educators, from Paulo Freire to John Taylor Gatto and Bob Moses, created curricula, scholarship, and initiatives illuminating the pitfalls and failures of compulsory education (Freire 1970; Gatto 2009). Their efforts would lay the foundation for future educators to tackle issues such as the Black achievement gap, the conspiracy to destroy Black boys, and the advocacy of African-centered education (Kunjufu 1985).

From Critical Theory to Black Power

Today, numerous educational paradigms are implemented to help solve the Black "achievement gap" (Montessori education, African-centered, multicultural, parochial, and charter). However, these educational paradigms, while laudable for expanding the educational possibilities of Black children, such as removing them from crowded, underfunded urban schools, particularly in a manner that allows an intellectual escape from the debilitating and racially disempowering effects of Eurocentric curricula, have failed to provide the education necessary to change the material conditions and social-political reality of Black America. For example, Blacks remain at the bottom of virtually every well-being metric in American society despite implementing numerous nontraditional educational theories and curricula (Johnson 2018) due in part to the lack of praxis in Black education and a curriculum that fails to center not only Black people but their experiences as well (Asante 1988).

For example, Critical Theory and its progeny of related postulations that critique systems of power, hegemony, societal institutions, and social structures have gained tremendous capital in intellectual, academic, and educational circles for its incisive ability to audaciously question societal inequity and power imbalances. Yet, Critical Theory is a beneficiary of the very inequity, privilege, and imbalances it professes to seek to critique. For example, Critical Theory has been criticized for being decidedly Eurocentric and has been called "a history of White men in conversation with themselves" (Yancy 1998: 3; see also Lumumba 2022). Thus, critical theorists and their canon are arguably palliative, ideological elixirs used to soothe the intellectual desires of bohemians at odds with contemporary society while concomitantly being unlikely to produce truly emancipatory discourse, literature, and action due to its inability or unwillingness to center the incisive views, thoughts, and experiences of the Black subaltern capable of inducing true liberation from white global hegemony (Lumumba 2022).

Moreover, Critical Theory and its ideological acolytes center the European-western sphere of influence as the epitome of educational excellence. For example, Critical Theory was forged in the academic cauldron of Marxism; its initial impetus was rooted in the fight for the rights of the proletariat and the eventual triumph of socialism over capitalism (Bronner 2017). Today, Critical Theory has expanded to address a broad range of issues that plague the culture, thought, and formation of Western democratic nation-states and institutions, including compulsory education (Freire 1970; Gatto 2009). Furthermore, "Critical Theory views thinking critically as being able to identify, and then challenge, and change, the process by which a grossly iniquitous society uses dominant ideology to convince people this is a normal state of affairs" (Brookfield 2005: viii). This position, while laudable, is not "critical" enough. The lack of praxis and inability to center the Black subaltern has failed to palpably change the conditions of a people suffering from the residual effects of chattel enslavement and second-class citizenship while concomitantly batting contemporary issues, such as the New Jim Crowism, police misconduct, extrajudicial violence, and a lack of adequate healthcare.

Thus, because of Critical Theory's tendency to intellectualize problems rather than solve them, an alternative educational model is paramount to ensuring Black people's survival. This educational model should infuse the scholarship of turn-of-the-twentieth-century Black educators such as Carter G. Woodson, W. E. B. Du Bois, and Anna Julia Cooper as a basis of a Black educational curriculum rooted in the acquisition and maintenance of power (social, political, economic, and cultural) to not only repel the insidious effects of anti-Black oppression but also restore African people to their traditional greatness as a free, proud, and productive people while fusing an African-centered curriculum rooted in the ethos of Black Nationalism.

The use of Woodson's, Cooper's, and Du Bois's scholarship is symbolic and substantial as they were and continue to be (through their scholarship) intellectual pillars of the African American community, who used their education and research to highlight racial inequity, anti-Black racism, and *misogynoir* in American society. For instance, Woodson's work championed the study of Black history (leading to the creation of Negro History Week and Black History Month), Black education, and miseducation. Du Bois's study "The Philadelphia Negro" (Du Bois et al. 1899), the first significant study of the Black community in America, and canonical sociological 1903 text *The Souls of Black Folks* (Du Bois 2014), which expounds on the Black experience of "double consciousness," have been a cause celebre for over a century, while Cooper's seminal text, *A Voice from the South: By a Black Woman of the South* (1892), highlighted the intersection of race, gender, and the socioeconomic realities of Black families during the late nineteenth century.

Their scholarship, fused with culturally specific programming, critical consciousness, and Afrocentric racial identity development, offers a compelling alternative to previous educational paradigms. As it centers and embraces the Black subalterns' history, culture, and experiences as the solution to their social, political, and economic quagmire, this educational paradigm focuses on inculcating racial pride, Afrocentric racial identity development (knowledge of one's history and culture), and a sense of critical consciousness to help foster academic achievement and Black student success. Moreover, culturally specific programming for students of African descent has been implemented at the K-12 level with excellent results concerning Black students' sense of self-worth, gaining of critical consciousness, and academic success (Aston and Graves 2018).

Furthermore, Afrocentric racial identity development, as a byproduct of culturally specific programming, can help Black students succeed in a hostile environment (the current American society), similar in manner to how people of Jewish descent have embraced Judaism as a historical, cultural, religious, and political identity—to have a positive self-concept despite the worldwide threat of anti-Semitism. This concept of racial pride as a catalyst for success and self-efficacy stems from the concepts and principles of Garveyism (Black Nationalism and Black Power) that flourished in the post–First World War era. The concepts of Garveyism (audacious Black self-assertion, racial pride, flamboyant rejection of white hegemony, and Black economic and institutional independence) served as the harbinger for African independence and decolonial movements while also serving as the template for the Black Power movement of the 1960s that led to the worldwide resistance of African people fighting against the triumvirate of anti-Black oppression (colonialism, apartheid, and Jim Crowism) (Garvey 1986).

Additionally, the use of critical consciousness, which involves engaging in critical analysis, what El-Almin et al. (2017) have called "knowledge about the systems and structures that create and sustain inequity" (20), can help Black students cultivate a sense of agency or awareness of their capability and power, in turn developing their ability to take critical action, which is a commitment to act against oppressive conditions. Moreover, El-Amin et al. (2017) suggested that Freire's concept of critical consciousness, defined as "the ability to recognize and analyze systems of inequality and the commitment to act against these systems," provided marginalized students an avenue "to academic motivation and achievement" (18). This research originated with the work of Brazilian educator Paulo Freire who conceived this concept while working with adult laborers in Brazil (Freire 1970). Furthermore, contemporary research has found that critical consciousness increases "young people's commitment to challenging pervasive injustice … but also increases academic achievement and engagement" (El-Amin et al. 2017: 20).

For example, I cite secondary education initiatives implemented "to develop critical consciousness have contributed to increased scholastic success and college enrollment" (20). This scholarship also implies that the use of critical consciousness about systems of oppression can inspire Black students to counter systems of injustices and oppression by "persisting in school and achieving in academics" (20). As research has shown, individuals who have an Afrocentric concept of racial identity development are known to have a strong racial identity, defined as the degree to which an individual feels a connection with and an attachment to their racial group based on a shared history and shared values, which has been shown to be a protective factor for people of color (Jones and Neblett 2016). Additionally, Black students who described having a positive view of their racial ethnic group were more likely to develop a stronger sense of belonging to other members of their group, which in turn allowed them to better cope with sociocultural stressors such as prejudice and discrimination (Jones and Neblett 2016).

Concluding Thoughts

In the massive treatise *Blueprint for Black Power: A Moral, Political, and Economic Imperative for the Twenty-First Century* (2011), Amos Wilson opined that the essence of African people's global quagmire is their lack of social, political, and economic power to effectively repel anti-Black domination. To address this issue, the ethos of Black Nationalism (audacious Black self-assertion, racial pride, flamboyant rejection of white hegemony, and Black economic and institutional independence) must be cultivated in Black youth during their formative educational years. This racial autonomy provides Black students with the emotional armor, intellectual vigor, critical consciousness, and skillset needed to combat a vehemently anti-Black world.

Furthermore, K-12 school leaders and administrators interested and invested in Black student success and Black community empowerment must provide a curriculum that aggressively confronts this reality while also providing the tools needed to overcome historical and contemporary barriers to Black nation-building. Such a curriculum requires scholars and practitioners to evaluate, challenge, and change how their current curricula and campus ecologies intersect with overarching systems of power and anti-Blackness to cloister Black educational achievement that renders Black liberation not only inconceivable but also virtually impossible.

Note

1 African American refers to one's ethnicity, which is a group of people with shared history, ancestry, and cultural traits, while Black refers to one's race, which is society's grouping of people based on shared physical and hereditary characteristics. While these terms are often used interchangeably, based on Cokley's (2007) distinction between the two terms and the presumption that race is a construct of society (Croom and Marsh 2016; Delgado and Stefancic 2017), I use the terms Black and African American interchangeably as the Black community consist of a multitude of African-descended ethnic groups, while noting that African Americans were the initial target of anti-Black violence in American education; that target has expanded to include all students of African descent.

References

Alexander, M. (2010), *The New Jim Crow: Mass Incarceration in the Age of Colorblindness*, New York: New Press.

Anderson, J. D. (1988), *The Education of Blacks in the South, 1860–1935*, Chapel Hill: The University of North Carolina Press.

Asante, M. K. (1988), *Afrocentricity*, Trenton, NJ: Africa World Press.

Brookfield, S. (2005), *The Power of Critical Theory for Adult Learning and Teaching*, Berkshire: Open University Press.

Bronner, S. E. (2017), *Critical Theory: A Very Short Introduction*, 2nd ed., Oxford: Oxford University Press.

Brooks, D., and R. Althouse (eds.) (2013), *Racism in College Athletics*, 3rd ed., Morgantown, WV: Fitness Information Technology.

Copper, A. J. (1892), *A Voice from the South by a Black Woman from the South*, London: The Aldine Printing House.

Cornelius, J. D. (1991), *When I Can Read My Title Clear: Literacy, Slavery, and Religion in the Antebellum South*, Columbia, SC: University of South Carolina Press.

Du Bois, W. E. B. (2014), *The Souls of Black Folk*, London: Millennium.

El-Amin, A., S. Seider, D. Graves, J. Tamerat, S. Clark, M. Soutter, I. Johannsen, and S. Malhotr (2017), "Critical Consciousness: A Key to Student Achievement," *Phi Delta Kappan* 98 (5): 18–23.

Ellis, N. T. (2022), "Experts Worry about a Heavier Police Presence in Schools: Black and Brown Children Bear the Brunt of Criminalization," CNN, June 9. www.cnn.com/2022/06/07/us/school-officers-impact-on-black-students/index.html.

Freire, P. ([1970] 2010), *Pedagogy of the Oppressed*, London: Continuum.

Garvey, A. J., and T. Martin (1986), *The Philosophy & Opinions of Marcus Garvey: Or, Africa for the Africans*, Baltimore, MD: Majority Press.

Gatto, J. T. (2009), *Weapons of Mass Instruction: A Schoolteacher's Journey through the Dark World of Compulsory Schooling*, Gabriola: New Society Publishers.

Glover, J. (2021), "Pushed Out: How Excessive School Discipline against Black Girls Leads to Dropout, Incarceration," ABC7News, March 10. https://abc7news.com/black-girls-suspended-more-than-white-pushed-out-school-to-prison-pipeline-school-pushout/10405118.

Graves, S., and C. Aston (2018), "A Mixed-Methods Study of a Social-Emotional Curriculum for Black Male Success: A School-Based Pilot Study of the Brothers of Ujima," *Psychology in the Schools* 55: 76–84.

Johnson, T. H. (2018), "Challenging the Myth of Black Male Privilege," *Spectrum: A Journal on Black Men* 6 (2): 21–42.

Jones, S., and E. Neblett (2016), "Racial-Ethnic Protective Factors and Mechanisms in Psychosocial Prevention and Intervention Programs for Black Youth," *Clinical Child and Family Psychology Review* 19 (2): 134–61.

Kunjufu, J. (1985), *Countering the Conspiracy to Destroy Black Boys*, Gilbert, AZ: African American Images.

Logan, R. (1965), *The Betrayal of the Negro, from Rutherford B. Hayes to Woodrow Wilson*, New York: Collier Books.

Lumumba, B. (2020), "Antiblackness in American Higher Education," *Journal of Blacks in Higher Education*. www.jbhe.com/2020/01/anti-blackness-in-american-higher-education.

Lumumba, B. (2022), "Why I Am 'Critical' of Critical Theory," *Journal of Blacks in Higher Education*. www.jbhe.com/2022/08/why-i-am-critical-of-critical-theory.

Mills, C. (1997), *The Racial Contract*, Ithaca, NY: Cornell University Press.

Painter, N. I. (2007), *Creating Black Americans: African American History and Its Meanings, 1619 to the Present*, Oxford: Oxford University Press.

Pearman, F. (2020), "Anti-Blackness and the Way Forward for K-12 Schooling," *Brookings*, July. www.brookings.edu/blog/brown-center-chalkboard/2020/07/01/anti-blackness-and-the-way-forward-for-k-12-schooling.

Perry, T., C. Steele, and A. G. Hilliard (2003), *Young, Gifted, and Black: Promoting High Achievement among African American Students*, Boston, MA: Beacon Press.

Seigel, R. (1997), "Why Equal Protection No Longer Protects: The Evolving Forms of Status-Enforcing State Action," *Stanford Law Review* 49: 1111–48.

Wilson, A. (1992), *Awakening the Natural Genius of Black Children*, New York: Afrikan World InfoSystems.

Wilson, A. (2011), *Blueprint for Black Power: A Moral, Political, and Economic Imperative for the Twenty-First Century*, New York: Afrikan World InfoSystems.

Woodson, C. (1933), *The Miseducation of the Negro*, New York: SoHo Books.

Yancy, G. (1998), *African American Philosophers: 17 Conversations*, New York: Routledge.

Zinn. H. (2003), *A People's History of the United States: 1492 to Present*, New York: Perennial Classics.

Conclusion: Fromm's Productive Love as a Syndrome of Attitudes for a Moral Care and Ethical Respect in Educational Leadership

Charles L. Lowery

To effectively and ethically engage, educational leaders are charged with adopting an ethic of care, responsibility, respect, and knowledge. This work is summed up in the critical theory of productive love. In *The Sane Society*, Fromm ([1955] 2008) discussed three basic types of love: brotherly love (or what he also called productive love), motherly love, and erotic love. Fromm explained that motherly love begins with oneness and leads to separateness, and erotic or physical love begins with separateness and ends in oneness. Contrary to both of these, "brotherly love," as Fromm suggested, is always about a positive and productive relationship of constant unity and equality.

Productive love is a concept developed throughout Fromm's work. As a concept, it is akin to creative activity—art and literature—and compliments reason and rationality—critical thinking and analytical skills. It provides a basis for a frame of orientation and devotion. Nonproductive love stands dialectically in opposition to its positive counterpart. We may tend to think of this nonproductive aspect of love as hate, or what Fromm might have been more inclined to call narcissism. This negative aspect of love gives way to destructiveness and irrationality. Productive love is formed in relatedness and being rooted; it is individuality with a sense of identity. Destructive love is narcissistic. It alienates and is ungrounded, promoting dysfunctional and fascist ideologies in its drive to oppress, control, and dominate. Destructive love is an individuation in which the individual has lost their identity in the need for conformity.

Therefore, the negative manifestations of selfishness, irrationality, and dysfunctional issues of control and submission are antisocial behaviors grounded not in healthy individualism but are due to an unhealthy individuation. The latter is the social process of becoming alienated. As Fromm (1947: 96) put it,

> Human existence is characterized by the fact that man is alone and separated from the world; not being able to stand the separation, he is impelled to seek for relatedness and oneness. There are many ways in which he can realize this need, but only one in which he, as a unique entity, remains intact; only one in which his own powers unfold in the very process of being related. It is the paradox of human existence that man must simultaneously seek for closeness and for independence; for oneness with others and at the same time for the preservation of his uniqueness and particularity. As we have shown, the answer to this paradox—and to the moral problem of man—is productiveness.

Fromm argued that we are innately and morally obligated to be productively engaged with life. The primary mode of this productiveness is brotherly love. First, it should be made clear that he distinguishes productive, brotherly love from maternal love (motherly love), physical love (or erotic love), and self-love (which he further distinguishes from selfishness).

Fromm also differentiates brotherly love from love of God (or religious love). These other forms of love are important to a deeper understanding of love—a theory of love—but these other types of expression are not explicitly a part of this analysis of productive love as an integral component of a spiritual democratic of the work of educational leadership. Second, in Fromm's view, productive love, as is the case with the power of reason, is the means by which we comprehend the world. It is neither emotional nor susceptible to shifts in a person's levels of dopamine and norepinephrine. Based on Fromm's concept of love, we can engage in loving another human being and the world in which we live, whether we feel like it or not. Third, as a form of human interactivity, we accept that love cannot be removed from any social activity, and therefore it is integral to all relationships, including teacher–student, leader–educator, and school–family.

An individual's ability to actively or productively love makes it possible "to break through the wall which separates [them] from another person" and therefore is a key to comprehending that other person (Fromm 1947). Productive love—also at times called brotherly love—is the only kind of love that fulfills "the condition of allowing one to retain one's freedom and integrity while being, at the same time, united with one's fellow man" (Fromm 2008: 35). Fromm referred to it in terms of a syndrome of attitudes. As such, this chapter will attempt to demonstrate how Fromm's ideals of "care, responsibility, respect and knowledge" are integral aspects of democratic education, such as defined by John Dewey (1916, 1927), and the ethic of care, such as developed by Nel Nodding (2006, 2015). To better establish a foundation for these attitudes as productive and nonproductive, we must wrestle with a critical understanding of love—not as it being positive or negative, but as it being both positive and negative.

The Dialectic of Productive Love

In Fromm's works, he is primarily concerned with two psychosocial aspects of humanity—being and loving. These refer to how we are (being) and how we relate to others (loving)—in other words, how we exist, and how we exist with the rest of the world. The productive and nonproductive forces of human being and loving are not pros and cons per se. One could easily categorize them as such. But they are forces that create a tension between them in much the same way Hegel viewed the tension between a despotic monarchy and a pure democracy. These forces tend toward a synthesis, what Hegel called a sublation. That is when these two opposing forces collapse into a new experience—an improvement that pushes us closer to a better society—such as a constitutional monarchy or a democratic republic.

For critical theorists like Fromm, this dialectical relationship between the positives and negatives is not "dualist separation," but instead they are "together as one holistic entity" (Dagostino and Lake 2014: 17). Our cultures and philosophies, particularly those of the United States and the UK that are influenced in large part by the philosophies of Aristotle and Rene Descartes, view them dualistically. But the dialectical thinking of critical theory is not dualistic. Human beings are products of both the things they desire and the things they avoid, both the things they love and the things they hate. Our societies and our experiences in those societies, as the Hegelian-influenced critical theorists would say, are formed by dueling forces of opposites.

In short, Fromm (1969) argued, humans experience both "the lust for power and the yearning for submission" (27). In other words,

> The most beautiful as well as the most ugly inclinations of man are not part of a fixed and biologically given human nature, but result from the social process which creates man. In other words, society has not only a suppressing function—although it has that too—but it has also a creative function. Man's nature, his

passions, and anxieties are a cultural product; as a matter of fact, man himself is the most important creation and achievement of the continuous human effort, the record of which we call history. (27)

For a modern day and readily available example, one only has to look to any social media platform. There you can find the "libertarian" tweeting about their rejection of all forms of government authority and power while simultaneously decrying any discussion of defunding the police or socialist efforts to share power with others. You may also stumble across the same individuals who post a meme demonizing the left wing for its overreach and regulatory controls, but in the very next post they share an ad depicting their right-wing candidate perpetually in power, or a video of them in a T-shirt proclaiming that candidate should be king. This contradiction would likely not be paradoxical to Fromm; given the social processes at work in the history of politics, it would be expected. For Fromm (2008: 24),

> The problem of man's existence ... is unique in the whole of nature; he has fallen out of nature, as it were, and is still in it; he is partly divine, partly animal; partly infinite, partly finite. The necessity to find ever-new solutions for the contradictions in his existence, to find ever-higher forms of unity with nature, his fellowmen and himself, is the source of all psychic forces which motivate man, of all his passions, affects and anxieties.

Mental unrest in our societies—anxiety and depression, or narcissism, personality disorders, dysfunctional relationships—stem from a failure to come to terms with the same social processes that relate to dialectical freedom. In essence, how the aspects of being and loving (how we live with ourselves and interact with others) present themselves in our lives determines how we view freedom and how we view ourselves as free.

In Fromm's view, as someone who had been exiled by the fascist German regime of his day, people had failed to understand the dialectical nature of being and loving in a world filled with others. Therefore, although people long for freedom, they simultaneously fear freedom. As Dagostino and Lake have stated,

> According to Fromm, our goal as humans is to be free and to live authentically. Historically, becoming free has meant being left alone to choose for ourselves; to have the right to think and act according to our own desires. Yet, what has happened is that even as modern man has achieved this negative freedom (freedom "from") he has failed to become fully free. This is because he has failed to appropriate both positive and negative freedom because, psychologically, he fears freedom. (18)

In this same line of thinking, American pragmatist and educational philosopher John Dewey (1989) stated:

> The serious threat to our democracy is not the existence of foreign totalitarian states. It is the existence within our own personal attitudes and within our own institutions of conditions which have given a victory to external authority, discipline, uniformity and dependence upon The Leader in foreign countries. The battlefield is also accordingly here—within ourselves and our institutions. (44)

But Fromm (1969) offered a point of hope—something of a solution. He said that we are not only shaped by history but also history is shaped by us. We can take a productive and active—or creative—participation in the events of history that are now playing out around us. We can overcome the tendency to look only at "how passions, desires, anxieties change and develop as a result of social processes" and start to see "how [our] energies thus shaped into specific forms in their turn become productive forces, molding the social process" (28).

Consider politics as a contextual means to situate school leadership as productive love. Local and organizational (and to a larger extent state) politics have always been a concern for school administrators. However, in recent years, national/federal politics are straining school relationships with parents and the community (Ujifusa 2022). It exposes the importance of having critical literacy skills to understand patterns and paradigms of social psychology and human behavior (for which both Fromm and others such as Dewey offer frameworks, arguably complementary lenses although distinct, temporally and culturally speaking). This also further speaks to the need to prepare politically literate citizens—future parents, business owners, and community members—who understand "disputes about transparency in curriculum and the role of the general public in what schools do every day have been supercharged by prominent politicians, the pandemic, divisions about race, and other factors" (Ujifusa 2022). But we must learn how—we must see it modeled in our role models and our leaders. It is both an educational concern—this ability to love and care for one another and not fear the responsibility freedom bestows upon us—and a concern of leadership.

Care Leadership

Care is an aspect—that is, "attitude"—of productive love that may seem obvious. However, in a consumer-capitalist society, care can perhaps become as trivial, as counterfeit, and as lifeless as the commercials that daily mediate and monopolize our primetime experiences. These types of expressions can distract us from important things—and understandably so. We spend a third or more of our days and a minimum of five-sevenths of weeks working to make a living. For some, these jobs are as monotonous as they are meaningless. For everyone, work can be draining—physically so for many and mentally for most. Although work and productivity are important and necessary, in the process our productive lives suffer. Downtime and personal space can become sacred and sensitive topics.

As a result, we get caught up in nonproductive activities. Our lives get filled with things we take for granted—important things that we just do not have the time for. Being civically engaged or actively concerned with the freedom and rights of anyone other than myself can be taxing. It isn't always the case that I "don't care." Often it is because I am unable to care—I lack the resources. And sometimes, I don't know how to care. At least, I did not learn and now cannot know how to productively care, given the frameworks in which we live and make a living.

In *Art of Loving*, Fromm (1962: 26) defined love as "the active concern for the life and growth of that which we love." He provided a concrete example: "If a woman told us that she loved flowers, and we saw that she forgot to water them, we would not believe in her 'love' for flowers" (26). To believe in her love for flowers, she has to take care of them. She must not only care about them (passively); she must also care for them (actively). However, she must also have both the resources and the understanding to care for her flowers.

So, how do educational leaders actuate productive love in caring for their students? Care becomes a primary concern for educational leadership on two levels. One, her or his own care of the students and all other stakeholders. The school leader must care about and care for others implicated in education (Jenlink 2014). Two, the modeling (i.e., teaching others through intentional activity) and mentoring (i.e., developing others through intentional sharing) are inherent to caring for those students and stakeholders. Both modeling and mentoring are forms of leadership involving teaching others through intentional moral activity and moral presence. The idea of leadership as caring and teaching is not new. Just as some critical pedagogy scholars, such as Nel Noddings, have viewed teaching as synonymous with caring (Monchinski 2010; Noddings 2015; Reed 2018), teachers are caring leaders (Noddings 2006). As Nodding points out, leaders, including classroom teachers, have to balance the objectives of higher authority with those of their staff; "caring leaders invite participation and responsible experimentation. They avoid coercion whenever possible. When a promising idea arises a caring leader may offer to support those who would like to try it" (344).

Key aspects of educational leadership depend fully on the obligation to care about and for others. For example, mentoring is moral care. Fostering relations, community connections, and executing legal and ethical duties may all be ways of exhibiting care for staff, students, and stakeholders. Similarly, the allocation of necessary resources as a form of support can be viewed as not only a type of care but also an act of responsibility.

Responsibility Leadership

Abdicating social and political responsibility is a common feature of representative nations (Parvin 2018). It was estimated that in the United States only slightly more 50 percent of the population voted in the 2020 national election (Desilver 2022), compared to 67 percent of citizens of the UK in the 2019 general election (Uberoi et al. 2020). Citizens tend to elect representatives and then, to some degree, disengage, returning to their day-to-day routines. In a sense, this aligns with Fromm's understanding of both human drives—to gain power and to submit to power. Through elected representatives, the citizens who voted for them gain a sense of control and may vicariously feel empowered by their candidates' policies and public statements. And yet, the citizen's personal political power is nonetheless handed over to her or his representative at the ballot box. Some become so accustomed to the politician making decisions and solving problems that the citizen disengages even more so, and this results in representatives becoming "career politicians," being elected indefinitely regardless of the good or bad they accomplish.

However, not all view nonparticipation as an abdication of responsibility, or as a negative form of citizenship (MacKenzie and Moore 2020). MacKenzie and Moore acknowledge that civic participation is "costly in terms of both time and effort and, as such, we must continually make choices about when to be politically active and when to refrain from participating. And even when we are willing and able to act, we may, instead, decide that nonparticipation is the better option" (2). They base their positive view of nonactivity in democracy on the premise that "we may decide not to participate for self-serving reasons, which might threaten the integrity of a democratic system or process," holding that "nonparticipation might, in certain circumstances, be desirable from a democratic perspective" (2). This view fails to acknowledge the extensive introduction of systems that might prevent participation from those who would otherwise vote. It also overlooks the apathetic conditioning or acculturation of individuals into a mindset that participation does not or will not matter.

Not participating to advance self-serving reasons may seem noble, but what to say of abstaining from voting in protest? When the lesser of two evils may be the best option to advance public good or the benefit of others, is there not a responsibility to one's community or country?

Nonetheless, as with caring, many obstacles can hinder our ability to respond to societal problems and issues that require informed decision-making. I am speaking here of a civic engagement that does not include the ballot box. Voting is widely held as a preeminent and predominant civic responsibility, but considering the vast efforts at voter suppression coupled with evidence that some residents are politically apathetic, voting may be a relatively "minor" way of being socially responsive and morally responsible. That is not to say that voting is not important (it is an incredibly important way to be involved); it is just not the only way. Voting can be thought of as the civic foundation of democracy—citizens must still build the house on that foundation.

Lack of access to reliable and vetted information is one such hindrance. Some citizens may not know where to go to get proper information or to become properly involved. Knowing when and how to respond is important. The call for educators to produce well-informed and well-educated citizens has long stood at the forefront of a moral education. But educators and students alike need to understand the rules of civic engagement. This requires political literacy. To develop one's ability to respond—and therefore be responsible—a politically literate citizen must have the knowledge of how to involve oneself and also be allowed to develop the social habits necessary to stay involved and be/become socially effective.

Fromm (2008: 32) defined responsibility as an individual's response to the needs of another, "to those [needs] he can express and more so to those he cannot or does not express." Schools are communities—microcosms of society—in which staff, students, and other stakeholders interact with one another to carry out the many facets of teaching, learning, and assessing. In many ways, where the student is concerned, this can be seen as a preparation for civic engagement. Educational leaders have an explicit responsibility to create spaces for the learning of language arts, fine arts, mathematics, the sciences, and social studies. Likewise, they have an implicit responsibility to assure that schools are incubators for the development of democratic efficiency.

Schools and the many classrooms are places where students first begin honing their social skills. Implied is a need to ensure these sites are democratic spaces. Civic engagement, as a means of increasing one's presence and purpose in their communities and countries, is first encountered in the democratic school. Students learn to seek out nonbiased information, sort out biases and types of propaganda, and develop their ability to think critically about their own opinions and to question their own views in the social studies classroom. Inferencing, making informed predictions, and drawing proper conclusions are commonly developed in the reading and language arts classroom. Probability and statistics as well as reasoning are typical to the mathematics course. In all subjects they ask, "Why?" But they must also learn how to question influence and the basis for all sorts of claims. When did these ideas and subjects develop? Who influenced these ideas? Why does the curriculum include what it does today?

Leaders also have a responsibility to ensure students learn about advocacy and activism, charity and care, and volunteering. These are foundational to demonstration, peaceable assembly, and grievance resolution as human rights. And in the course of learning how and when to do these, they should perhaps learn more about getting involved in local government, attending city councils and town halls, and the concept of placemaking.

Responsibility as the ability to respond implicates the school leader in the obligation to ensure our young citizens (i.e., the students or the learners) know how to educate themselves and others about their constitutional freedoms and how to dialogue with others about their nation's framers of policy and liberties. In doing so, students may learn that human rights, such as exercising one's freedom of speech, is not solely about expressing opinion, and that it is most importantly a means of generating democratic ideas and speaking out in opposition to oppressive ideas. Likewise, to engage in the freedom of press is not simply the right to propagandize one's own ideologies but serves to give voice to truth and respect for fellow humans by writing in opposition to propaganda that promotes authoritarianism.

Respect Leadership

Fromm (2008) defined respect in terms of how we see others, or how we are mindful of them, or how we regard them. He stated, "I respect him, that is (according to the original meaning of *respicere*) I look at him as he is, objectively and not distorted by my wishes and fears" (32). The Latin *respicere* connotes to care for, to consider, and to consult or seek the counsel of another. Implied are the ideas of both reflection and circumspection or prudence in the way we see others. Respect gives no place to bias, prejudice, or discrimination.

Disrespect is present in all forms of bias, prejudice, and intolerance. These are forms of false relatedness. In the introduction to the second edition of Fromm's *The Sane Society*, Ingleby (1991) wrote, "For Fromm false relatedness is as bad as none at all. True relatedness—love—is essentially symmetrical, based on equality and respect, in contrast to sadistic or masochistic relationships in which either the subjectivity of the other, or one's own, is denied" (xxviii). False relatedness is simply a mode of disrespect. Disrespect and divisiveness can be political or personal, cultural or social. Divisiveness is detrimental to families, communities, and nations. In fact, any organization can be hindered or even dismantled under the weight of divisive situations—whether it comes in the form of toxic relations between individuals, or wars between factions.

Division occurs when disrespect allows wedges to be inserted. The wedges of disrespect can be driven in when individuals or groups of individuals are isolated. Schools are social settings that have developed and now designed to bring multiple learners and multiple educators together in one microcosm of society. Staff, students, and stakeholders need to have respect demonstrated at all times and during all situations. Only by giving respect and modeling respect can we expect others to show us respect. Our native tendencies toward grasping for power or yielding vicariously to the powers of others diminish our capacity to respect ourselves and others.

Fromm (2008) stated, "Productive love when directed toward equals may be called brotherly love" (32). This authentic recognition of equality is essential to Fromm's concept of respect and how it relates to education and educational leadership.

> Man has to relate himself to others; but if he does it in a symbiotic or alienated way, he loses his independence and integrity; he is weak, suffers, becomes hostile, or apathetic; only if he can relate himself to others in a loving way does he feel one with them and at the same time preserve his integrity. Only by productive work does he relate himself to nature, becoming one with her, and yet not submerging in her. As long as man remains rooted incestuously in nature, mother, clan, he is blocked from developing his individuality, his reason; he remains the helpless prey of nature, and yet he can never feel one with her. Only if he develops his reason and his love, if he can experience the natural and the social world in a human way, can he feel at home, secure in himself, and the master of his life. (66)

Disrespect and division impede the development of the very skills that businesses and industry are asking schools to provide their future employees. Collaborative problem-solving and cooperative decision-making are all dependent in various ways on regard and thoughtfulness as well as coalition and integration. Problem-solving, communication (including dialogue and debate), creativity or innovation, compromise or negotiation, and leadership all require fundamentally a productive respect for those with whom you are interacting. Even sales and management when properly and ethically executed require respect as an introspective skill. It impedes our very endeavors of inquiry and dialogue and therefore hinders our pursuits of shared knowledge.

Knowledge Leadership

In large part, knowledge—ways of knowing, the acquisition of knowledge, the application of knowledge, the adjustments we make to how and what we know— is all a part of our "becoming" (Freire 1970). Freire stated:

> Education is thus constantly remade in the praxis. In order to be, it must become. Its "duration" (in the Bergsonian meaning of the word) is found in the interplay of the opposites permanence and change. The banking method emphasizes permanence and becomes reactionary; problem-posing education—which accepts neither a "well-behaved" present nor a predetermined future—roots itself in the dynamic present and becomes revolutionary. (84)

However, Fromm not only implied knowledge in the sense of being educated. As with Freire, he also wholly means knowledge of one's fellow man. Fromm asserted, "I know him, I have penetrated through his surface to the core of his being and related myself to him from my core, from the center, as against the periphery, of my being" (32). Without care, responsibility, and respect, it is impossible to know others in our communities. We may see examples of this in the public politics of many nations. For example, currently in the United States, it is difficult to identify individuals from either polarized party legitimately wanting to know the views of those on the other side.

Right-leaning values may overemphasize a permanence of the past—a glorification of history and national myths over the recognition of an opportunity to improve and advance. This can lead to a dangerous stagnation of social progress—it could prevent or at least slow our becoming. It educates for the transmission of former ideals and a homogenous identity. Knowledge is used as either cautionary (e.g., the tree of the knowledge of good and evil) or reactionary (such as the long-established anti-intellectualism or antiscientific movement witnessed during the Covid-19 pandemic when citizens around the world rebelled against wearing masks and vaccinations).

Similarly, those with left-leaning values may lose sight of the revolutionary work of becoming by falling into a change-everything (or change-for-the-sake-of-change) mindset. This type of knowledge lodges itself in the recognition and emphasis of symptoms and outwardly visible concerns. It fails to delve effectively into the underlying rhizomatic issues that cause the symptoms and social ills. For example, we often fail to see that race is a man-made social construction that connects to and/or intersections with many other social ills. It can be difficult to understand that when dealing with social conflict, our opposition's view is often a product of one's failure to recognize that individual problems or obstacles are products of that same social construction that shapes their view of their adversary. To do so, they may be prone to attack the "racist" and not the systemic and institutional policies that dominate the society in which systemic racism is instituted. It may be much easier to dehumanize individuals who engaged in a failed coup against the US Capitol on January 6, 2020, than to engage in a quest for knowledge that reveals deeper-seeded problems that should be blamed for the conditions that led to a people's extreme distrust and hatred of their own government.

In either case, our ability in becoming fully human is halted by the inability to see critically into the democratic nature of our social problems. Both views are reactionary and not revolutionary in the Freirean sense. Both are immature, in that they represent a type of knowledge that is not rooted in care, responsibility, or respect. Both present a false unity of concerns and a dividedness of ourselves. Both hinder the Hegelian idea of sublation—that is, integration—necessary for social and individual growth. According to Freire,

> The individual is divided between an identical past and present, and a future without hope. He or she is a person who does not perceive himself or herself as becoming; hence cannot have a future to be built in unity with others. But as he or she breaks this "adhesion" and objectifies the reality from which he or she starts to emerge, the person begins to integrate as a Subject (an I) confronting an object (reality). At this moment, sundering the false unity of the divided self, one becomes a true individual. (1970: 173)

But to see becoming as purely a traditional view of immaturity is not a critical view. Immaturity is not simply a lack of something else—becoming does not imply that we are caterpillars that will one day become butterflies. For Freire, becoming is a natural and necessary—an integral—part of the human experience. The problem is not that we are becoming—the things Freire wants us to problematize are the ones that prevent the process of becoming, that stagnate it. Similarly, Dewey is instructive in this concept in the vein of American pragmatic thought. Dewey (1916) captured the idea of becoming in his parallel concepts of growth and habits. He stated:

> The primary condition of growth is immaturity. This may seem to be a mere truism—saying that a being can develop only in some point in which he is undeveloped. But the prefix "im" of the word immaturity means something positive, not a mere void or lack. It is noteworthy that the terms "capacity" and "potentiality" have a double meaning, one sense being negative, the other positive. Capacity may denote mere receptivity, like the capacity of a quart measure. We may mean by potentiality a merely dormant or quiescent state—a capacity to become something different under external influences. But we also mean by capacity an ability, a power; and by potentiality potency, force. Now when we say that immaturity means the possibility of growth, we are not referring to absence of powers which may exist at a later time; we express a force positively present—the ability to develop. (41)

This same possibility of growth as an ability is inherent in Freire's idea of becoming. It does not have to do with qualities that are lacking—but qualities that are growing or engaged in a process of becoming developed. As Dewey went on to elaborate, immaturity was not simply a state of being in need or lacking. Likewise, growth in the Deweyan sense did not mean that the individual was in need of being filled up (here again is an echo of Freire's banking concept of education). Because we use adulthood as the standard, there is a tendency to only see the child in terms of what she or he does or will not have until they too are adults.

According to Dewey, "There is excellent adult authority for the conviction that for certain moral and intellectual purposes adults must become as little children" (1916: 42). Dewey, though not a critical theorist in the Frankfurtian sense, presents an argument well aligned with Fromm's and Freire's. If we assume the "fulfillment of growing" to mean achieving the accomplishment of being an adult, then this would mean that adults "have no further possibilities of growth" (42).

Fromm, on the other hand, saw this as *a giving birth to ourselves*. Education is a process of giving birth to oneself. As with Dewey and Freire, Fromm's notion of becoming is not a passive, unengaged process. We are actively giving birth while simultaneously being born. However, education as a process needs an environment. Schools are the incubators of this process of becoming or being born—a place where we can grow in knowledge-about as well as knowledge-for life. It is a lifelong learning process.

The foundations are laid as developing infants, but the fundamental formation of this process occurs when we are school-age children. Fromm ([1955] 2008) stated:

> The child begins to recognize outside objects, to react affectively, to grasp things and to co-ordinate his movements, to walk. But birth continues. The child learns to speak, it learns to know the use and function of things, it learns to relate itself to others, to avoid punishment and gain praise and liking. Slowly, the growing person learns to love, to develop reason, to look at the world objectively. He begins to develop his powers; to acquire a sense of identity, to overcome the seduction of his senses for the sake of an integrated life. Birth then, in the conventional meaning of the word, is only the beginning of birth in the broader sense. The whole life of the individual is nothing but the process of giving birth to himself. (25)

The abilities to learn to love, develop reason, and analyze the world objectively—to interact socially, think critically (and creatively), and evaluate and critique our surroundings and problems—are foundational. Leadership that is prepared and equipped to engage with others in care, responsibility, respect, and knowledge is required to create a learning environment where becoming can be optimal.

Problems of Individuation and Alienation

Fromm and other critical theorists might argue that the necessary models and frameworks needed to make capitalism an unquestioned success drive a problem of individuation that causes human beings to be divided, and resultantly alienates us from nature and others. Current neoliberal metrics applied to contemporary education systems, which can be seen in the reforms that fail to prepare learners for life and citizenry in local or global communities (e.g., businesses, cities/towns, cultures, political arenas), create systems of individuation and alienation. Fromm (1973) asserted that humankind

> must overcome the market-oriented and passive attitudes which dominate [us] now, and choose a mature productive path. [We] must acquire again a sense of self; [we] must be capable of loving and of making [our] work a meaningful and concrete activity. [We] must emerge from a materialistic orientation and

arrive at a level where spiritual values—love, truth, and justice—truly become of ultimate concern to [us]. (102)

Fromm warned that "any attempt to change only one section of life, the human or the spiritual, is doomed to failure" (102). Drawing from historical examples of this one-sided failure, he cited, "The gospel, concerned only with spiritual salvation, led to the establishment of the Roman Catholic Church; the French Revolution, with its concern exclusively with political reform, led to Robespierre and Napoleon; socialism, inasmuch as it was concerned only with economic change, led to Stalinism" (102).

Neoliberalism (arguably a driver behind contemporary systems in consumer curriculum and, by extension, markets directed at educational leadership) creates environments of learning that drive dedemocratization, political divisiveness, and loss of the ability to recognize commonalities through individualistic separation in our various social settings as human beings. Individualism, or what Fromm calls alienation or separateness, leads to aggression and destruction, be it symbolic or otherwise. This is an issue of integrity. Unless citizens are integral to a community, there is no connectedness or completeness. Integrity implies soundness of moral principle and character—entire uprightness or fidelity, especially in regard to truth and fair dealing (etymology). Fundamentally, integrity then replies to wholeness. Therefore, my application extends this to include closeness—not only closeness in proximity, such as a neighbor, but closeness in the sense of affection or care for others. I also hold that this is why Fromm interchanges the terms "brotherly love" with "productive love."

Fromm wrote, "Man is created in the likeness of God; hence all men are equal—equal in their common spiritual qualities, in their common reason, and in their capacity for brotherly love" (51). This aligns quite expressly with Dewey's (1916) concept of democracy and social efficiency—community, common goals, and communication. In alignment with this, democratic K-12 educational leaders are positioned to generate and foster climates and cultures of productive love, or moral care, in their schools. As such, this chapter will present a discussion on the relationship of Fromm's "productive love" with Jenlink's (2014) moral care and Nodding's ethics of care and how the interplay between these concepts can be instructive to the work of democratic educational leaders in K-12 schools. Therefore, critical theory like educational leadership seeks to create "a society bound by the bonds of brotherly love, justice and truth, a new and truly human home to take the place of the irretrievably lost home in nature" (Fromm [1955] 2008: 346).

School leaders must recognize their role as metaphorical mental health providers. They must lead their schools in becoming spaces of care and creativity, respect and spirituality, and knowledge and acknowledgment. They must work to make schools places for the process of becoming and to foster an education for that very process. Fromm ([1955] 2008) stated:

> Mental health is characterized by the ability to love and to create, by the emergence from incestuous ties to clan and soil, by a sense of identity based on one's experience of self as the subject and agent of one's powers, by the grasp of reality inside and outside of ourselves, that is, by the development of objectivity and reason. (67)

Educational leaders must also learn to recognize the ways in which controversy, conflicts, and crises shape the culture and climate of their schools. In their book *Shaping School Culture*, Deal and Peterson (2016) asserted:

> Cultural patterns and traditions evolve over time. They are initiated and formed as the school is founded and thereafter shaped by critical incidents, forged through controversy and conflict, and crystallized through triumph and tragedy. Culture takes form over the years as people cope with problems, stumble onto routines and rituals, and create traditions and ceremonies to reinforce underlying values and beliefs. (55)

This acknowledgment of the role critical incidents and crises have in shaping school culture requires a critical eye and critical forms of thought to address. The psychosocial concerns that underlie the controversies, conflicts, and crises of the twenty-first century are not new to humanity. The way in which they present themselves is new, but the basic human needs that underscore our desires to have power and control over our own lives, and our willingness to submit to others whom we view as having the power to protect our values, have not changed. The same de-democratizing effects we witness in the global shift to hyper-conservatism and alt-right-wing authoritarianism are seen as well in the regressive efforts of the left. These opposing forces can pull us further from the Hegelian collapses and ruptures that lead to synthesis. We may miss opportunities to recognize the sublation (i.e., integration) of progress that carries us forward, in a Hegelian sense, to where we find ourselves now.

A need exists for school leaders as curricular and instructional decision-makers to acknowledge this and advocate for socially efficient and politically literate citizens. They must see their roles as community liaisons and resource allocators through a similar critical lens. School leadership is a commitment and a calling. Individuals taking up the mantle of educational administration are committed to not only preparing individuals for reading, mathematics, social studies, and the sciences but also ensuring that students learn democratic values. This requires leaders to understand that students are not lacking intelligence or competence in their immature stage, but that the young are instead actively becoming the integrated individuals of the future who can decode moral and intellectual information and take well-informed and autonomous steps in their lives. The expectations that leaders set for teachers and the democratic spaces they create for learners can play a major role in shaping as well as advancing this critical framework. Doing so through a lens of productive love—of care, responsibility, respect, and knowledge—is at the heart of critical leadership. As Fromm wrote, "To practice the spirit of brotherly love, truth and justice, [is] hence to become the most radical critics of present-day society" (343).

For example, the person on the "left" who attacks the man advocating for the worker (regardless of the worker's profession) because they assume the advocate represents support for the product (such as coal) or profit of the industry (as a capitalist system) does not understand true leftist ideals. Supporting coal miners does not mean the advocate supports coal (in fact by supporting coal miners you may very well be supporting miners of metallurgical resources used in making wind turbines and other alternative fuel efforts). Failing to make this association exposes an absence of critical thinking. Advocating for the freedom of others to protest does not mean you are disavowing what they are protesting or the cause behind their activism. Likewise, acknowledging and allying with the frustrations and fears of the Black community over the shooting and killing of an unarmed African American citizen should give us pause to consider problems of authority and unregulated power. Instead, as a public we get blinded by the media's efforts to distract us from underlying social issues by pitting "Blue Lives" against "Black Lives."

Similarly, recognizing that there are corrupt, prejudiced, or poorly prepared individuals serving as police officers does not mean that one must think everyone called to serve and protect is evil or racist. Authoritarian personalities can exist in all positions wielding power—we would be foolish to refuse to believe that any apparatus of the government, the police force included, would have an issue with this problem. Students tend to graduate as citizens and community members who anecdotally struggle with a profound understanding of the left-right and authoritarian-libertarian (or "order-freedom") matrix—or any profound mapping of political nuances. We are programmed in a society and system that only presents a dual and dichotomous way of thinking and fails to fully grasp the plurality of thought that goes unrecognized and unrepresented.

Perhaps Fromm would attribute this to our separation from our true selves—our natural selves. Leadership that understands the issues relating to alienation and will seek out ways to combat it by connecting students to one another democratically. They do this by creating spaces of community in schools that are grounded in inquiry and dialogue, rooted in understanding one another and opening lines of communication between the various stakeholders. Schools under a critical-oriented leadership can foster the democratic spaces to learn what it means to be an individual without falling victim to the individuation that divides us and separates us from our causes, communities, and colleagues. Leadership that models and mandates a deeper understanding of the importance of being authentically connected can help others see how to practice care, responsibility, respect, and knowledge as productive love.

Conclusion: Leading as Thinking for Doing (aka Praxis)

School leaders have two roles in this: the first is her or his practice. They must recognize factions and divisions in their schools and districts/communities. They lead knowing that their decisions will be questioned or challenged. The allocation of resources, even if just and equitable, will create concerns with some. But they also must lead in ways that bring these factions together and engage them in consensus-building and the politics of schooling and shaping educational policy. Where the first role concerns their practice, the second role deals with the preparation of others to be democratically equipped. They must foster models of schools as democratic spaces where not only teachers and parents are engaged but also students are able to hone their political skills—that is, learn how to interact with others as caring and respectful individuals (a social aim) and develop as individuals who must use their experiences in life as responsible and knowledgeable individuals (a cultural aim). For this reason, I find the critical literacies, such as political, moral, spiritual, and cultural literacy, are inherent to the application of productive love as critical educational leadership.

Fromm's productive love represents positive power and positive submission as well. Through love we have the power to not only passively care about others but also engage in actively caring for them. It is the power to engage in a response to their needs—it enables us to respond with class-conscious, culturally relevant, and socially just decisioning. Productive love is the school leader's praxis—it is the footbridge connecting theory and practice. We engage in the praxis of productive love by combining reflective thinking with positive doing—or rather *converting* purposeful reflection into productive doing. This is done by acknowledging a need for improvement and by acting in a critically conscious manner to achieve the aims and goals we set for our staff, students, and selves.

However, achievement is not determined by a standardized measure or legislated mandate. Achievement tests and standardized assessments only provide one data point on the educational trajectory of any one student or school. The critical educational leader endeavors to understand and respond to underlying problems that hinder personal success and academic achievement all along an individual's educational arch. Whether it is the care needed in addressing the crises, conflicts, and controversies that challenge and shape school culture and our communities, or it is our active response of allocating assets and resources purposefully and equitably to empower teachers, productive love is the praxis of the critical educational leader.

References

Dagostino, V., and R. Lake (2014), "Fromm's Dialectic of Freedom and the Praxis of Being," in S. J. Miri, R. Lake, and T. M. Kress (eds.), *Reclaiming the Sane Society: Essays on Erich Fromm's Thought*, 17–30, Rotterdam: Sense.

Deal, T. E., and K. D. Peterson (2016), *Shaping School Culture*, 3rd ed., Hoboken, NJ: Jossey-Bass.

Desilver, D. (2022), "Turnout in the U.S. Has Soared in Recent Elections but by Some Measures Still Trails That of Many Other Countries," *Pew Research Center*, 1 November. www.pewresearch.org/short-reads/2022/11/01/turnout-in-u-s-has-soared-in-recent-elections-but-by-some-measures-still-trails-that-of-many-other-countries.

Dewey, J. (1916), *Democracy and Education*, New York: Free Press.

Dewey, J. ([1927] 1954), *The Public and Its Problems*, Denver, CO: Alan Swallow.

Dewey, J. ([1939] 1989), *Freedom and Culture*, Seattle, WA: Promethean Books.

Freire, P. (1970), *Pedagogy of the Oppressed*, London: Continuum.

Fromm, E. ([1941] 1969), *Escape from Freedom*, New York: Avon.

Fromm, E. (1947), *Man for Himself: An Enquiry into the Psychology of Ethics*, London: Routledge.

Fromm, E. ([1955] 1973), *The Dogma of Christ and Other Essays on Religion, Psychology and Culture*, Robbinsdale, MN: Fawcett Premier.

Fromm, E. ([1956] 1962), *The Art of Loving: An Enquiry into the Nature of Love*, New York: Harper & Row.

Ingleby, D. (1991), "The Argument of the Sane Society," in *The Sane Society*, 2nd ed., xxiv–xxxvii, London: Routledge.

Jenlink, P. M. (ed.) (2014), *Educational Leadership and Moral Literacy*, Lanham, MD: Rowman & Littlefield.

MacKenzie, M. K., and A. Moore (2020), "Democratic Non-Participation," *Polity* 52 (3): 430–59.

Monchinski, T. (2010), "Critical Pedagogies and an Ethic of Care," *Counterpoints* 382 (1): 85–135.

Noddings, N. (2006), "Educational Leaders as Caring Teachers," *School Leadership and Management* 26 (4): 339–45.

Noddings, N. (2015), "Critical Thinking," *Journal of Educational Controversy* 10 (1): art. 1.

Parvin, P. (2018), "Democracy without Participation: A New Politics for a Disengaged Era," *Res Publica* 24: 31–52.

Reed, C. D. (2018), "Critical Pedagogy and the Ethics of Care: How Values Affect the Classroom Dynamic," PhD thesis, Oxford, MI: University of Mississippi.

Uberoi, E., C. Baker, R. Cracknell, G. Allen, N. Roberts, C. Barton, G. Sturge, S. Danechi, R. Harker, P. Bolton, R. McInnes, C. Watson, N. Dempsey, and L. Audickas (2020), *General Election 2019: Results and Analysis—Briefing Paper No. CP 8749*, 2nd ed., London: House of Commons Library.

Ujifusa, A. (2022), "How Politics Are Straining Parent-School Relationships," *Education Week*, February. www.edweek.org/leadership/how-politics-are-straining-parent-school-relationships/2022/02.

Index

achievement gap 26, 27–8, 32, 216
a priori 3, 39, 81, 99, 115, 122, 165
Adorno, T. 5, 9, 17, 57–8, 59, 62, 64, 66, 68, 70, 118, 134, 144, 146, 157, 159
aesthetics 86, 108, 161
African American 85, 136, 201, 205, 207, 209, 239
   Afrocentric racial identity, 218
alienation 4, 9, 98, 134, 138, 236–40
   becoming alienated 224
   individuation 6
   opposed to productive love 224
   oppression 96
   problems of 236
   psychological effects of isolation 148
   separateness 7, 138, 237
anthropology 8, 37, 41, 140, 144, 207
   new anthropological type 133, 139, 145–6
Aristotle 18, 114, 115, 126, 129, 225
Art of Loving 228
authoritarian(ism) 133
   alt-right wing 3, 238
   anti-authoritarianism 30
   characteristic of culture 145
   egoistic 45, 51, 54
   fascist 142
   personality type 146, 239
   stereotypical categorizing 145
   ticket thinking 145
Authoritarian Personality 133, 334, 144–5
Awakening the Natural Genius of Black Children 213

Bass, B. M. 18, 77, 85
Benjamin, W. 5
biopolitics/biopower 57, 58, 62–4, 68, 70
Black Critical Theory (BlackCrit) 136
Black codes 206
Black education 136, 203, 205, 206, 213, 215, 216
   Black Power 216–20

Black schools 210
   children's intellectual capacity 216
   community empowerment 220
   history of 215–16
   leadership 135, 207, 208, 210, 214, 220
   quality 208, 214
   racial pride 218, 220
   social-political context 214–15
   teachers 207, 209
Black Lives 201, 239
Blue Lives 239
Blueprint for Black Power 220
Brecht, B. 9
Brown v. Board of Education 209–11, 213, 216
bureaucracy 38, 121, 142, 145, 150, 207
   authoritarian bureaucracy 144–7
   characteristic of schooling 49
   characteristic of institutions 145, 149
   characteristic of power 121
   characteristic of society 145
   hegemonic 38
   mechanization 49
   monopolistic 144
   multi-agencies 207
   technological 142
Burns, J. M. 76, 77

capitalism 5, 9, 43, 45, 46, 63, 70, 133, 145, 147, 156, 158, 159, 165, 190, 217, 244
   bourgeoisie, 46
   characteristic of consumer industry, 57
   characteristic of modern state, 43
   characteristic of society, 134
   driver of alienation, 236
   imperialism, 162
   morally unmoored, 46
   neoliberal, 244
   system, 12, 17
   technology, 165
class(ism) 23, 27, 46, 119, 136, 155, 157, 182, 215, 240

blue collar, 146
characteristic of society, 4
class conscious, 136, 240
 exploitation, 156
 relation to racism, 214–17
 socio-economic status, 25
 stratification, 89, 162
 working class, 4, 158
citizenship/citizenry 4, 10, 27, 34, 91, 104, 121, 137, 138, 161, 163, 167, 186, 191, 197, 206, 214, 215, 217, 234, 236
 agency 229
 citizen agency 135, 164
 civic 5, 101, 165, 231
 democratic 91, 161, 214, 230
 educated 104, 163, 166, 197, 230
 engagement 231
 first-class 216
 global 167
 informed 121
 integral to community 138, 237, 239
 participation 5, 229
 politically literate 227, 230, 238
 responsibility 5, 101, 229
 second-class 214, 216–17
 working class 4
communicative action 11, 51, 120
conflict 27, 208, 234, 238, 241
conscientização see Freirean critical theory
controversy 8, 27, 33, 238, 241
Cooper, A. J. 218
covid 27, 114, 140, 147, 148, 167, 172, 234
crisis 4, 27, 38, 45, 83, 208, 210, 234, 238, 241
critical media literacy 134, 155, 160, 163, 165, 167
Critical Race Theory 85, 162, 163
culture 3, 4, 40, 49, 59, 61, 65, 67, 75, 86, 99, 125, 137, 138, 189, 191, 192, 193, 194, 195, 197, 217, 218, 225, 237
 change 79, 88
 chattel 201
 counterculture 162
 localized 127
 mass(produced) 9, 10, 59, 70, 133, 158
 material 160
 media 159, 161
 organizational 77, 87
 peace 17, 54
 plantation

popular culture 10
 predatory 101
 silence 183
 subcultures 127, 165
 see also culture industry
 see also school culture
cultural dominance *see* hegemony
Culturally Relevant Practice 192, 194, 197
 critical theory 195
culture industry 5, 134, 149, 158–9
 consumerism 17, 58, 66–9, 158
 education policy 61
 leadership industry 61
 mass-distributed 144
 mass-produced 58–9, 158–9
 media 156, 159
 psychopower 64
 sameness 59
 specialization 60–1
curriculum 7, 10, 16, 29, 31, 32, 50, 54, 101, 135, 136, 151, 160, 165, 173, 184, 192, 196, 214, 217, 218, 220, 227, 231, 237

democracy 8, 10, 11, 37, 42, 91, 155, 161, 164, 166, 174, 189, 191, 194, 196, 197, 208, 225
 characterized by justice 42
 dangers to 22, 45
 democratic efficiency 230
 democratic values 48, 195, 239
 Deweyan 137–8
 Habermasian 121
 more than government 11, 38
 pluralistic 43
Deleuze, G. 58, 64
Derrida, J. 58, 59, 64, 65
Dewey, J. 11, 30, 37, 41, 137, 225, 227, 235
dialectic(al) 12, 96, 99–101, 156
Dialectic of Enlightenment 59, 61, 159
dialogic 22, 45, 180, 184
 incivility 45, 54
 reflection 184
dialogue 10, 22, 30, 51, 70, 121, 135, 171, 173, 175, 177, 183, 185, 231, 240
disenfranchisement 5, 214
Du Bois, W. E. B. 214, 218

economic(s) 9, 10, 18, 22, 26, 28, 29, 33, 38, 44, 46, 60, 63, 66, 96, 98, 100, 124,

127, 159, 186, 190, 203, 211, 218, 219, 237
  agency 142
  conditions 210
  exploitation 214
  inequalities 202
  justice 181
  literacy 12
  needs 5
  power 202
  wellbeing 140
education 15, 22, 29, 33, 37, 43, 48, 50, 62, 64, 76, 91, 95, 134, 140, 143, 148, 151, 160, 165, 168, 174, 180, 181, 186, 194, 205, 217, 228, 233, 235, 236
  adult education 171, 184
  American system 136, 213
  Australian system 69
  backbone of democracy 190
  beyond the classroom 98
  bildung 164
  bureaucratization 49
  commodification 46–7, 53
  connection to critical theory 2
  critical literacies 12
  critical theory 22–3, 41–2
  curricular vehicle/venue 191
  dialectic 96
  education research(ers) 78, 83
  emancipatory 38, 44, 48, 52, 101
  ethical 38, 197
  existing social order, 89
  holistic 49
  liberating 96, 214
  neoliberal attacks 104, 162
  political dimension 98
  remote platforms 139
  role in freedom 100
  schooling 10
  self-actualization 7
  shift 80
  socializing role 165
  space of resistance 46–7
  standardization 50
  systemic 18, 27, 33, 99, 166, 190, 193
  technologically mediated 139, 143
  tool for social change 29, 166, 181
  traditional concepts 98, 179, 183
  transformative 166
  type of praxis 30

  see also Black education
educational leadership 38, 54, 57, 64, 71, 80, 98, 135, 164, 176, 179, 185, 224, 228, 230, 237, 238, 240
  care leadership 227–9
  critical educational leader 1, 11, 12, 16, 33, 96, 97, 99, 101, 102, 104, 241
  discourse 58, 60, 62, 70
  emancipatory 42
  industry 58, 61, 66–9
  knowledge leadership 233–6
  preparation 172
  professional experience 172
  respect leadership 231–3
  responsibility leadership 229–31
  specialization 60
  transformative 172
education research(er) 75, 83, 84, 88, 89, 90
emancipation/emancipatory 16, 38, 41, 43–6, 48, 50, 52, 88, 97, 100, 102, 104, 136, 158, 160, 163, 202, 206, 213
Emancipation Proclamation 205
enlightenment 23, 47, 59, 120, 178
  end 118
  era/time 115
  Greeks 159
  reason 159
enslavement 16, 42, 50, 213, 215, 216, 217
  see also slavery
equity 8, 16, 24, 28, 30, 31–3, 34, 38, 78, 80, 87, 114, 137, 166, 172, 176, 178, 185, 190, 191, 193, 194, 196, 197, 201, 202, 208, 210, 240

F-scale 144
fascism 3, 6, 142, 145, 156
feminist theory 85, 162
  see also women's studies
Foucault, M. 16, 57, 62–4, 66, 70, 120, 122–3, 126, 129
Frankfurt School 18, 37, 86
  authoritarianism 144
  capitalism 134, 144
  conditions of modernity 144
  critical philosophy 41
  critical theorists 8, 16, 59, 75, 95, 118, 156
  critique of society 86, 140, 158
  critique of technology 160

history 156–8
sociological project 144
spirit 2
totally administered society 159
Freire, P. 104, 135, 165, 172–4, 176, 178, 179, 181, 183, 185, 216, 219, 233, 235
Freirean critical theory 30, 184, 216, 234
   banking concept of education 136, 179, 180, 183, 233, 235
   becoming 172, 235, 238
   critical consciousness 135, 202, 219, 220
   culture of silence, 183
   emancipatory theorist 177
   Freirean beliefs 175–7
   impact on educational leadership 182–5
   message of hope 181
   model for reflective practice 179
Freud, S. 9, 158, 160, 161, 162
Fromm, E. 5, 6, 7, 10, 11, 137, 138, 157, 223–5, 226, 228, 232, 233, 236, 237, 240

Garvey/Garveyism 219
Gatto, J. T. 136, 216
gender 8, 23, 25, 26, 27, 85, 89, 119, 166, 182, 208, 218
Giroux, H. 102, 244
government 11, 27, 32, 38, 67, 106, 114, 121, 122, 127, 205, 208, 209, 216, 226, 231, 234, 239
governmentality 62

Habermas, J. 11, 16, 22, 37, 38, 41, 43, 50, 114, 120, 121, 122, 137, 191, 193
Hannah-Jones, N. 207
Hegel(ian) 9, 58, 156, 158, 160, 225, 234, 238
hegemony, 18, 27, 37, 44, 53, 97, 100, 104, 124, 155, 161, 190, 193, 217, 219, 220
   characteristic of bureaucracies 38
   characteristic of enslavement 50
   characteristic of knowledge reproduction 48
   characteristic of neoliberalism. 102, 162
   characteristic of school structures 54
   characterized by control 53
   characterized by neo-conservative 161
   epistemological assumptions 193
   form of leadership 51
   hallmarked by forms of power 104

ideology 97, 102, 155
   Orwellian 18, 100
   power-knowledge structures 44
   repressive 37
   societal institutions 217
   status quo 18
   subjugation 50
   whiteness 220
Heidegger, M. 158
History of Sexuality 62
Holocaust 136, 214
hope 91, 102–3, 126, 161, 165, 174, 175, 176, 181, 184, 227
Horkheimer, M. 3, 9, 23, 37, 42, 43, 59, 60, 61, 64, 66, 118, 119, 129, 134, 156, 157, 158, 159
Hume, D. 16, 37, 39, 40, 41, 115, 116, 117

individuality 142, 143, 145, 224, 232
   individualization 6, 7
   individuation 6, 65, 223, 224, 236, 240
   liberal individualism 45
   social withdrawal 149
inequality 15, 22, 24, 25, 29, 44, 166, 177, 182, 202, 210, 219
inequity 30, 33, 44, 54, 85, 89, 184, 187, 192, 193, 195, 216, 217, 219
   economic 44, 89
   educational 27, 32, 48, 50
   (post)modernity 16, 37, 45, 48
   racial 218
   structural 17
injustice 24, 26, 30, 157, 172, 175, 184, 219
intellectual 22, 26, 29, 77, 95, 102, 160, 216, 217, 220, 235, 239
   anti-intellectualism 8, 234
isolation *see* alienation
Institut für Sozialforschung see Frankfurt School

juridification 46, 49, 53

Kant, I. 18, 37, 39, 40, 41, 58, 114, 116, 117, 118, 120, 121, 123, 125, 129, 158

Ladson-Billings, G. 137, 192, 195, 197
leadership 12, 16, 17, 19, 22, 23, 33, 37, 44, 54, 57, 58, 63, 66, 69, 75, 81, 85, 88, 97, 102, 134, 190, 193, 208

deliberative collective leadership 50–1, 52
distributed 7, 59, 61
hegemonic leadership 51
ideologies of 60
knowledge 233–6
leadership style 79
Multifactor Leadership Questionnaire 77
transformative 3, 16, 172
zombie leadership 68
see also educational leadership
see also transformational leadership
Leadership and Performance beyond Expectations 77
learning 2, 10, 12, 16, 21, 25, 27, 29, 30, 32, 34, 38, 43, 45, 48, 49, 52, 53, 70, 96, 101, 136, 139, 140, 142, 149, 161, 165, 171, 173, 175, 176–7, 182, 185, 191, 193, 195, 197, 205, 230, 236
Leibniz, G. W. 115, 116
LGBTQIA+ 25, 162, 208
  antigay campaigns 208
  gay and lesbian studies 162
  heteronormativity 155
  homophobia 162
liberation *see* emancipation
Lincoln, A. 206
Lonely Crowd 146
love 6, 10, 11, 31, 50, 52, 137, 175, 176, 178, 180, 183, 225, 228, 232, 236, 237
  characteristic of solidarity 44, 49, 52, 54
  see also productive love
Lukács, G. 9
Lyotard, J. 58, 64

Marcuse, H. 5, 18, 38, 44, 46, 75, 80, 83, 86–8, 91, 96, 97, 98, 99, 100, 102, 104, 134, 140, 141, 143, 145, 151, 157, 158, 160, 162, 164, 167
marginalization 15, 21, 23, 25, 27, 31, 49, 50, 60, 70, 85, 87, 136, 162, 176, 180, 190, 193, 219
Marx, Karl 9, 22, 37, 53, 95, 158, 160
Marxism 46, 62, 64, 137, 156, 158, 159, 161, 174, 217
mass media 64, 67, 70, 134, 141
  see also social media

mediated education 10, 45, 48, 127, 142, 144
  technologically 134, 139, 141
meme 5, 226
Mills, C. W. 133, 144, 146
Mills, Charles M. 214
miseducation 99, 216, 218
misinformation 1, 167
misogyny 155
moral(ity) 15, 40, 90, 95, 117, 119, 120, 230
  characteristic of individualism 43
  characteristic of moral 40
  characteristic of solidarity 38, 41
  dimension of education 98

neoliberal(ism) 48, 53, 66, 68, 80, 89, 137, 162, 163, 167, 236, 237
Nietzsche, F. 9, 158
nihilism 65, 162

One-Dimensional Man 18, 75, 141, 157, 160
one dimensionality 18, 76, 87, 88, 89, 96, 97
opinion *see* public opinion
opioid crisis 4

partisanship 5, 10, 11
Party Government 11
pedagogy 2, 7, 16, 22, 28, 49, 91, 163, 164, 166, 168, 177, 182, 192, 194
  critical pedagogy 29–30, 183, 228
  culturally relevant pedagogy 137, 197
Pedagogy of the Oppressed 177, 182
Plato 158
polarization 167, 233
policy/policies 41, 61, 63, 240
  neoliberal policies 48, 53
  racist 28
political 1, 3, 5, 9, 11, 16, 18, 28, 64, 86, 95, 104, 158, 196, 220, 229, 239
  acumen/literacy 10, 12, 98, 227, 230
  agency 96, 160, 229, 240
  conflicts 208
  dimension 98, 137, 151
  discourses 27
  dispositions 197
  divisiveness 37, 44, 138, 232, 237
  domination 99, 103, 104

economy 156, 165, 167
identity 218
ideologies 103
mechanizations 102
reproduction/socialization 38, 101
responsibility 229
subordination 216
violence 123
postmodern 9, 37, 43, 45, 47, 49, 51, 53, 54
poststructuralists 58, 64, 66
praxis 12, 24, 30, 96, 97, 98, 103, 122, 163, 178, 182, 190, 217, 240
  action 172
  alternative pedagogy 163
  contemplative 99–101
  critical thought 96, 101
  definition 172, 179
  educational 30
  emancipatory 104
  form of leadership 96–7, 178, 240
  overcoming injustice 182
  public acts 120–1
  reflection 98, 172
  restorative 49
  self-understanding 173
productive love 10, 224, 237, 239, 240
  brotherly love 11, 137, 138, 223, 232, 239
  dialectic 225–7
  form of praxis 241
  nonproductive love 223
  opposite of destructive love 223
problem-posing 31, 172, 233
propaganda 7, 161, 231
psychopower 64–6
public opinion 9, 118, 147, 231

race 6, 8, 23, 24, 25, 27, 89, 119, 136, 166, 172, 186, 203, 208, 209, 213, 214, 216, 218, 234
racism 28, 90, 99, 162, 214, 220
  abolitionism 211
  anti-Black 214, 218, 220
  anti-racism 211
  apartheid 219
  caste system 214
  inequity 218
  institutional 28
  misogynoir 218
  racial retrenchment 215

systemic 135, 234
rationality 18, 43, 80, 102, 114, 115, 117, 120, 125, 126, 140, 151, 223
  Aristotelian 128
  cultural 127, 129
  positive 133
  practical 127
  technological 140–3, 144
reflection 3, 29, 179, 181, 184–5, 196, 232, 241
  critical reflection 175
  essential to action 172
  praxis 98
reflexivity 3, 16, 29, 89, 192, 197
relatedness 6, 7, 138, 223, 224, 232
rhizome 5, 6, 234
Riesman, D. 144, 146, 147
Rousseau, J. 158

Sane Society 137, 223, 232
Scheler, M. 37, 41, 44, 45, 47, 52
school culture 18, 23, 24, 25, 26, 135, 136, 214, 238, 241
  cultivation 100
  democratic 29
  educational 90, 194
  equity-focused 32
  learning 113
  toxic 32
separateness *see* alienation
sexual assault 204, 213
sexuality 8, 26, 62, 63, 203, 204
Shaping School Culture 238
slavery 27, 136, 202, 203, 204, 205, 206, 207, 211, 213, 215, 216
social justice 16, 22, 24–7, 31, 33, 37, 54, 156, 165, 168, 181, 185, 192
social media 5, 8, 58, 65, 147–8, 150, 151, 165
social science 3, 39, 42, 49, 105, 119, 125, 129
socialization 135, 164, 189, 195, 196, 201, 202, 209, 211
  agents 8, 158
solidarity 37, 38, 41, 42, 43, 44, 45, 46, 48, 49, 50, 51, 99
status quo 6, 18, 25, 46, 48, 100, 119, 123, 137, 152, 183, 191, 192, 193, 195, 197, 205, 206
Stiegler, B. 57, 58, 62, 64, 65, 66, 68, 69, 70

structures 24, 26, 29, 37, 46, 51, 54, 97, 102, 121, 134, 140, 148, 150, 165, 173, 185, 190, 193, 195, 211, 213, 219
   Black perspective, 203
   bureaucratic 207
   discursive 84
   familial 204
   hidden 179
   organizational 85
   oppressive 16, 21, 29, 39
   political 15, 22
   power/knowledge 17, 22, 37, 44, 51, 53
   relationship 207
   repressive 49
   social structures 134, 148, 217
   structural domains 12, 22
   superstructures 44
   visible 179

Taking Care of Youth 64
technology 8, 10, 64, 105, 134, 139, 140, 142, 160, 164, 168
   assistive 29
   information communication 155

hallucinatory worlds 151
   material dimension 150
   STEM 166
Theory of Communicative Action 50
totalitarian(ism) *see* authoritarian(ism)
transformational leadership 17, 18, 59, 75, 77, 79, 81, 83, 87, 89, 137, 179
   promise 76–8
   transformational theory 76
Transformative Practice in Critical Media Literacy 244
Voice from the South 218

violence 23, 136
   anti-Black 136, 220
   political 123
Virginia Slave Codes 205

Weber, M. 9
white supremacy, 155, 165, 205
Wilson, A. 213, 220
Woodson, C. G. 218
women's studies 163

Young Radicals 96